KT-497-360

AROUND PARLIAMENT
See pages 104–119.

Around Városliget

Central Pest

AROUND VÁROSLIGET
See pages 140–151.

CENTRAL PEST
See pages 120–139.

EYEWITNESS TRAVEL GUIDES

BUDAPEST

EYEWITNESS TRAVEL GUIDES

BUDAPEST

Main contributors:
BARBARA OLSZAŃSKA, TADEUSZ OLSZAŃSKI

LONDON, NEW YORK,
MELBOURNE, MUNICH AND DELHI
www.dk.com

Produced by Wydawnictwo Wiedza i Życie, Warsaw
SERIES EDITOR Ewa Szwagrzyk
CONSULTANTS András Hadik, Małgorzata Omilanowska,
Katalin Szokolay
EDITORS Joanna Egert, Anna Kożurno-Królikowska,
Bożena Leszkowicz
DESIGNER Paweł Pasternak

Dorling Kindersley Ltd
PROJECT EDITOR Jane Oliver
EDITORS Felicity Crowe, Nancy Jones

MAIN CONTRIBUTORS
Tadeusz Olszański, Barbara Olszańska

TRANSLATORS
Magda Hannay, Anna Johnson, Ian Wisniewski

PHOTOGRAPHERS
Gábor Barka, Dorota and Mariusz Jarymowiczowie

ILLUSTRATORS
Paweł Mistewicz, Piotr Zubrzycki

Printed and bound in China by South China Printing Co. Ltd

First published in Great Britain in 1999
by Dorling Kindersley Limited
80 Strand, London WC2R 0RL
Reprinted with revisions 2000, 2001, 2004

Copyright 1999, 2004 © Dorling Kindersley Limited, London
A Penguin Company

ALL RIGHTS RESERVED. NO PART OF THIS PUBLICATION MAY BE
REPRODUCED, STORED IN A RETRIEVAL SYSTEM, OR TRANSMITTED IN ANY
FORM OR BY ANY MEANS, ELECTRONIC, MECHANICAL, PHOTOCOPYING,
RECORDING OR OTHERWISE, WITHOUT THE PRIOR WRITTEN PERMISSION
OF THE COPYRIGHT OWNER.

A CIP CATALOGUE RECORD IS AVAILABLE FROM THE BRITISH LIBRARY.

ISBN 0 7513 6880 6

FLOORS ARE REFERRED TO THROUGHOUT IN ACCORDANCE WITH BRITISH
USAGE; IE THE "FIRST FLOOR" IS THE FLOOR ABOVE GROUND LEVEL.

**The information in this
Dorling Kindersley Travel Guide is checked regularly**.
Every effort has been made to ensure that this book is as up-to-date
as possible at the time of going to press. Some details, however, are
liable to change. The publishers cannot accept responsibility for any
consequences arising from the use of this book, nor for any material
on third party websites, and cannot guarantee that any website
address in this book will be a suitable source of travel information.
We value the views and suggestions of our readers very highly.
Please write to: Publisher, DK Eyewitness Travel Guides,
Dorling Kindersley, 80 Strand, London WC2R 0RL, Great Britain.

◁ **The Parliament building** *(see pp108–9)*, **standing on the Danube**

CONTENTS

HOW TO USE
THIS GUIDE *6*

Pallas Athene on the Old Town Hall

INTRODUCING
BUDAPEST

PUTTING BUDAPEST ON
THE MAP *10*

THE HISTORY OF
BUDAPEST *16*

BUDAPEST
AT A GLANCE *36*

BUDAPEST THROUGH
THE YEAR *58*

**Hungarian crest adorning a wall
close to the Tunnel *(see p100)***

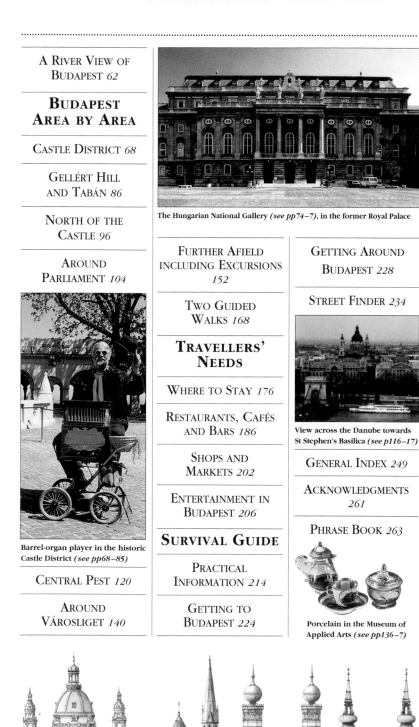

The Hungarian National Gallery *(see pp74–7)*, in the former Royal Palace

Barrel-organ player in the historic
Castle District *(see pp68–85)*

View across the Danube towards
St Stephen's Basilica *(see p116–17)*

Porcelain in the Museum of
Applied Arts *(see pp136–7)*

The landmark domes and towers of four of Budapest's most striking places of worship

HOW TO USE THIS GUIDE

THIS EYEWITNESS Travel Guide helps you get the most from your stay in Budapest with the minimum of difficulty. The opening section, *Introducing Budapest*, locates the city geographically, sets modern Budapest in its historical context and describes events through the entire year. *Budapest at a Glance* is an overview of the city's main attractions. *Budapest Area by Area* starts on page 66. This is the main sightseeing section, which covers all of the important sights, with photographs, maps and illustrations. It also includes day trips from Budapest and two walks around the city. Information about hotels, restaurants, shops and markets, entertainment and sports is found in *Travellers' Needs*. The *Survival Guide* has advice on everything from using the postal service and telephones to Budapest's public transport system and medical services.

Plotting the route

FINDING YOUR WAY AROUND THE SIGHTSEEING SECTION

Each of six sightseeing areas in Budapest is colour-coded for easy reference. Every chapter opens with an introduction to the area of the city it covers, describing its history and character, and has one or two *Street-by-Street* maps illustrating typical parts of that area. Finding your way around the chapter is made simple by the numbering system used throughout. The most important sights are covered in detail in two or more full pages.

Each area has colour-coded thumb tabs.

Locator map

The area shaded pink is shown in greater detail on the *Street-by-Street* map.

A suggested route takes in some of the most interesting and attractive streets in the area.

1 Introduction to the area
For easy reference, the sights in each area are numbered and plotted on an area map. To help the visitor, this map also shows underground stations, main bus and tram stops and parking areas. The area's key sights are listed by category: Museums and Galleries; Churches; Historic Streets and Squares; Palaces and Historic Buildings; Hotels and Baths and Parks and Gardens.

A locator map shows where you are in relation to the other areas in the city centre.

2 Street-by-Street map
This gives a bird's-eye view of interesting and important parts of each sightseeing area. The numbering of the sights ties up with the area map and the fuller description on the pages that follow.

The list of star sights recommends the places that no visitor should miss.

BUDAPEST AREA MAP

THE COLOURED AREAS shown on this map *(see inside front cover)* are the six main sight-seeing areas used in this guide. Each is covered in a full chapter in *Budapest Area by Area (pp66–167)*. They are highlighted on other maps throughout the book. In *Budapest at a Glance*, for example, they help you locate the top sights. They are also used to help you find the position of the two walks *(pp168–73)*.

Numbers refer to each sight's position on the area map and its place in the chapter.

Practical information provides everything you need to know to visit each sight. Map references pinpoint the sight's location on the *Street Finder* map *(pp234–47)*.

Façades of important buildings are often shown to help you recognize them quickly.

The visitors' checklist provides all the practical information needed to plan your visit.

3 **Detailed information on each sight**
All the important sights in Budapest are described individually. They are listed in order following the numbering on the area map at the start of the section. Practical information includes a map reference, opening hours, telephone numbers and admission charges. The key to the symbols used is on the back flap.

4 **Budapest's major sights**
Historic buildings are dissected to reveal their interiors; museums and galleries have colour-coded floorplans to help you find important exhibits.

Stars indicate the features no visitor should miss.

A timeline charts the key events in the history of the building.

INTRODUCING BUDAPEST

CONRAFACTVR. DER HAVBTSTAD OPEN IN VNGERN WIE DIE VON DEN CHRISTE BELEGERT GEWEST. AÑO.1598

Putting Budapest on the Map

The capital of the Republic of Hungary, Budapest has over 1.8 million inhabitants, a fifth of the country's total population. The city is situated on the Danube and covers an area of 525 sq km (200 sq miles). One third of the city is taken up by hilly Buda and Óbuda, on the western bank of the Danube, and the remaining two thirds by flat Pest, on the eastern bank. Budapest has a pivotal location at the heart of central Europe. From here one can easily reach other major cities such as Vienna, Zagreb, Bratislava, Belgrade, Bucharest and Prague.

Hungary in Europe
Hungary is entirely landlocked within central Europe. Budapest's passenger airport, Ferihegy 2, has two terminals and there are numerous connections by road and rail to neighbouring countries (see pp224–7).

BUDAPEST AND ENVIRONS

ESZTERGOM
VÁC
SZENTENDRE
GÖDÖLLŐ
ÉRD
See next page
ÜLLŐ
SZÁZHALOMBATTA
Ferihegy Airport

0 kilometres 15

0 miles 15

Budapest and Environs

Most of the city's tourist attractions are found on Castle Hill in Buda and in the central part of Pest. These are described on pages 66–151. Sights outside the centre, including day trips, are covered on pages 152–67. Two suggested walk routes are given on pages 168–73.

TATRAS
RUDOHORIE
Salgótarján
Miskolc
BÜKK
Eger
MÁTRA
Tisza
Szolnok
Kecskemét
Körös
Békéscsaba
ROMANIA
Szeged
Arad
Mures
Subotica

KEY

▢	Greater Budapest
–·–	Country boundary
✈	Airport
▭	Motorway
▬	Major road
—	Railway

0 kilometres 50

0 miles 25

SERBIA AND MONTENEGRO

Novi Sad

An aerial view over Castle Hill and central Budapest

Greater Budapest

BUDAPEST WAS FOUNDED in 1873 after the unification
of three separate towns: Buda, Óbuda and Pest
(see p32). The western part of the city stands on nine
hills, the highest of which is János (St John's) Hill *(see
p161)*. Greater Budapest is divided into 23 districts
numbered in the Roman numeral system *(see p223)*.
Districts I, II, III, XI, XII and XXII are found on the
western side of the Danube, District XXI on Csepel
Island, and the rest on the eastern side. Greater
Budapest is surrounded to the north and west by
beautiful recreational areas and the resort towns of
Szentendre, Visegrád and Esztergom. Located in the
Danube Bend, these towns are popular destinations
for day trips out of the city *(see pp164–7)*.

Vác
DUNAKESZI
FÓT
MOGYORÓD
E71 M3
Miskolc
Mogyoródi-patak
GÖDÖLLŐ
Gödöllő
Rákos-
palota
Hungaroring
▲ BOLNOKA
KEREPES
XV
Újpalota
Szilas-patak
CSÖMÖR
KISTARCSA
KÜDŐI-HEGY ▲
Pest-
újhely
Árpádföld
NAGYTARCSA
XIV
Zugló
Rákos-
szentmihály
XVI
Cinkota
Sashalom
Mátyásföld
PÉCEL
Józsefvárosi
pu.
X
Rákos-patak
Rákosliget
Kőbánya
Kőbánya-kertváros
Rákos-
keresztúr
XVII
Rákoscsaba
Jászberény
31
XIX
Erzsébettelep
Rákoshegy
Rákoskert
Kispest
XX
Pesterzsébet
✈ 1
Ferihegy Airport
✈ 2
ECSER
Pestszentlőrinc
XVIII
E60 4
Debrecen
Soroksár
Pestszentimre
VECSÉS
XXIII
Ráckevei-Dunaág
GYÁL
Gyáli-patak
E75 M0
E75 M5
DUNAHARASZTI
51
50
Baja
Kecskemét
Szeged

KEY

■	Central Budapest
□	Greater Budapest
□	Outer suburbs
✈	Airport
🚉	Train station
🚌	Coach station
	Motorway
■	Major road
	Minor road
	Railway

Central Budapest

Detail on the Stock Exchange

THE CENTRE OF TOWN includes Castle Hill (district I) on the western bank of the Danube and districts V, VI, VII, VIII and IX of Pest on the river's eastern bank, bounded by the city's original tram line. The Roman numerals denote the official administrative districts *(see p223)*. For the purposes of this guide, the centre is divided into six areas. Each area has its own chapter containing a selection of sights that convey its character and history. Sights on the outskirts of the city, and suggested day trips and walks, are covered in separate chapters.

Calvinist Church
Situated close to the Danube, this church is distinguished by its eye-catching, poly-chromatic roof (see p100).

Royal Palace
The Royal Palace has been destroyed and painstakingly rebuilt many times. It was last meticulously reconstructed after World War II, to the form that the Habsburgs had given it (see pp70–71).

Liberation Monument
This statue of a woman holding aloft the palm of victory was created by the Hungarian sculptor Zsigmond Kisfaludi Stróbl. Situated in a park on Gellért Hill, the monument is visible from all over the city. It is now one of the symbols of Budapest (see p92).

NORTH OF THE CASTLE

CASTLE DISTRICT

GELLÉRT HILL AND TABÁN

0 metres   500
0 yards   500

Parliament
This magnificent building hosts the sessions of the National Assembly. It is also the location of Hungary's most important government offices, including those of the prime minister (see pp108–9).

KEY

▪	Major sight
Ⓜ	Metro station
⚓	River boat boarding point
🅿	Parking
ⓘ	Tourist information
🚓	Police
✝	Church
✡	Synagogue

Váci Street
This pedestrianized street is a banking centre as well as a shopping venue with souvenir shops, cafés and pubs (see p127).

THE HISTORY OF BUDAPEST

AS EARLY AS THE Palaeolithic era, there were settlements in the area of Budapest: the narrowing of the Danube made the crossing of the river easy at this particular spot. In around AD 100, the Romans established the town of Aquincum here. Their rule lasted until the early 5th century AD, when the region fell to Attila the Hun. It was subsequently ruled by the Goths, the Longobards and, for nearly 300 years, by the Avars.

The ancestors of modern Hungarians, the Magyars, migrated from the Urals and arrived in the Budapest region in 896. They were led by Prince Árpád, whose dynasty ruled until the 13th century. At the turn of the first millennium, St István, whose heathen name was Vajk, accepted Christianity for the Hungarians. As their first crowned king, István I also laid the basis of the modern Hungarian state.

It was Béla IV who, in 1247, after the Mongol invasion, moved the capital to Buda. Much of the expansion of Buda took place under kings from the dynasty of the Angevins. Buda reached a zenith during the reign of Mátyás Corvinus in the 15th century, but further development was hindered by the advancing Turks, who took the region and ruled Buda for 150 years.

Crest of the Hunyadis

Liberation by the Christian armies resulted in the submission of the country as a whole to the Habsburgs. They suppressed all nationalist rebellions, but at the same time took care of economic development. Empress Maria Theresa and Archduke Joseph, the emperor's governor, made particular contributions to the modernization of both Buda and Pest. Yet, the slow pace of reforms led to an uprising in 1848, which was brutally crushed by Franz Joseph I. Compromise in 1867 and the creation of an Austro-Hungarian Empire stimulated economic and cultural life once more. Soon after, in 1873, Buda and Pest were united to create the city of Budapest.

Following World War I, the monarchy fell and Hungary lost two thirds of its territory. The desire to regain this contributed to its support of Germany in World War II. However, Budapest was taken by Russian troops in 1945 and large sections of it levelled. Under the subsequent Communist rule, the popular uprising of 1956 was ruthlessly suppressed by Soviet tanks but it initiated a crisis that shook the regime. Free elections took place in 1990, resulting in the victory of the democratic opposition, and the emergence of a new bourgeoisie.

Dating from 1686, when the Turks were expelled, this map shows the fortified towns of Pest and Buda

◁ Gyula Benczúr's *The Baptism of Vajk*, displayed in the Hungarian National Gallery *(see pp74–7)*

The City's Rulers

IN THE 13TH CENTURY, Béla IV built a castle in Buda and designated the town as his new capital. Until that time, the Árpád dynasty, the first family of Hungarian kings, had ruled their domain from elsewhere. When, at the beginning of the 14th century, there were no male heirs to the Árpád throne, Hungary began a long period during which it was mainly ruled by foreign kings including the French Angevins and the Polish Jagiełłos. Under Mátyás Corvinus, a great Hungarian king, Buda became one of Europe's most impressive cities. The Habsburgs, while suppressing national insurrections, rebuilt Buda and Pest after the devastation left by the Turks, adding fine pieces of architecture.

1440–44
Władysław (Ulászló) I
of Poland

1301–5
Wenceslas II of Bohemia

1541–66
Sultan Süleyman,
"the Magnificent"

1385–6
Charles II
of Durazzo

1490–1516
Władysław
(Ulászló) II

1386–95
Maria
(crowned)

1526–64
Ferdinand I

1272–90
Ladislas IV,
"the Cuman"

1437–9
Albert of
Austria

1270–72
István V

1307–42
Charles I Robert
of Anjou

1200	1300	1400	1500	
ÁRPÁDS	**ANGEVINS**		**JAGIEŁŁOS**	**OTTOMAN**
1200	1300	1400	1500	

1445–57
Ladislas V,
"Posthumus"

1290–1301
András III

1382–5
Maria (un-
crowned)

1235–70
Béla IV

1458–90
Mátyás I, "Corvinus"

1516–26
Louis II

1342–82
Louis I (Lajos),
"the Great"

1526–40
János I
Zápolyai

1564–76
Maximilian I

1305–7
Otto Wittelsbach
of Bavaria

1387–1437
Sigismund of Luxemburg
(initially as Maria's consort)

1576–1608
Rudolf I

1990–2000 President Árpád Göncz

1950–56
Secretary Mátyás Rákosi

1608–19
Mátyás II

1740–80
Maria Theresa

1637–57
Ferdinand III

1919–44
Admiral
Miklós Horthy

1848–9 Lajos Kossuth

1918–19
President
Mihály Károlyi

1705–11 Joseph I

1790–92
Leopold II

1835–48
Ferdinand V

	1700	1800	1900	2000
HABSBURGS			HEADS OF STATE	
	1700	1800	1900	2000

1711–40
Charles III

1792–1835
Franz I

1916–18
Charles IV

1657–1705
Leopold I

1946–8
President
Zoltán Tildy

2000
President
Ferenc Mádl

1948–50
President
Árpád
Szakasits

1780–90 Joseph II

1619–37
Ferdinand II

1848–1916
Franz Joseph I

1957–89
Secretary János Kádár

Early Settlers

Traces of settlements in the region by the Scythians and the Celtic Eravi date from around 400 BC onwards. In the 1st century AD, the Romans conquered the area as their province of Pannonia and soon established Aquincum *(see pp162–3)* within the limits of the modern city. Little evidence remains of the next rulers, the Huns, who were followed by the Goths and the Longobards. For nearly three centuries, starting in around AD 600, the Avars were pre-eminent. In 896, the Magyars swept into the region and laid claim to what would later become the Hungarian state.

Bronze Age vessel

Locator Map

■ *AD 300* ☐ *Today*

Bronze Decorations
In the 2nd century AD, Roman carts were often decorated with bronze plaques. This example depicts (from left): a satyr, Bacchus, god of wine and Pan, god of shepherds, under a palm frond. It was found in Somodor.

Workshops and shops, known as *tabernae*, were enclosed and faced onto the street.

The Sun God Mithras
The Persian god Mithras was adopted by the Eravi and his cult survived into the Roman period. This bronze image dates from 2nd–3rd centuries AD.

Reconstruction of the Macellum
This solidly built, square market hall was the focus for trade in the Roman town of Aquincum. At its centre was a courtyard with stalls, shops and workshops built around.

Timeline

10,000 BC Remains dating from the Palaeolithic era indicate the existence of a settlement in the Remeda Cave in Buda.

Silver Celtic coin dating from the 4th century BC

c. 50 BC Celtic Eravi settlement on Gellért Hill *(see pp88–9)*

c. AD 100 The town of Aquincum is established by the Romans

800 BC Tombs with Iron Age urns at Pünkösdfürdő.

400 BC Scythians in the region

10,000	5000	1000	AD 1

5000 BC Stone Age settlements in Talxina and along the Danube

Scythian ornamental gold stag

AD 89 Romans establish a permanent army camp in modern-day Óbuda

AD 106 Aquincum becomes the capital the Roman province of Lower Pannon

Sacrificial Altar
This altar, decorated with rams' heads, dates from the Neolithic era. It was found in Segedyna.

Shell Necklace
Dating from the Neolithic era, some 5,000 years ago, this necklace was found in Kisköre. It provides evidence of the early migration of tribes and their developed trade activities.

Butchers' stalls
faced onto the courtyard.

The rotunda
housed the weights and measures.

Silver Augur's Rod
This instrument was used by Roman priests for divination purposes. This one was found near Komárom, the site of a 3rd-century Roman town.

WHERE TO SEE THE EARLY CITY

Some quite considerable relics of the Roman legions that were once stationed here can be seen in modern Óbuda. The remains of an amphitheatre are near an unusual underground museum *(see p170)*, while magnificent mosaics adorn the Hercules Villa *(p171)*. Further up the Danube are the ruins of Aquincum itself *(pp162–3)*. Here visitors can wander around the remains of various buildings and enter a museum. On the Pest side of the river, just to the north of the Inner City Parish Church, there is a small, open-air section of remains from Contra Aquincum *(p122)*.

This Roman amphitheatre, one of two in Aquincum, indicates the status of the town.

The mosaic of Hercules and Diana, which survives at the Hercules Villa, was probably imported from Alexandria during the 2nd or 3rd century AD.

. 140–60 Two amphi-heatres are built to erve Aquincum's growing population

409 The Huns, under Attila, conquer Aquincum

c. 600–896 The Avars rule the region

Ornate earring from the 7th century AD

| 200 | 400 | 600 | 800 |

194 Aquincum is promoted to the status of a Roman colony

294 Contra Aquincum is founded on the eastern bank of the Danube

453 Collapse of the Huns' domination

Carving of the Sun God Mithras

896 Magyar (Hungarian) tribes take over Pannonia

The Árpád Dynasty

Hair clasp from the 9th century

AFTER A LONG JOURNEY beginning in the Urals region in Russia, nomadic tribes of Magyars eventually settled in Pannonia in AD 896. Following a period of internal disputes, the tribes made a blood-bonded alliance and chose one leader, Árpád. While Géza I made contact with missionaries, it was his son, István I, who accepted Christianity for his people. Their first crowned king, István organized the state according to the European, feudal model. Initially under the Árpáds, Esztergom *(see p164)* was the country's capital and later Székesfehérvár. The development of Buda, Pest and Óbuda began in the second half of the 12th century, but was interrupted by the Mongol invasion of 1241.

EXTENT OF THE CITY

☐ 1300   ☐ *Today*

Christ is depicted twice in the middle section of the coat; in each case He is larger than the surrounding figures.

Trinity of Hungarian Saints
The figures of three saints, King István, his son Imre and Bishop Gellért, are presented on this colourful triptych in the Chapel of St Imre in Mátyás Church (see pp82–3).

Figures of the Apostles

King Géza
Géza I, the father of King István, is represented on an enamel plaque decorating the Crown of the Árpáds.

CORONATION COAT
This silk coronation coat was made in 1031 for the Árpád kings. It has a pearl-beaded collar and is embroidered with the figures of Christ, Mary, the Apostles and the Prophets.

TIMELINE

c.900 Árpád settles on Csepel Island (in modern-day Budapest) and his brother Kurszán in Óbuda

Sword of an Árpád king

850	900	950	1000	1050

973 King Géza invites missionaries into the region

Sculpture of King István I by Imre Varga

1001 Coronation of István (Stephen) I

1046 Revolt by pagans and the martyr's death of Bishop Gellért, thrown in a barrel into the Danube

Crown of the Árpáds

This gold crown, ornamented with jewels, pearls and enamel, was created by joining two existing crowns. The lower, Byzantine one was known as the "Greek crown" and the upper one as the "Latin crown".

Bone artifacts

Bone items such as shepherds' staffs often had carved handles.

Figures of the Prophets

King István's coin

The first Hungarian coin, the denar, *was produced soon after AD 1000, during King István's reign.*

Tympanum

This 11th-century church tympanum, from Gyulafehérvár in modern Romania, is in the Hungarian National Gallery (see pp74–7).

WHERE TO SEE THE MEDIEVAL CITY

Only a few monuments survive from the Middle Ages. Among the notable ones that still remain are the crypts in Mátyás Church *(see pp82–3)*, and the elevations and cellars of some historic houses in the Castle District (a few of which are now converted into wine bars). The reconstructed lower chambers of the Royal Palace *(pp70–71)* and parts of its fortifications also date from the medieval era.

This 19th-century copy of the Romanesque Ják Chapel (see p143) reveals how the Árpáds adopted European styles.

Gothic niches can be seen by the entrances to many houses in the Old Town (see pp78–9).

1188 Béla III moves his headquarters to Óbuda and sets out on Frederick Barbarossa's crusade

1222 "Golden Bull" grants nobility privileges including tax exemption

1241 Mongol invasion

1247 Béla IV builds castle in Buda, which becomes capital of Hungary

1267 Béla IV announces new "Golden Bull"

1100	1150	1200	1250	1300

Magyar belt buckle dating from the 10th century

1244 The citizens of Pest are granted civic rights

1255 The citizens of Buda get civic rights

1301 Death of King András III, last king of the Árpád dynasty

Gothic and Renaissance Eras

Tabernacle of the Inner City Parish Church

A S A RESULT of the efforts of the Angevins and Sigismund of Luxembourg, the Gothic style reached Buda in the 14th century. Buda's palace and the summer palace in Visegrád were both extensively rebuilt. Shortly after defeat by the Turks at Varna, Hungary regained control of Belgrade and, for a while at least, halted their invasion. Mátyás Corvinus, the son of hetman János Hunyadi, the victor of Belgrade, became king. Under Mátyás's rule Hungary was turned into the greatest monarchy of Middle Europe, and, as a result of his marriage to Beatrice, a Neapolitan princess, the Renaissance began to blossom in the country.

EXTENT OF THE CITY

■ *c. 1480*   □ *Today*

Castellan Ferenc Sárffy was the commander of Győr Castle.

Illuminated letter from the Philostratus Codex
This illuminated letter depicts King Mátyás I after he took Vienna. Part of his own library, it is today housed in the Széchenyi National Library (see p72).

Hungarian soldier

Royal Medallion
An unknown master from Lombardy commemorated King Mátyás I in this marble silhouette dating from the 1480s.

Gold Seal
This gold seal, which belonged to King Mátyás I, is indicative of the affluence enjoyed by Hungary while he was on the throne.

Ulrik Czettrich, an officer of the royal household, discovered the body of Louis II on the marshy bank of the Csele river.

TIMELINE

Ciborium dating from the 14th century

1355 Óbuda's citizens gain civic rights	**1370** Louis I enters a political union and becomes king of Poland	**1385** Sigismund of Luxembourg marries Maria	
		1395 University established in Óbuda	
1350	**1375**	**1400**	**1425**
1342 Louis I, "the Great", becomes king		**1387–1437** Rule of Sigismund of Luxembourg. He enlarges the Royal Palace *(see pp70–71)*	
1335 Treaty on co-operation and succession signed by the kings of Hungary, Poland and Czechoslovakia in Visegrád		**1382** After death of Louis I, one daughter, Maria, becomes queen of Hungary and another, Jadwiga, queen of Poland	

Wine Cups

This pair of elaborate Renaissance wine cups, dating from the 16th century, is designed to fit together to form a covered receptacle.

Crest of King Mátyás Corvinus

Inscribed with the date 1470, this crest commemorates the building of significant additions to Mátyás Church (see pp82–3), which was then renamed after the king.

WHERE TO SEE THE GOTHIC AND RENAISSANCE CITY

The full bloom of the Gothic period took place in Hungary in the 14th century. Mátyás Church (see pp82–3) has portals that survive from this era. Renaissance art reached Hungary thanks to Italian masters brought by Mátyás's second wife, Beatrice. Both the Royal Palace (pp70–71) and the summer palace at Visegrád (p164) were outstanding pieces of Renaissance architecture. Since the storming of Buda by the Turks, only a few remnants of the former splendour have remained.

A royal chamber from the period of Angevin rule can be seen in the Budapest History Museum (see p72).

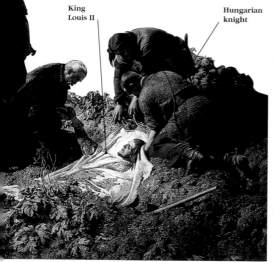

King Louis II

Hungarian knight

THE DISCOVERY OF LOUIS II'S BODY

At the Battle of Mohács, on 29 August 1526, King Louis II lost his life together with thousands of Hungarian and Polish knights. The tragic scene of the finding of his body was recreated by Bertalan Székely in 1859.

This portal of Mátyás Church dates from the 14th century. In the 19th century, a Neo-Gothic porch was built around it.

1440 Władysław III of Poland is Władysław I of Hungary

1456 Victory over Turks at the Battle of Belgrade

1473 *Chronica Hungarorum*, the first book to be published in Hungary, is printed by András Hess

1514 Peasant revolt under György Dózsa

Sword of Władysław II

1450	1475	1500	1525	1550

1458–1490 Reign of Mátyás Corvinus

1444 Władysław I is killed during the Battle of Varna

1478 Law is passed threatening landlords who fail to maintain their buildings with dispossession

1526 Defeat by the Turks at the Battle of Mohács. King Louis II perishes during the fighting

Shield of soldier in the army of Mátyás Corvinus

The Turkish Occupation

Ottoman plate

AFTER THE BATTLE OF MOHÁCS, the Turks razed Buda, but they temporarily turned their attention elsewhere and did not return to occupy it until 1541. When they then moved into the Royal Palace *(see pp70–71)*, Buda became the capital of Ottoman Hungary, while eastern Hungary and Transylvania were feudal suzerains. The Ottomans soon converted the city's churches, including Mátyás Church, into mosques and also built numerous Turkish baths *(see pp50–53)*. The Habsburgs tried relentlessly to recover Buda during this period. Their sieges destroyed the city progressively and when, in 1686, the Christian armies eventually recovered it the scene was one of devastation.

EXTENT OF THE CITY

▪ *1630*   ☐ *Today*

The Liberation of Buda in 1686
After a bloody siege, the Christian army, led by Prince Eugene of Savoy, entered Buda and liberated it from the Turks. This painting by Gyula Benczúr, dating from 1896, depicts the event.

Turkish fortress on Gellért Hill   **The Rudas and Rác Baths**

Ottoman Tombstones
A few inscribed Ottoman tomb-stones, topped by distinctive turbans, remain to this day in Tabán (see p94).

PEST AND BUDA IN 1617

Georgius Hurnagel's copperplate print shows the heavily-fortified towns of Pest and Buda in a period when much of Hungary was firmly under Turkish rule.

TIMELINE

1526–41 Turks conquer Buda on three occasions

1529 János I Szapolyai, the Hungarian monarch, pays homage to Sultan Süleyman I

1541–66 Reign of Sultan Süleyman I, "the Magnificent", who considered himself the Turkish king of Hungary

1602–3 Austrians, led by General Herman Russworm, fail in attempts to storm Pest and Buda

1525	1545	1565	1585	1605

1530–40 János I Szapolyai rebuilds Buda

1542 The Austrians lay siege to Buda

1594 Bálint Balassi, Hungary's first great lyric poet, is killed taking part in a battle against the Turks at Esztergom *(see p164)*

Austrian siege of Buda

Campaign Tent

Taken during the siege of Vienna in 1683, this Turkish leader's tent is decorated with appliqué work. It is on show in the Hungarian National Museum (see pp130–33).

Mátyás Church *(see pp82–3)* was converted into a mosque.

Ottoman Coat

This 16th-century leather coat was supposedly taken from the battlefield of Mohács (see p25).

Ottoman Jug

Dating from the 17th century, this copper vessel was found in Buda during the reconstruction of the Royal Palace (see pp70–71).

WHERE TO SEE THE TURKISH CITY

Almost all Turkish buildings were razed by their successors, the Habsburgs, during or after the recapture of the city. Churches which the Turks had used as mosques were converted back again, although some *mihrabs*, the niches pointing towards Mecca, were left. These can be seen in the Inner City Parish Church *(see pp124–5)* and in the Capuchin Church *(p100)*. Among the few wonderful examples of classical Ottoman architecture to survive are the Rudas, Rác *(p95)* and Király Baths, and the Tomb of Gül Baba, a Turkish dervish *(p101)*.

The Király Baths, built in the 16th century by Arshlan Pasha, remain an impressive Ottoman monument (see p101).

The Rudas Baths have an original Turkish dome covering their central chamber (see p93).

Ottoman tablet with calligraphy

1634 György I Rákóczi, prince of Transylvania, joins an anti-Habsburg alliance with France and Sweden

1684 Start of ultimately successful siege of Buda by the Austrians

Viennese sword dating from the 17th century

1625	1645	1665	1685

1624 Signing of the Treaty of Vienna

Gold five-ducat coin from 1603, showing the prince of Transylvania's crest

1648 Death of György I Rákóczi

1686 Christian troops enter Buda. The end of Turkish rule in Hungary

Habsburg Rule

Order created by Maria Theresa

IN ORDER TO GAIN CONTROL of Hungary, the Habsburgs encouraged foreign settlers, particularly Germans, to move into the country. This policy led to a national uprising in 1703–11, led by the prince of Transylvania, Ferenc II Rákóczi. Only in the second half of the 18th century, particularly under Empress Maria Theresa, did the reconstruction of Buda, Óbuda and Pest begin in earnest. This was accompanied by economic development and a further increase in the country's population. The university at Nagyszombat (now Trnava in the Slovak Republic) moved to Buda in 1777, and subsequently to Pest in 1784, and was an important factor in their expansion.

EXTENT OF THE CITY

☐ *1770* ☐ *Today*

Maria Theresa holds the infant Joseph, the successor to her throne.

The Return of the Crown to Buda *(1790)*
A vast ceremonial procession of commissioners marked the arrival in Hungary of royal insignias from Vienna, a sign of peace between the two countries.

Ferenc II Rákóczi
This fine portrait by Ádám Mányoki depicts Ferenc II Rákóczi, the leader of the national uprising of 1703–11 and a figure much loved by the Hungarian people.

"VITAM ET SANGUINEM"
In 1741, the Hungarian states swore on "life and blood" their loyalty to the Habsburg Empress Maria Theresa. This copperplate print by Joseph Szentpétery depicts the scene of the oath-taking.

TIMELINE

1687 Under Austrian pressure, the Hungarian parliament gives up its right to elect a king and accedes to the inheritance of the throne by the Habsburgs

1702 The Jesuits open a college and theological seminary

1703 The Prince of Transylvania, Ferenc II Rákóczi, leads a rebellion by the Hungarians against the Habsburgs

1729 The start of the reconstruction of Pest's suburbs

1690	1705	1720	1735

1689 Bubonic plague devastates the population of Buda and Pest

Royal postal carriage

1711 Suppression of Rákóczi's rebellion; a second bubonic plague decimates the city

1724 The population of Buda and Pest reaches 12,000 people

1723 Great Fire of Buda

Triple-jug of the Andrássy family

These silver jugs are joined by a miniature of the castle belonging to the Andrássy family, at what is now Krásna Hŭrka in the Slovak Republic.

Hungarian aristocrats

swear on their lives to protect Maria Theresa's throne.

Dress *(c. 1750)*

This dress, typical of Hungarian style with its corset which was tightened by golden cords, was worn by a lady from the noble Majtényi family.

Ferenc II Rákóczi's Chair

Richly upholstered, this graceful 18th-century chair from Regéc Castle is typical of the style of the period.

WHERE TO SEE THE HABSBURG CITY

Having taken Buda and Pest from the Turks in the late 17th century, the Habsburgs set about rebuilding them in the 18th century, mainly in the Baroque style. Famous buildings from this era include the Municipal Council Offices, St Anne's Church *(see pp102–3)*, St Elizabeth's Church *(p101)* and the University Church *(p139)*.

***St Anne's Church**, which was built between 1740–1805, astonishes visitors with its magnificent Baroque interior.*

***The Municipal Council Offices** in the heart of Pest have a portico decorated with allegorical figures by Johann Christoph Mader (see p127).*

5–71 Building of the
.sburg Royal Palace

The magnificent Habsburg Royal Palace

1788 First Hungarian newspaper, *Magyar Merkurius*, begins printing

A hussar, or soldier

1778 Roman remains are discovered in Óbuda

1750	1765	1780	1795

1752 A regular postal service operates between Buda and Vienna

1766 A floating bridge links Buda and Pest

1792 Convocation of parliament and the coronation of Franz I

46–57 Construction of the
hy Palace in Óbuda *(see p171)*

1777 University moves from Nagyszombat to Buda; later relocates to Pest

1784 Establishment of Ferenc Goldberger's textile factory in Óbuda

National Revival and the "Springtime of Revolutions"

Hungarian crest

THE DYNAMIC ECONOMIC development of Buda and Pest began at the start of the 19th century. Pest, in particular, benefited from favourable circumstances for the grain trade and became, in the Napoleonic Wars, an important centre for the Habsburg monarchy. A national revival and rekindling of cultural life took place after the Napoleonic Wars. The Hungarian National Museum and many other public and private buildings were built at this time. Yet, Hungarian reformers were hampered by the Viennese royal court and an uprising erupted in the spring of 1848. This rebellion was suppressed by the Habsburgs, with the help of the Russian army, and a period of absolutism followed.

EXTENT OF THE CITY

■ 1848   □ Today

Count György Andrássy, offered 10,000 forints towards the building of the Hungarian Academy of Sciences.

The Advance of the Hussars
In this watercolour, painted in 1850, Mór Than depicts fighting in the Battle of Tápióbicske of 1849. The Hungarian side was led by a Polish general, Henryk Dembiński.

The Great Flood
This bas-relief, made by Barnabás Holló in 1900, shows a heroic rescue by Count Miklós Wesselényi during the Great Flood of 1838.

THE FOUNDING OF THE ACADEMY

In 1825, István Széchenyi put up 60,000 forints towards the building of Hungarian Academy of Sciences *(see p114)*, a move which led to a national effort to collect funds for it. Barnabás Holló created this bas-relief depicting the major donors.

TIMELINE

1802 Count Ferenc Széchenyi donates collections which will form the basis for Széchenyi National Library *(see p72)* and Hungarian National Museum *(see pp130–33)*

1809 Royal court moves from Vienna to Buda as Napoleon advances. Despite his offer of Hungarian independence, the Hungarians back the Habsburgs

1817 First steamboat sails on Danube in the environs of Buda and Pest

| 1800 | 1805 | 1810 | 1815 | 1820 |

1808 Establishment of the Embellishment Commission, led by Governor Archduke Joseph

Boats on the Danube

Lajos Batthyány Eternal Flame
This lamp, designed by Móric Pogány, has burnt since 1926 in Liberty Square (see p110). It was there that the Austrians shot Lajos Batthyány, the first prime minister of liberated Hungary, on 6 October 1849.

Count István Széchenyi, an energetic force for change, is regarded as the one of the greatest Hungarians.

National Song
The 1848 uprising was sparked on 15 March when Sándor Petőfi recited his poem, Nemzeti Dal (National Song), outside the Hungarian National Museum.

WHERE TO SEE THE NEO-CLASSICAL CITY

In the early 19th century, the Embellishment Commission, set up by Archduke Joseph and led by architect János Hild, prepared a plan for the development of Pest in which its centre was redesigned on a pattern of concentric streets. Monumental Neo-Classical buildings were built here and to this day they form the heart and the character of this area. Structures to look for in particular include the Hungarian National Museum, the Chain Bridge and several houses located on József Nádor Square *(see p126).*

György Károlyi

***The Hungarian National Museum**, which was built in 1837, is among Hungary's finest examples of Neo-Classical architecture (see pp130–31).*

Buda and Pest in 1838
Seen here in the year before the construction of the Chain Bridge, the Danube was an important means of transport.

***The Chain Bridge**, the first permanent bridge over the Danube, was built by Adam Clark in 1839–49 (see p63).*

1825–48 Period of major projects: establishment of the Hungarian Academy of Sciences, Hungarian National Museum and National Theatre

Poet Sándor Petőfi (1823–49)

1840 Language Act: Hungarian takes over from Latin as the official language of the nation

15 March 1848 Uprising begins

1847 Death of Archduke Joseph, emperor's governor

1825	1830	1835	1840	1845

1830 István Széchenyi publishes his book, *On Credit*. It is seen as the manifesto for the fight for modern Hungary

The Great Flood

1838 Catastrophic Great Flood results in destruction of half of Pest's buildings

1846 First railway line in the city, linking Pest and Vác

1849 After stout resistance, the Russian army, under the command of General Ivan Paskievicz, suppresses uprising

Compromise and the Unification of Budapest

Maria Theresa

A FTER SUFFERING A DEFEAT by Prussia in 1866, the Habsburgs realized the necessity of reaching an agreement with Hungary and the Compromise brokered in 1867 proved to be of tremendous importance for the future of Buda and Pest. The option of uniting the two cities had been considered since the opening of the Chain Bridge in 1849. It eventually came about in 1873 and Budapest soon found itself among Europe's fastest growing metropolises. In 1896, Városliget was the focal point for Hungary's Millennium Celebrations *(see p142)*.

EXTENT OF THE CITY
▨ *1873*   ☐ *Today*

The Citadel *(see p92)* on Gellért Hill

Castle District

Hungarian Wine Cup
This 19th-century wine cup is embellished with the Hungarian crest, which incorporates the Crown of the Árpáds (see p23).

Ferenc Deák
(1803–76)
A great statesman, Deák was an advocate of moderate reforms. He argued persuasively in favour of accepting the Compromise reached with the Habsburgs in 1867.

Today's Boráros tér, where goods were once traded.

Decorative Pipe *(1896)*
Made in the year of Hungary's Millennium Celebrations, this pipe of "heavenly peace" includes figures of the Árpád kings and Emperor Franz Joseph.

TIMELINE

1854 Martial law ends five years after 1848–9 uprising

1856 Tunnel *(see p100)* built by Adam Clark under Castle Hill
Entrance to the Tunnel

1875 Opening of the Franz Liszt Academy of Music *(see p129)*, with the composer as its principal

| 1850 | 1860 | 1870 | 1880 |

1859 Synagogue on Dohány utca *(see p134)* completed

1864 Opening of the Great Market Hall *(see p203)*

1873 The unification of Buda, Óbuda and Pest as one city, with a total of 300,000 inhabitants

1867 Compromise with Austria, giving Hungary independence in its internal affairs. Creation of the Dual Monarchy; Emperor Franz Joseph accepts the Hungarian crown

Monument to Hungarian Soldiers Killed in World War I
This bas-relief, by János Istók, commemorates the dead of World War I, in which Hungary fought on the German side. It is located next to the main entrance to the Servite Church (see p128).

"Handcuff" Bracelet
Following the defeat of the national uprising of 1848–9, Hungarians sought to symbolize their oppression even in pieces of jewellery.

WHERE TO SEE THE HISTORICIST CITY

Historicism had a profound influence on the form of the rapidly developing metropolis at this time. A wonderful example of the style is the Hungarian Academy of Sciences. Among others are Parliament (see pp108–9), St Stephen's Basilica (pp116–17), the Museum of Fine Arts (pp146–7), the New York Palace (p129) and many of the buildings that stand on Andrássy Street (p144).

***The Hungarian Academy of Sciences** is housed in this fine Neo-Renaissance palace dating from 1864 (see p114).*

***St Stephen's Basilica** was built over a period of 60 years by three architects. It was finished in 1905 (see pp116–17).*

TRADING ON THE PEST EMBANKMENT
Completed in 1887, this painting by Antal Ligeti shows the Pest embankment at a time when the city was booming. Manufactured goods and grain were sent along the Danube for sale in Germany and the Balkans.

1894 Body of Lajos Kossuth (see p106) is returned from Turin

1904 Grand opening of Parliament (see pp108–9)

Congress Hall in Parliament

1916 Franz Joseph dies and Charles IV becomes king of Hungary

| 1890 | 1900 | 1910 | 1920 |

1896 First metro line and several museums opened

1909 Airport opened in Rákos, now Kőbánya

1900 With a population of 773,000, Budapest is Europe's fastest growing city

1914 Hungary enters World War I on the German side

1918 Abdication of Charles IV marks end of the Austro-Hungarian Empire

Modern Budapest

Poster for Unicum liqueur *(see p193)*

Hungary paid a high price for its alliances first with Austria and later with Nazi Germany. Following defeat in both World Wars, the country had lost a large portion of its territory. As a result of the Yalta Agreement of 1945, it then found itself within the Soviet-controlled zone of Europe. Stalinism took on a particularly ruthless form here and led to the 1956 Uprising, which was brutally put down by Soviet tanks on the streets of Budapest. Efforts towards reform, undertaken by János Kádár, brought some changes but political opposition was not tolerated. In 1989, the Communists were ousted and Hungary at last regained control of its own affairs.

1944 Efforts to withdraw from World War II end with German troops entering the country. A ghetto is established in Budapest and the extermination of Hungarian Jews begins. As the Russian army approaches the city, all bridges across the Danube are blown up

1945 After a siege lasting six weeks, the Russian army takes Budapest

1946 Proclamation of Republic of Hungary. Smallholders' Party wins elections

1919 Communists take over government and declare the Hungarian Soviet Republic

1922 Reopening of the State Opera House *(see pp118–19)* after World War I

1928 Budapest is a free port on Danube

1941 Hungary enters World War II on Germany's side

1939 Hungary neutral at beginning of World War II. Accepts refugees after capitulation of Poland

1937 Sixth and last visit of author Thomas Mann

1947 After falsification of election results, Communists control the whole country

1957 János Kádár is first secretary of Hungarian Socialist Workers' Party

1949 Stalinist terror prevails. Cardinal Mindszenty *(see p111)* goes on trial. László Rajk, secret police chief, sentenced to death by Moscow loyalists

1920	1930	1940	1950

1920	1930	1940	1950

1935 Tabán *(see p94)* levelled and transformed into a park

1938 Eucharistic Congress

1953 The national football team beats England 6–3 at Wembley

1925 Radio Budapest broadcasts its first programme

1948 Mátyás Rákosi leads Hungarian Socialist Workers' Party, created by Communists

1919 Admiral Miklós Horthy enters Budapest; many killed in the period of "White Terror". Horthy becomes regent

1945–1 August 1946 Monetary reform. Banknotes valued at one billion pengő are printed during rampant inflation. There is not enough room for all the zeros to be shown on the notes

1918 Democratic revolution; Hungary declared a republic. Mihály Károlyi selected as the country's first president

1956 National uprising is suppressed through Soviet intervention

1958 The leader of the 1956 Uprising, Prime Minister Imre Nagy, is executed

1960–66 Rebuilding of Castle District *(see pp68–85)*, including Royal Palace, and the Danube bridges

October 1989 Republic of Hungary is proclaimed once more. The national emblem is changed

September 1989 Hungary opens its borders to allow refugees to flee from East Germany to the West

February 1989 Round-table talks between opposition parties and ruling socialist government

1991 Warsaw Pact is dissolved. Russian army leaves Hungary

1994 Elections won by Socialist Hungarian Party. Coalition government led by Gyula Horn

1998 Elections won by Viktor Orbán of the Citizens' Party

2002 Elections won by Péter Medgyessy of the Hungarian Socialist Party. Imre Kertész receives a Nobel prize for Literature

1964 The Elizabeth Bridge *(see p63)* reopens to traffic, having been totally reconstructed

1981 Director István Szabó receives an Oscar for his film *Mefisto*

2004 Hungary becomes member of the EU

1970 1980 1990 2000

1970 1980 1990 2000

1968 Introduction of new economic system known as "goulash-Communism"

1987 UNESCO places the historic Castle District and the Banks of the Danube on its list of world monuments

June 1989 Ceremonial funeral for Imre Nagy and rehabilitation for other leaders of 1956 Uprising

1990 The Democratic Hungarian Forum wins free elections. József Antall becomes the first prime minister to be elected in a democratic process; Árpád Göncz is elected president

1993 Pope John Paul II visits Hungary

1970 Opening of a new metro line

1991 Václav Havel, József Antall and Lech Walesa sign an agreement in Visegrád *(see p164)* between Czechoslovakia, Hungary and Poland

BUDAPEST AT A GLANCE

O FTEN DESCRIBED as the "Little Paris of Middle Europe", Budapest is famous not only for the monuments reflecting its own 1,000-year-old culture, but also for the relics of others who settled here. Remains from both Roman occuption, and, much later, rule by the Turks can still be seen in the city. After Turkish rule, union with Austria had a particular influence on the city's form and style. Descriptions of nearly 150 places of interest can be found in the *Area by Area* section of the book. However, to help you make the most of your stay, the following 20 pages are a guide to the best Budapest has to offer. Museums and galleries, churches and synagogues, palaces and historic buildings, baths and pools are presented, together with the influence of Secession in the city. Each sight is is cross-referenced to its main entry. Below are the sights not to be missed.

BUDAPEST'S TOP TEN SIGHTS

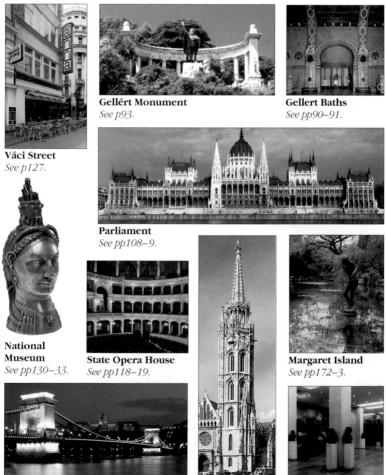

Gellért Monument
See p93.

Gellert Baths
See pp90–91.

Váci Street
See p127.

Parliament
See pp108–9.

National Museum
See pp130–33.

State Opera House
See pp118–19.

Margaret Island
See pp172–3.

Danube and Chain Bridge
See p62.

Mátyás Church
See pp82–3.

National Gallery
See pp74–7.

◁ The Neo-Renaissance façade of the City Council Chamber *(see p138)* in the centre of Pest

Budapest's Best: Museums and Galleries

U NLIKE MANY OTHER European cities – such as
Paris with the Louvre and Madrid with the
Prado – Budapest does not have a museum
founded from a royal treasury because Hungary
was for so long ruled by foreign powers. In
the early 19th century, however, the modern
aristocracy, backed by an increasingly affluent
middle class, began to take an interest in pre-
serving historic objects for the nation. Today,
there are over 60 museums and galleries in
Budapest, ranging from those with collections
of international significance to others of much
more local interest. For more information on
museums and galleries see pages 40–41.

Museum of Military History
*This museum has interesting
displays illustrating the history of
Hungarian weaponry.*

Hungarian
National Gallery
*The Hungarian art
displayed here dates
from the Middle Ages
right through to the
20th century. The
Yawning Journeyman
(1868), by the great
Mihály Munkácsy, is
among the highlights
of the collection.*

North of
the Castle

DANUBE

Castle District

Budapest History Museum
*This Gothic work is one
of the medieval treasures
of the Budapest History
Museum. The oldest ex-
hibits are located in the
original, lower-floor
rooms of the Renais-
sance Royal Palace.*

Gellért Hill
and Tabán

| 0 metres | 500 |
| 0 yards | 500 |

**Semmelweis Museum of
Medical History**
*Doctor Ignác Semmelweis,
famous for his discovery of the cure for
puerperal fever, was born in 1818 in the
house where the museum is now situated.*

Ethnographical Museum

Among the exhibits at this museum illustrating the material culture of the Hungarians is this jug, dating from 1864, made by György Mantl. There are also impressive displays concerning tribal societies in other parts of the world.

Museum of Fine Arts

The wonderful Portrait of a Man *(c.1565), by Paolo Veronese, is one of many Old Masters in this splendid collection of paintings and sculpture.*

Around Parliament

Around Városliget

Central Pest

Jewish Museum

Located in several rooms beside the Great Synagogue, this museum covers the Holocaust in this country and displays religious objects.

Hungarian National Museum

Beautiful frescoes by Károly Lotz and Mór Than decorate the elegant staircase of Budapest's oldest museum.

Museum of Applied Arts

Precious ceramics, porcelain and furnishings are housed in a building that is itself a work of art, surmounted by a magnificent, oriental-style dome.

Exploring the Museums and Galleries

Crest of the
Museum of
Commerce

MOST OF the city's museums and galleries are located in historic buildings. These include the spacious chambers of the restored Royal Palace, which in the 1970s and 1980s were designated as the premises of several museums, including the Hungarian National Gallery. The largest museums – including the Hungarian National Museum and Budapest History Museum – also stage temporary exhibitions that are popular with both locals and tourists.

Sculpture of Imre Varga at the gallery named after him *(see p171)*

HUNGARIAN PAINTINGS AND SCULPTURE

THERE ARE TWO important venues that should be on the itinerary of anyone interested in viewing the finest examples of Hungarian art.

At the **Hungarian National Gallery**, seven chronological sections present paintings and sculpture dating from the Middle Ages up until modern times. The sequence begins in the Lapidarium, where fragments of recovered medieval stone sculptures from the castles of the first Hungarian kings are exhibited.

As a rule, very few examples of Gothic and Renaissance art survive in Budapest because of the pillage inflicted by the Turks during their rule. However, a fine collection of altar retables from the 15th and 16th centuries are on display

in the Hungarian National Gallery. In the 19th century, Hungarian painting developed and flourished, at the same time reflecting all the major international modern art movements. The Hungarian style can be seen particularly in the works of Pál Szinyei-Merse, Mihály Munkácsy and László Paál. For sculpture, meanwhile, the main names to look out for are István Ferenczy, Zsigmond Kisfaludi Stróbl and Imre Varga.

It is portraits, rather than paintings and sculpture, that are shown at the **Hungarian National Museum**. These provide a fascinating insight into the country's history.

The **Vasarely Museum** has a collection of 300 works by Hungarian-born artist Victor Vasarely. He moved to Paris in 1930 and became famous as one of the main exponents of the Op Art movement.

EUROPEAN PAINTINGS AND SCULPTURE

MASTERPIECES BY the finest European artists, from medieval times to the modern day, are also divided between two museums in Budapest.

The **Museum of Fine Arts** has a magnificent collection of Italian paintings, dating from the 14th century up to the Baroque period, by masters such as Titian, Antonio Correggio, Paolo Veronese, Giambattista Tiepolo and Jacopo Tintoretto. However, it is the *Esterházy Madonna* (1508) by Raphael, that is the jewel of the Italian collection. Equally splendid is the exhibition of Spanish paintings, which is one of the largest in the world. Works by Goya include *The Water Carrier* (c.1810). There are seven canvases by El Greco and others by Francisco de Zurbarán and Bartolomé Esteban Murillo. Other galleries within the museum represent artists of the Netherlands and Germany, as well as British, French and Flemish masters. The museum also owns more than 100,000 drawings and engravings by the Old Masters, while its modern art collection includes some notable works.

Modern European paintings can also be viewed in the **Ludwig Museum Budapest-Museum of Contemporary Art**. All the canvases belong to the Peter Ludwig Foundation of Germany. Highly prized works here include two paintings by Pablo Picasso, *Mother and Child* and *Musketeer*.

Pablo Picasso's *Musketeer* (1967), in the Ludwig Collection

The Jewish Museum, located
beside the Great Synagogue

HISTORY

THE HISTORY of Budapest,
and that of Hungary as a
whole, is illustrated in several
museums. Relics from the
Roman era can be found at
the **Aquincum Museum** and
at a handful of museums,
including the **Roman Camp
Museum**, in Óbuda.

The most important national
historic treasures are housed
in the **Hungarian National
Museum**. The Coronation
Mantle, dating back to the
11th century, is included in
this collection.

Medieval seals and Gothic
statuary are among the exhibits at **Budapest History
Museum**. At the **Museum of
Military History**, displays
chart various Hungarian strug-
gles for liberty, including the
1956 Uprising *(see p34)*.

The **Jewish Museum** has a
room covering the Holocaust,
as well as many ritual objects.
The collection of the **Lutheran
Museum**, situated next to the
Lutheran Church, includes a
copy of Martin Luther's will.

MUSIC

TWO OF the museums
featured in this
book are dedicated
to internationally re-
nowned composers:
the **Franz Liszt
Museum** and the
**Zoltán Kodály
Museum**. In each
case, the apartment
where the composer

lived and worked is the
setting, and visitors can see
the musical instruments that
they played, scores, photographs and correspondence.

A more general view of
Hungarian music is on offer
at the **Museum of Musical
History**, located in a Baroque
palace. Displays feature the
development of instruments,
folk music and the musical
scene of the 18th and 19th
centuries; a special section is
dedicated to Béla Bartók.

ETHNOGRAPHY AND ORIENTAL CRAFTS

LAVISH FOLK costumes,
as well as many other
everyday items that be-
longed to the people of
the region, can be viewed
in the beautiful interiors
of the **Ethnographical
Museum**. The museum
also has a section that
focuses on the primitive
tribes of Africa, America
and, particularly, Asia. It is
in Asia that the Hungarians
seek their roots as it is from
there that the Magyars are
thought to have come.

This fascination with
the Orient has led to
the foundation of two
other museums display-
ing Eastern artifacts. The
György Rath Museum has
items such as fans and combs
from China and Japan, while
the **Ferenc Hopp Museum**
has assorted Indian objects.

DECORATIVE ARTS

HOUSED IN an extraordinary
building designed by
Ödön Lechner *(see p56)*, the
Museum of Applied Arts

Roling pin at
the Museum
of Commerce

gives an impressive
overview of the devel-
opment of crafts
from the Middle
Ages onwards.
Meissen porce-
lain is exhibited
alongside oriental
carpets and Hungarian
pieces. The display re-
lating to the Secession
(see pp54–7) is striking
and there are usually
also temporary shows.

Beer mug at the
Lutheran Museum

The decorative arts, paintings
and architectural plans that
are gathered at the **Kiscelli
Museum** give a flavour of life
in Budapest in the 18th and
19th centuries. Other exhibits
in this varied museum include
an antique printing press.

SPECIALIST MUSEUMS

ANYONE INTERESTED in the
history of gastronomy
should head for one of
Budapest's more unusual
museums, the **Museum of
Commerce and Catering**.
It boasts a varied selection
of exhibits connected
with the food trade.

The **Semmelweis
Museum of Medical
History** explores the
work of a doctor called
Ignác Semmelweis, who
discovered the cure for
puerperal fever. This
affliction had previously
been a serious threat for
women who had recently
given birth. The **Golden
Eagle Pharmacy Museum**
is situated in a building that
first opened as a pharmacy
in 1681. Many original
fixtures are intact and
pharmaceutical exhibits
are displayed.

Railway enthusiasts
will appreciate the **Transport
Museum** with its enormous
collection of model trains.

WHERE TO FIND THE MUSEUMS AND GALLERIES

Aquincum Museum *pp162–3*
Budapest History Museum *p72*
Ethnographical Museum *p110*
Franz Liszt Museum *p144*
Jewish Museum *pp134*
Hungarian National Gallery
pp74–7
Hungarian National Museum
pp130–33
Kiscelli Museum *p170*
Ludwig Museum Budapest *p73*
Museum of Applied Arts
pp136–7
Museum of Commerce and
Catering *p84*
Museum of Fine Arts *pp146–9*
Museum of Military History *p85*
Semmelweis Museum of Medical
History *p95*

Budapest's Best: Churches and Synagogues

THERE ARE VERY FEW medieval and Renaissance churches still standing in Budapest. This is mainly due to the fact that the Turks, during their 150-year rule, turned all churches into mosques, which were later destroyed during the attacks on Buda and Pest by the Christians. The reconstruction of old churches and the building of new ones started in the late 17th century, hence the prevalence of Baroque and Neo-Classical styles.

Capuchin Church
Two Turkish windows remain from the time when this church was used as a mosque, alongside fragments of its medieval walls.

St Anne's Church
Built in the mid-18th century, this is one of the most beautiful Baroque churches in the city. The joined figures of St Anne and Mary decorate the centre of its façade.

North of the Castle

Castle District

DANUBE

Mátyás Church
Romanesque and Gothic styles are both evident in the coronation church of the Hungarian kings. The Neo-Gothic altar dates from the 19th century.

Gellért Hill and Tabán

Cave Church
In the rocky interior of St István's Cave, on the south side of Gellért Hill, the priests of the Pauline order established a church in 1926. It was designed to imitate the holy grotto at Lourdes.

| 0 metres | 500 |
| 0 yards | 500 |

St Stephen's Basilica
A bas-relief by Leó Feszler, representing the Virgin Mary surrounded by Hungarian saints, decorates the main tympanum of St Stephen's Basilica. This imposing church was built between 1851–1905.

Lutheran Church
This Neo-Classical church was completed by Mihály Pollack in 1808. The impressive façade was added half a century later by József Hild.

Around Parliament

Around Városliget

Central Pest

Great Synagogue
Two Moorish-style minarets, each topped by an onion-shaped dome, dominate the exterior of the largest synagogue in Europe.

Franciscan Church
The magnificent 19th-century paintings that decorate the interior of this Baroque church are by Károly Lotz.

Inner City Parish Church
Dating from 1046, this church is Pest's oldest building. A figure of St Florian, the patron saint of fire fighters, was placed on the wall beside the altar after the church survived the great fire of 1723.

Exploring the Churches and Synagogues

MOST OF THE CITY'S churches are found around the centres of Buda and Pest. Only a few sacred buildings of architectural interest are situated on the outskirts of the city. The greatest period of construction took place in the 18th century, after the final expulsion of the Turks. Another phase occurred in the second half of the 19th century, producing two of Budapest's grandest places of worship: St Stephen's Basilica and the Great Synagogue. Religious buildings were neglected after World War II, but thanks to restoration some have now regained their former splendour.

Detail on St Elizabeth's Church

Reconstructed Gothic window of the Church of St Mary Magdalene

MEDIEVAL

BOTH **Mátyás Church** and the **Inner City Parish Church** date originally from the reign of Béla IV in the 13th century. Glimpses of their original Romanesque style can be seen, although each church was subsequently rebuilt in the Gothic style. After being sacked by the Turks in 1526,

Mátyás Church was given a Baroque interior by the Jesuits who had at that time taken it over. Finally, the church was returned to a likeness of its medieval character between 1874–96, when all Baroque elements were systematically removed and it was given a Neo-Gothic shape.

The **Church of St Mary Magdalene**, built in 1274 in the Gothic style, was almost completely destroyed in 1945. All that remains intact today is the 15th-century tower with its two chapels. A Gothic window has also been rebuilt.

St Michael's Church, founded in the 12th century on Margaret Island, was completely destroyed by the Turks. However, in 1932 it was reconstructed from its original Romanesque plans.

BAROQUE

IN THE 18TH CENTURY, 17 churches were built in Pest, Buda and Óbuda, all of them in the Baroque style. The influence of the Italian architectural school is visible in many of them, although only

University Church was built by an Italian architect, Donato Allio. Under Habsburg rule, the leading architects working in the city, András Meyerhoffer, Mátyás Nepauer and Kristóf Hamon, often chose to follow Austrian examples.

University Church and **St Anne's Church** are generally considered to be the most beautiful buildings in the city dating from this era. The former astonishes visitors with its beautifully carved stalls and pulpit, and with the paintings by Johann Bergl adorning its vaults. St Anne's Church has a magnificent Baroque façade and reveals the influence of southern German Baroque in its oval floor plan. Inside, there is a lavish altar and pulpit designed by Károly Bebó.

The **Franciscan Church**, which is situated in the centre of Budapest and dates from 1758, has a wide Baroque nave and a main altar created by Antal Grassalkovich.

The interior of the Servite Church (1725), with its Baroque altar

SPIRES AND DOMES

The Gothic spire belonging to the Church of St Mary Magdalene and the Neo-Gothic spire of Mátyás Church are among Budapest's main landmarks. The twin Baroque towers of St Anne's Church and the soaring spire of the Calvinist Church rise above the Danube in Buda. On the Pest side, the dome of St Stephen's Basilica and the minarets of the Great Synagogue dominate.

Gothic spire of the Church of St Mary Magdalene

Baroque towers of St Anne's Church

Neo-Gothic spire of the Calvinist Church

NEO-CLASSICAL AND HISTORICIST

I N 1781, JOSEPH II passed an edict permitting the building of Protestant churches. The city already had many Catholic churches and Protestant communities now started to build their own places of worship in the prevailing style of the time, Neo-Classicism.

One of the first to go up was the **Lutheran Church**, on Deák Ferenc tér, completed in 1808 by Mihály Pollack, a gifted master of Neo-Classical architecture. The white, ascetic interior of the church, with its two-floor gallery, was ideally suited to the nature of this place of worship. The majesty and simplicity of the Neo-Classical style corresponded with the more austere nature of Protestant belief. József Hild, another master of the style, later extended the church. He added the portico with its Doric columns, linking the church with the presbytery and a school. The complex as a whole is one of the best examples of Neo-Classical architecture in Budapest.

On a more modest scale is the **Calvinist Church**, built in the Neo-Gothic style between 1893–6.

When plans for it were drawn up by József Hild in 1845, **St Stephen's Basilica** was intended to be the pinnacle of Neo-Classical architecture. However, several delays, including the collapse of its dome at one point, meant

Baptismal font at the Lutheran Church

that the realization of the original design was impossible. Following Hild's death in 1867, Miklós Ybl continued the project. He departed from Hild's plan, incorporating Renaissance-style features. The Basilica was finally completed by a third architect, József Kauser, in 1905.

LATE 19TH- AND 20TH-CENTURY

T HE TWO MOST stunning synagogues in Budapest were designed by Viennese architects in the second half of the 19th century.

Ludwig Förster constructed the **Great Synagogue** in Byzantine-Moorish style in 1859 and Otto Wagner, an important Secession architect (*see pp54–7*), realized one of his first projects in 1872. This was the **Orthodox Synagogue** on Rumbach utca, which also incorporated Moorish ideas.

Closely linked to the Secession style is the Hungarian National Style, based on an idiosyncratic combination of ethnic motifs and elements from folk art. This style is most visible in two churches by Hungarian architects. Ödön Lechner, the originator of the Hungarian National Style, completed **Kőbánya Parish Church**, on the outskirts of Budapest, in 1900. Meanwhile, Aladár Árkay built **Városliget Calvinist Church** in 1913. These two churches display a striking combination

Carvings and an inscription adorning the Great Synagogue

of colourful ceramics, Eastern-style ornamentation and also Neo-Gothic elements.

WHERE TO FIND THE CHURCHES AND SYNAGOGUES

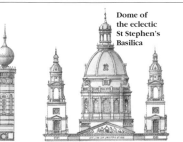

Moorish-style towers of the Great Synagogue

Dome of the eclectic St Stephen's Basilica

Budapest's Best: Palaces and Historic Buildings

Detail on the façade of Károly Palace

BUDAPEST boasts historic buildings and palaces in a broad range of architectural styles. The majority represent the Neo-Classicism, Historicism and Secession of the 19th and early 20th centuries, when a dynamic development of the capital took place. All but a few Gothic and Renaissance details were lost in the destruction of Buda and Pest by Christian troops in 1686, but some examples of its Baroque heritage remain. This map gives some highlights, with a more detailed look on pages 48–9.

Royal Palace
This palace has a turbulent history dating back to the 13th century. Its present form, however, reflects the opulence of the 19th century. Today the palace houses some of the city's finest museums.

North of the Castle

Castle District

DANUBE

Houses on Vienna Gate Square
This charming row of four houses was built in the late 18th and early 19th centuries on the ruins of medieval dwellings. The houses are adorned with decorative motifs in the Baroque, Rococo and Neo-Classical styles.

Gellért Hill and Tabán

Sándor Palace
The original friezes that decorated this 19th-century palace were recreated by Hungarian artists as part of its restoration. The palace is now the headquarters of the President of the Republic of Hungary.

Várkert Casino
This Neo-Renaissance pavilion was built by Miklós Ybl (see p119) as a pump house for the Royal Palace. It now houses the luxurious Várkert Casino.

Hungarian Academy of Science
The façade of the academy is adorned with statues by Emil Wolff and Miklós Izsó, symbolizing major fields of knowledge: law, natural history, mathematics, philosophy, linguistics and history.

Gresham Palace
Now housing a Four Seasons Hotel, this splendid example of Secession design was built in 1905–7 by Zsigmond Quittner.

0 metres 500
0 yards 500

Around Parliament

Around Városliget

Central Pest

Pallavicini Palace
Gustáv Petschacher built this Neo-Renaissance mansion on Kodály körönd in 1882. The inner courtyard was copied from the Palazzo Marini in Milan.

Ervin Szabó Library
The grand, Neo-Baroque palace that now houses this library was originally built in 1887 for the Wenckheims, a family of rich industrialists.

Péterffy Palace
This plaque, commemorating a flood of 1838, was placed on one of the few Baroque mansions that remain in Pest. The house was built in 1756.

Exploring the Palaces and Historic Buildings

LITTLE MORE THAN FRAGMENTS remain of Budapest's Gothic and Renaissance past. However, some Baroque buildings have survived in Buda's Castle District and Víziváros. Neo-Classicism, on the other hand, has a much wider presence; there are many apartment buildings, palaces and secular monuments built in this style, especially around the old fortification walls of Pest on the eastern side of the Danube. Historicism dominated the architecture of the second half of the 19th century. It played a vital role in the enlargement of the city as it expressed and celebrated the optimism of the era.

Façade of the Gross Palace, built by Jószef Hild in 1824

BAROQUE PALACES AND BUILDINGS

MANY BUILDINGS in the Castle District and neighbouring Víziváros, around Fő utca, have retained their original Baroque façades. The main entrance of the **Hilton Hotel**, formerly a 17th-century Jesuit college, is a fine example.

Other outstanding instances of this style are the four houses on **Vienna Gate Square**, the **Batthyány Palace** on Parade Square and the **Erdődy Palace** on Mihály Táncsics Street, now the Museum of Musical History.

The **Zichy Palace** in Óbuda is a splendid Baroque edifice, and the buildings of the former **Trinitarian Monastery**, now the Kiscelli Museum, stand as significant models of the style.

There are only two Baroque monuments remaining in Pest. The **Péterffy Palace**, a mansion that stands below the current street level, dates from 1755. Pest's other Baroque edifice was, however, the first to be built in either Buda or Pest. The huge complex of the **Municipal County Offices**, formerly a hospital for veterans of the Turkish wars, was constructed by the Italian master Anton Erhard Martinelli. It was greatly admired by Empress Maria Theresa, who declared it to be more beautiful than the Schönbrunn Palace in Vienna.

NEO-CLASSICAL PALACES AND BUILDINGS

NEO-CLASSICISM, influenced by ancient Greco-Roman design, was popular in the first half of the 19th century as it reflected the confidence of this period of national awakening and social reform. Many monumental Neo-Classical structures were produced, including the Chain Bridge, built in 1839–49. The leading Neo-Classical architect was Mihály Pollack, who built the **Hungarian National Museum**.

Two stunning Neo-Classical palaces deserve particular mention – **Sándor Palace** in Buda and **Károlyi Palace** in Pest. The first stands on Castle Hill, by the top of the funicular railway, and impresses visitors with its harmonious elegance. The second, now housing the Petőfi Literary Museum, gained its present form in 1834 after considerable reconstruction.

A group of particularly attractive Neo-Classical houses is situated on **József Nádor Square**. Some of their features, such as the pillars, projections and tympanums, merit individual attention.

In 1808, the Embellishment Commission was set up by the Austrian architect János Hild to develop Pest. He and his son, József Hild, who built the **Gross Palace** in 1824, were both involved in the general restoration of the city. Having studied architecture in Rome, they created many splendid Italianate buildings.

Baroque balcony and carved crest above the entrance to Erdődy Palace

HISTORICIST PALACES AND BUILDINGS

IN THE SECOND HALF of the 19th century, Historicism took precedence over Neo-Classicism. After the unification of Buda, Óbuda and Pest in 1873, Historicism had a significant influence on the city's architectural development. In this period Budapest gained an eclectic mix of new apartment buildings and palaces, as Historicist architects sourced different genres for inspiration. Miklós Ybl, whose work includes the **State Opera House** and the expansion of the **Royal Palace**, looked to the Renaissance, while Imre Steindl designed a Neo-Gothic **Parliament** (to which a Neo-Renaissance dome was added). Frigyes Schulek's **Fishermen's**

Sculptures on the Vigadó façade

Bastion features Neo-Gothic and Neo-Romanesque designs.

The **Vigadó**, a concert hall built by Frigyes Feszl between 1859 and 1864, is often thought of as the most magnificent Historicist building, with its façade richly decorated with relief sculptures and busts of the great Hungarians. However, the complex of three French-style, Neo-Renaissance palaces, Festetics, Károly and Esterházy, in **Mihály Pollack Square**, is also considered by many to be a fine example.

The **Drechsler Palace** in Andrássy út is a marvellous model of Neo-Renaissance design, while the **Divatcsarnok** department store features Lotz's Hall, stunningly decorated with paintings and gold. The twin apartment buildings known as the **Klotild Palaces** incorporate Spanish-Baroque motifs

Beautiful Neo-Baroque interior of the New York Palace

and can be admired near the Elizabeth Bridge. Perhaps one of the most extravagant of all the examples of Historicism in the city is the Neo-Baroque **New York Palace** by Alajos Hauszmann, which has a luxurious interior of marble columns and rich colour.

DECORATIVE FEATURES

The façades of many palaces and buildings still display the rich sculptural decoration characteristic of the various styles of architecture prevalent in the city. These features include coves, cartouches, finials, relief sculptures and ornamental window frames.

Regrettably, almost no original Gothic detail remains in Budapest, but niches or pointed arches decorating old apartment buildings can be spotted in the Old Town.

Baroque elements are still evident in fine buildings such as the Zichy Palace and the Erdődy Palace.

Decorative Neo-Classical features, such as borders and tympanums, are visible on many buildings from the first half of the 19th century.

A finial with cartouche on the Neo-Classical Károlyi Palace

Relief on the Hungarian National Bank (1905)

Cove detail on the façade of the Staffenberg House

Ornate window frame adorning the house at 21 József Nádor utca

Budapest's Best: Baths and Pools

BUDAPEST IS ONE OF the great spa cities of Europe. Numerous natural hot springs pour out over 80 million litres (18 million gal) of richly mineralized water every day. The greatest concentrations of natural springs are situated in Óbuda, near Gellért Hill, on the Buda embankment near Margaret Bridge and on Margaret Island itself. Baths have existed here since Roman times, but it was the Turks who best exploited Budapest's natural resources. Today there is a wide choice of therapeutic and recreational baths and pools.

Palatinus Strand
With seven swimming pools, hot springs, water slides and a restful location on Margaret Island, this spa is perhaps the most beautiful in Europe.

Hajós Olympic Pool
The pool was designed by Alfréd Hajós, who won Hungary's first Olympic gold medal for swimming in 1896, and on the walls of the swimming hall hang gold-engraved marble plaques citing Hungary's numerous Olympic champions.

North of the Castle

Castle District

DANUBE

Lukács Baths
These 19th-century thermal pools are open all year round, and attract both tourists and the locals of Budapest.

Gellért Hill and Tabán

Király Baths
Dating from 1566, these baths were built by the Turks and have many authentic Ottoman features.

Rác Baths
An ornate side room at these baths has been turned into a gymnasium.

Dagály Strand
Half a century ago, it was discovered that the water in a pond on this site was beneficial to health. Now a huge open-air complex of swimming pools, children's pools and a hydrotherapy and fitness centre is located here.

Around Városliget

Around Parliament

Central Pest

Széchenyi Baths
This spa has the hottest thermal baths in Budapest and the added attraction of magnificent Neo-Baroque architecture. The warmth of the water is such that these baths are popular even during the winter season.

Rudas Baths
The most famous of the Turkish baths were constructed during the 16th century. They still have an original Ottoman cupola and octagonal pool.

Gellért Baths
The main indoor swimming pool of this popular Buda spa delights bathers with its beautiful Secession interior, marble columns and colourful mosaics.

| 0 metres | 500 |
| 0 yards | 500 |

Exploring Budapest's Baths and Pools

Heated DEEP INSIDE THE EARTH, the waters of the mineral-rich hot springs which bubble up through fractures in the rocky hills of Buda and Óbuda have given the city a Turkish-influenced bathing culture which has survived even the rigours of Communism. A total of 31 spa-water pools and thermal baths, with entrance fees kept low by generous government subsidies, make taking the waters an unmissable treat for visitors to Budapest.

THE TURKISH INFLUENCE

Although THE ruins of Roman thermal baths dating from the 2nd century AD have been found in Óbuda, it was only under the Ottoman occupation of the 16th–17th centuries *(see pp 26–7)*, that the bathing culture really took hold in Budapest.

Four stunning Turkish-built baths, some of the few remaining examples of Ottoman architecture in Budapest, are still in operation. The **Rudas**, the **Rác**, the **Király** and the **Komjády** (formerly known as Császár) were all built in the 16th century, and are constructed on a single model. A marble staircase leads into a chamber containing a dome-topped, octagonal thermal pool, which is surrounded by smaller dome-covered pools at temperatures ranging from icily cold to roastingly hot. The most beautiful are almost certainly the Rudas Baths, followed closely by the Király Baths. Though not without their charms, the Rác Baths have been heavily restored and are less spectacular than the Rudas and Király Baths. The Császár Baths have been absorbed into the Lukács Baths complex *(see below)*.

Many of the city's newer baths are for both men and women. The Turkish baths, however, owe much of their unique atmosphere to the fact that they remain resolutely single-sex. The Rudas Baths are for men only, while the Rác and the Király Baths are open to men and women on alternate days. There is no need to wear a bathing suit, as a small apron is provided.

AFTER THE TURKS

THE LATE 19TH and early 20th century was a new golden age for Budapest *(see pp32–3)*, and saw the building of a number of splendid baths. Many have spring-water swimming pools attached.

Opened in 1894 the Neo-Classical **Lukács Baths** offer two outdoor swimming pools as well as the 16th-century Császár thermal pool. The **Széchenyi Baths**, opened 20 years later on the Pest side of the river, make up the biggest bathing complex in Europe. In addition to the usual indoor thermal pools, they also boast outdoor thermal and swimming pools, complete with sun terraces. With the hottest spa-water in the city, the outdoor thermal pool is popular even in the depths of winter.

As well as the thermal pools, Budapest's bathing establishments also include a steam room and sauna. Professional massages are almost always available for a small fee. Some places offer medicinal mud and sulphur baths. You will be invited to take a shower, and a short nap in the rest room before you leave.

Swim in style at the Gellért Hotel

SPA HOTELS

Nestling AT THE foot of Gellért Hill, the beautiful **Gellért Hotel and Baths Complex** is the oldest and most famous of a handful of luxury hotels in Budapest offering swimming and thermal pools, steam rooms, sauna and massage. The renowned Gellért Baths were opened to the general public in 1927, and include a fabulous, marble-columned indoor swimming pool, a labyrinth of thermal baths (one set for men and one for women), single-sex nudist sun-bathing areas and an outdoor swimming pool. A hugely popular wave machine is switched on in the latter for ten minutes in every hour.

A second wave of spa-hotels were built in the 1970s and '80s. Set on Margaret Island, the modern, squeaky-clean and extremely luxurious **Thermal Hotel Margitsziget**, is linked by an underground passage to the older **Grand Hotel Margitsziget**. In addition to the usual range of baths and pools, services on offer here

Outdoor pool at the Gellért Hotel and Baths Complex

Széchenyi Baths, the biggest bathing complex in Europe

include manicure, pedicure and a solarium. The late 1980s saw the arrival of two new spa hotels, the **Thermal Hotel Helia** not far from the Pest riverbank and, on the Buda side, the **Corinthia Aquincum**, facing north towards Óbuda. Both make use of the hot springs on Margaret Island, and offer gyms, bars and restaurants as well as swimming pools and thermal baths.

THE HEALING WATERS

The citizens of Budapest are great believers in the medical benefits of the thermal baths. Most of the baths employ staff who can offer advice on the most appropriate pools and special treatments for a particular ailment. The spa waters are extremely good for general relaxation. They can also be helpful in the relief of a number of specific complaints, including post-traumatic stress, joint and muscle damage, rheumatism and menstrual pain.

An ornamental tap, typical of the architectural detail found in Budapest's historic baths

SWIMMING AS SPORT

Many Hungarians are excellent swimmers, and the country has achieved great success in competitive water sports. In addition to Budapest's many recreational pools, sports pools include the **Hajós Olympic Pool** complex on Margaret Island. The complex consists of three sports pools, two outdoor, including one at full Olympic size, and one indoor. The pools are used for professional training, but are also open to the public. Together with the Komjádi Béla Swimming Stadium on Árpád Fejedelem útja, the Hajós Olympic Pool is the place to go to see professional swimming, diving or water polo.

Sculpture at the Római Strand

A DAY AT THE STRAND

Designed as a complete bathing day out, the strands of Budapest are a phenomenon not to be missed. A total of 12 strands in the city testifies to their popularity. Outdoor swimming and thermal pools are surrounded by grassy sunbathing areas. Trampolines and ping-pong and pool tables offer a change from the water, while ice creams, beers and hot dogs add to the summer-holiday atmosphere.

The lovely **Palatinus Strand**, set in a large area of

parkland on Margaret Island, boasts seven outdoor pools, some thermal and some for swimming, complete with water slides and wave machines. Just east of the Pest river bank is the vast, modern **Dagály Strand** complex. Built after World War II, it includes 12 pools, with space for up to 12,000 people. Other strands worth visiting include **Római Strand** in Óbuda in the north of the city. Three pools have been carefully rebuilt here, on the site of some Roman baths, together with a not-so-Roman water chute. To the north of the city at Csillaghegy on the HÉV suburban train line, **Csillaghegy Strand** consists of four pools set in picturesque grounds, and includes a popular south-facing nudist beach.

WHERE TO FIND THE BATHS AND POOLS

Corinthia Aquincum *p185*
Komajády Baths, part of Lukács Baths *p101*
Gellért Hotel and Baths Complex *pp90–91*
Hajós Olympic Pool *p172*
Király Baths *p101*
Lukács Baths *p101*
Palatinus Strand *p172*
Rác Baths *p94*
Grand Hotel Margitsziget *pp 173, 185*
Rudas Baths *p93*
Széchenyi Baths *p151*
Thermal Hotel Margitsziget *p173*
Thermal Hotel Helia *p185*

Budapest's Best: the Secession

VISITORS TO BUDAPEST are often impressed by its wonderful late 19th and early 20th century buildings. The majority of these are found in central Pest and around Városliget; Buda was already developed at this stage and so boasts few examples. The movement started among groups of avant-garde artists in Paris and Vienna, from where the term Secession comes. In Budapest, the Secession style was also the inspiration for the development of the Hungarian National Style. Further details are given on pages 56–7.

Decoration on a house on Áldás utca

The School on Rose Hill
Károly Kós and Dezső Zrumeczky used motifs from village houses in Transylvania to give this building on Áldás utca its character.

Woman with a Birdcage (1892)
This painting by József Rippl-Rónai has an atmosphere of mystery and intimacy typical of Hungarian art of the period. It hangs in the Hungarian National Gallery (see p77) today.

North of the Castle

Castle District

DANUBE

Ironwork Gates of Gresham Palace
Two intricately crafted peacocks, a classic Secession motif, decorate the wrought-iron gates of Gresham Palace. This block of offices was built by Zsigmond Quittner and the Vágó brothers between 1905–7.

Gellért Hill and Tabán

Gellért Hotel and Baths Complex
Supported by flattened arches, a glass roof adds to the tranquil appeal of this hall in the famous spa at the Gellért Hotel. The Secession interiors created here are among the most splendid to be found in Budapest.

Post Office Savings Bank
The main staircase of this building by Ödön Lechner is embellished by fine balusters, rounded lamps and decorative windows.

Entrance to the Zoo
Kornel Neuschloss made ingenious use of elements of Hindu architecture when he created this amusing gate guarded by two elephants.

Around Parliament

Around Városliget

Central Pest

Sipeky Balázs Villa
Built between 1905–6, this fanciful villa is perhaps the most representative example of the Secession style in Budapest. It was designed by Ödön Lechner.

Philanthia Florist's
This extraordinary florist's is on Váci utca. The interior of the shop is in the Secession style, while the building itself is Neo-Classical.

| 0 metres | 500 |
| 0 yards | 500 |

Apartments on Bartók Béla utca
Ödön Lechner was the leading exponent of the Hungarian National Style. He built this apartment block, with a studio for himself on the fourth floor, in 1899. The block is at 40 Bartók Béla utca.

Exploring Secession Budapest

THE SECESSION MOVEMENT crossed artistic boundaries, influencing painting and the decorative arts as well as architecture. Colourful, sometimes fantastical designs are instantly recognizable hallmarks of the style. The Hungarian National Style drew heavily on this general trend, incorporating motifs from old Hungarian architecture, particularly that of Transylvania, folk art and even oriental features.

Secession ornament

Vase designed by István Sovának, in the Museum of Applied Arts

József Rippl-Rónai's *Lady in Red* (1899), in the Hungarian National Gallery

The work of János Vaszary was heavily influenced by both German and English art. His finest pictures, which include *Gold Century* and the mysterious *Adam and Eve*, can be admired in the Hungarian National Gallery. Lajos Gulácsy was influenced by the Pre-Raphaelite movement and his pictures are often symbolic. Many of his paintings, too, can now be viewed in the Hungarian National Gallery.

The artists' colony based at Gödöllő was an important centre for painters working in the new Secession style. Its founder, Aladár Körösfői-Kriesch, created numerous works, including a fresco entitled *The Fount of Youth* which decorates the **Franz Liszt Academy of Music**.

DECORATIVE ARTS

NEW IDEAS in the decorative arts at this time were closely related to architectural developments. Ödön Lechner

began to make use of colour-ful ceramic tiles, acquired from his father-in-law's brickyard in Pécs in southern Hungary, not only to cover roofs but also as a decorative element.

The owner of this brickyard, Vilmos Zsolnay, discovered an innovative method of glaz-ing tiles and ceramics. This proved so successful that the the brickyard was turned into a factory specializing in their production. Zsolnay's factory eventually made most of the vivid and distinctive ceramic tiles covering the Secession buildings in the city.

Zsolnay also employed leading designers to create ranges of dinner services, vases and candlesticks. For these he was awarded the Gold Medal of the Legion of Honour at the World Fair in Paris. A wonderful collection of his Secession china is dis-played in the Museum of Applied Arts, where beautiful

PAINTINGS AND DRAWINGS

THE MAIN EXPONENTS of Secession art in Hungary were József Rippl-Rónai, János Vaszary and Lajos Gulácsy.

Rippl-Rónai spent many years in Paris, at the time when the Art Nouveau movement was beginning to flourish. *Lady in Red*, which he painted in 1899, was the first Hungarian painting in the Secession style. Many of Rippl-Rónai's works are on show in the **Hungarian National Gallery**. There is also a tapestry version of *Lady in Red* in the **Museum of Applied Arts**.

ÖDÖN LECHNER (1845–1914)

The most influential architect of the Hungarian Secession, Ödön Lechner trained in Berlin before completing his apprenticeship by working in both Italy and France. His quest was to create an iden-tifiable Hungarian National Style, by combining Secession motifs with elements from Hungarian folk art and Hindu designs. The colour-ful ceramics that he often used

Portrait of Lechner

became his signature. Among the buildings that Budapest owes to him are the Museum of Applied Arts, the Post Office Savings Bank and the Institute of Geology. Behind the ingenious and fantastic exteriors, Lechner's buildings have wonderfully simple, functional and superbly lit interiors.

Secession glass, lamps and decorative ironwork are also exhibited. **Gresham Palace** and the **Gellért Hotel and Baths Complex** are among the many buildings in the city that are embellished by ornamental wrought-iron gates, gratings and banisters that incorporate Secession motifs.

INTERIOR DECORATION

AMONG THE INTERIORS of the era, those of the **New York Palace** are a real jewel. Ostentatiously decked out in the best materials, including bronze and marble, they retain the splendour of their original, Neo-Baroque form.

Also worth visiting are the **Hungarian National Bank** and the **Post Office Savings Bank**, with their furnished secure rooms and ornate door and window frames. The interior of Philanthia, a florist's shop, is another wonderfully

A Secession cabinet, displayed in the Museum of Applied Arts

Window created by Miksa Róth, at the Hungarian National Bank

preserved example of decor from the Secession.

Exhibitions of attractive Secession furniture are a feature of both the Museum of Applied Arts and also the **Nagytétény Palace**.

ARCHITECTURE

HUNGARIAN architecture of the *fin de siècle* is characterized not only by decorative forms using glazed ceramics, but, more fundamentally, by the implementation of modern technical solutions. Reinforced concrete, steel and glass were used together, and large, light-filled interiors were often achieved. The central hall of the Museum of Applied Arts is a fine example of this.

Aside from Ödön Lechner, the most important of the Hungarian Secession architects, others who contributed significant buildings in the prevailing style included Béla Lajta, Aladár Árkay, Károly Kós and István Medgyaszay.

Béla Lajta, a pupil of Lechner, designed the **Rózsavölgyi Building**, with its distinctive geometrical ornamentation, on Martinelli tér. Also among his buildings is the extraordinary former **Jewish Old People's Home**, at No. 57 Amerikai út. With sophisticated ornamental details based on folk designs, **Városliget Calvinist Church** was the creation of Aladár Árkay.

Károly Kós was a highly original member of this set. Fascinated by the traditional architecture of Transylvania, he trawled the whole of that region, making drawings of the village churches and manor houses he encountered. Motifs from these buildings were later transferred to the aviary at Budapest's **Zoo** and the houses of the **Wekerle Estate**.

Frieze on the Rózsavölgyi Building

DECORATIVE MOTIFS

Stylized folk motifs derived from embroidery and also oriental patterns were often employed in Budapest's decorative arts during this period. Secession motifs such as feline forms, based on Viennese and Parisian examples, also feature.

Sunflower motif adorning the Post Office Savings Bank

Secession lettering on the sign of Philanthia Florist's

Colourful mosaic at No. 3 Aulich utca

BUDAPEST THROUGH THE YEAR

SET IN THE MIDDLE OF the Great Hungarian Plain, Budapest enjoys a continental climate with sharply defined seasons, each of which brings its own attractions, from traditional feast days to cultural and sporting events. Historically a centre of cultural, and especially musical, activity, Budapest continues the tradition

Spring Festival logo

with many musical events including the Spring Festival, an international celebration of classical music and ballet, and the smaller Budapest Contemporary Music Weeks, devoted to contemporary classical music. Many hotels and tourist offices provide a programme of the events taking place in the city, as do English-language weeklies.

SPRING

SPRING MAKES A welcome return to the city in March, with sunshine and fresh, warm days. Budapest turns green and the Spring Festival sees the arrival of some of the year's first tourists.

MARCH

The Spring Uprising *(15 Mar).* A public holiday marks the day in 1848 when the youth of Buda, led by the poet Sándor Petőfi, rebelled against the Habsburg occupation of Hungary *(see pp30–31).* Thousands of people take to the streets to lay wreaths and light eternal flames, wearing the national colours of red, white and green. There are speeches and street theatre, especially in front of the Hungarian National Museum *(see pp130–33).*

Spring Festival *(last two weeks of Mar– mid-Apr).* Top musicians from Hungary and

Parade in the Castle District during the Spring Festival

the rest of the world gather in Budapest for several weeks of music and dance in churches and concert halls all over the city. The emphasis of the festival is on the classical tradition, but also in evidence are folk music and dance, as well as pop and jazz.

APRIL

Easter is an important religious event in Hungary and the Easter service is well worth attending in one of the city's many churches. On the

morning of Easter Monday young men roam the streets, spraying girls and young women with perfume or water, a ritual which is said to keep them beautiful until the following year. Painted eggs are given in return.

World Dance Festival *(29 Apr).* The National Dance Theatre and the Association of Hungarian Dance Artists organize this festival every year, with participation from top Hungarian dance groups and foreign guest artists. Castle Theatre, Erkel Theatre, the Light Opera Theatre and the Hungarian State Opera House hold the events.

Horse Racing *(Sun, Apr–Oct).* April sees the beginning of the flat-racing season. Place your bets every Sunday at the busy and charmingly down-at-heel Kincsem Park race course on Albertirsai út.

Budapest International Book Festival. Organised in co-operation with the Frankfurt Book Fair, this festival is the most important event in Hungary's publishing year, both for the publishing industry and for the general public. It is held in the Budapest Congress Centre.

MAY

May Day *(1 May).* No longer a compulsory display of patriotism, May Day celebrations take place in public parks all over the city and involve craft markets, street performers and sausage and beer tents. A dip in the local thermal bath or swimming pool *(see pp50–53),* is another popular May Day tradition.

Springtime magnolia blossom on Margaret Island

AVERAGE DAILY HOURS OF SUNSHINE

Hours
12 –
9 –
6 –
3 –
0 –
Jan Feb Mar Apr May Jun Jul Aug Sep Oct Nov Dec

Sunshine Chart
Budapest enjoys some of the sunniest weather in Europe, with an average of eight hours of sunshine each day from April to September. During the sticky months of high summer (June, July and August), the Buda hills provide a welcome refuge from the heat of the city.

SUMMER

THE LONG HOT DAYS of summer are made for relaxing on Margaret Island or sun-bathing at some of the city's twelve open-air pools.

JUNE

Open-Air Theatre Festival *(Jun–Aug)*. Margaret Island and Óbuda Island provide two of the major venues for this summer-long, open-air arts festival.
Budapesti Búcsú *(last weekend in Jun)*. A mixture of music, dance and theatre celebrates the departure of Soviet troops in 1991.
Danube Carnival International Cultural Festival. Various venues host music and dance events.
Danube Water Carnival. Kayak, canoe and motor-boat racing take place between

Formula One racing in the Hungarian Grand Prix

Margaret Bridge and Chain Bridge.
Hungarian Formula 1 Grand Prix Power Boat World Championship Race *(22 Jun)*. This is held on the Danube.

JULY

Concerts in St Stephen's Basilica *(Jul–Aug)*. Monday evening organ concerts in

the city's largest church *(see pp116–17)* provide a perfect opportunity to study the lavish interior decoration of this extraordinary building.
Budapest Summer Opera and Ballet Festival *(Jul or Aug)*. Look out for the ten-day series of shows that makes up the summer season at the State Opera House *(see pp118–19)*.

AUGUST

Hungarian Grand Prix *(2nd Sun in Aug)*. This, the biggest event in the Hungarian sporting calendar, takes place east of the city, at the Mog-yoród race track.
St István's Day *(20 Aug)*. St István, the patron saint of Hungary, is celebrated with mass in St Stephen's Basilica followed by a huge procession. The day ends with fireworks on Gellért Hill *(see pp88–9)*.
Sziget Festival *(1st week in Aug)*. Ten stages and a camp site are set up on Óbuda Island for this popular week-long festival of rock, folk and jazz.
Budapest Parade *(end of Aug)*. This end-of-summer carnival takes place between Roosevelt Square and Hősök tere.

Fireworks on Gellért Hill to celebrate St István's Day

AVERAGE MONTHLY RAINFALL

mm — Inches

Jan Feb Mar Apr May Jun Jul Aug Sep Oct Nov Dec

Rainfall Chart
*Budapest is a fairly dry
city. Typically, it rains
very heavily for two
days or so, then is dry
for several weeks.
June is the wettest
month, with May, July,
August and November
only slightly drier.
Autumn is usually the
driest season, while
there is some snowfall
in the winter months.*

AUTUMN

O NE OF THE MANY TREATS of
autumn in Budapest is a
visit to one of the city's fruit
and vegetable markets, where
you can feast your eyes on a
vast array of jewel-coloured
vegetables and fruit.

SEPTEMBER

Budapest Wine Festival
(2nd week of Sep). After the
late-August grape harvest,
wine makers set up their stalls
for wine tastings and folk
dancing on Mihály Vörösmarty
Square *(see p126)* and other
squares around the city.

**Budapest Contemporary
Music Weeks** *(25 Sep–end
Oct).* The anniversary of the
death of the great Béla Bartók
marks the start of this festival
of 20th-century classical music.
**Jewish Summer Cultural
Festival**. This multicultural
festival includes a Jewish
book fair, an Israeli film
festival, art exhibitions, and
cuisine presentations.
**Kaiser's Plus Budapest
International Marathon and
Running Festival**. As well as
the classic marathon, a marathon relay race, a mini-mara-
thon, and a family running
competition await participants.
Concerts and events are also
held for the spectators.

**A colourful food stall in one of
Budapest's covered markets**

OCTOBER

Autumn Festival *(late Sep–
mid-Oct).* Several weeks of
contemporary film, dance and
theatre at a number of venues
across the city.
**Vienna-Budapest Super
Marathon Running Com-
petition**. This competition
aims, through sport, to streng-
then ties between central
European countries, particularly those of Austria and
Hungary, and celebrates
open European borders.
Remembrance Day *(23 Oct).*
This is a national day of mourning to remember the 1956
Uprising, when 30,000 people
were killed by Soviet tanks
and 200,000 fled the country.
Wreaths are laid in Municipal
Cemetery *(see pp158–9)*, on
the grave of the executed
leader Imre Nagy *(see p34)*.

NOVEMBER

Vox Pacis *(Nov).* A festival of
choral music featuring choirs
from all over the world.

Performers take part in the Open-Air Theatre Festival

AVERAGE MONTHLY TEMPERATURE

Temperature Chart
*Seasons in Budapest
are sharply defined.
Daytime temperatures
rise rapidly from
March onwards. By
June, the thermometer
often reaches 30°C
(90°F) and more.
September sees cooler
weather, with temper-
atures falling rapidly
to lows of well below
freezing in January.*

WINTER

DESPITE THE COLD weather,
winter can be an exciting
time to visit Budapest. Open-
air ice-skating takes place from
November, roast-chestnut sel-
lers appear on the streets and
a Christmas tree is erected in
Mihály Vörösmarty Square.

DECEMBER

Silver and Gold Sunday
*(2nd-to-last Sunday before
Christmas).* All the city's shops
stay open for this Sunday of
serious Christmas shopping.
Mikulás *(6 Dec).* On *Mikulás,*
or St Nicholas Day, children
leave their shoes on the window sill for Santa Claus to fill.
Christmas *(25–26 Dec).* The
city shuts down for two days.
Celebrations begin with a
family meal of carp on 24 Dec.
Szilveszter *(31 Dec).* The
whole of Budapest celebrates
in style on New Year's Eve.
Public transport is free and
runs all night.
Budapest Christmas Fair.
Artists and craftsmen display
and sell their work in
Vörömarty Square.

**Seeing in the New Year, a stylish
affair in Budapest**

**Christmas tree in Mihály
Vörösmarty Square**

JANUARY

New Year's Gala Concert
(1 Jan). Held in the Vigadó
concert hall *(see p208),* this
cheerful occasion is an
excellent way to start the new
year. Outstanding Hungarian
and foreign artists perform
excerpts from European
opera and musicals, providing
a lively evening of music.

FEBRUARY

Hungarian Film Festival
(early Feb). This two-day
celebration of Hungarian
film has been run by the
Magyar Filmszemle since
1969, in an attempt to attract
funding to a hard-pressed
industry. Many of the films
are subtitled.
Masked-Ball Season *(Feb).*
Budapest forgets the cold
weather to welcome the

coming of spring, and the
arrival of the *farsang,* or
fancy dress masked-ball
season, with many companies
holding their own event.
The climax of the season is
a masked procession on
Carnival Sunday, which is the
last Sunday before Lent.

Shopping for Christmas

PUBLIC HOLIDAYS

Public holidays mainly
follow the Christian calendar. Two days mark cata-
clysmic events in Magyar
history, while one, May
Day, is a reminder of the
country's socialist past.

New Year's Day (1 Jan)
Spring Uprising (15 Mar)
Easter Sunday (variable)
Easter Monday (variable)
Whit Monday (variable)
May Day (1 May)
St István's Day (20 Aug)
Remembrance Day
(23 Oct)
Christmas Day (25 Dec)
Boxing Day (26 Dec)

Margaret Bridge to Elizabeth Bridge

Crown on Elizabeth Bridge

A TRIP ON A river boat along the Danube provides a unique panorama of the city. Most major cities have a river at their heart. However, the Danube historically played a different role in this case, for centuries dividing the separate towns of Buda and Pest. Several road bridges today link the two halves of the modern city. All had to be reconstructed this century after being destroyed by the retreating Nazi army towards the end of World War II.

Centenary Monument
This momument was erected in 1973 to commemorate the centenary of the joining of Buda, Óbuda and Pest as Budapest. It stands on Margaret Island (see pp172–3), close to Margaret Bridge.

St Elizabeth's Church
This Baroque church was built for an order of nuns, with its front facing away from the Danube. The hospital and hostel run by the sisters face the river (see p101).

Mátyás Church
With medieval origins, the tower of this church has been rebuilt several times. It overlooks the Hilton Hotel and the Fishermen's Bastion (see pp82–3).

St Anne's Church can be recognized by its twin, slender Baroque towers.

Chain Bridge was built between 1839–49 at the inititiative of Count István Széchenyi *(see p31)*. It was designed by Englishman William Tierney Clark and built by the unrelated Scot, Adam Clark. The bridge extends for 380 m (1,250 ft), supported by two towers – a major feat of engineering at the time.

KEY

M	Metro
	River boat boarding point

Margaret Bridge was built by the French engineer Ernest Gouin, at the point where the Danube becomes a single body once more after dividing to flow around Margaret Island. The bridge is distinguished by its unusual chevron shape. It was erected in 1872–6, and between 1899–1900 access from the bridge onto the island was added. Sculptures by Adolphe Thabart decorate its columns.

Parliament
The magnificent, high dome of the Parliament building is visible from every point along the Danube in central Budapest (see pp108–9).

Much of the eastern bank of the river is characterized by fairly uniform architecture. Variation is provided here by the dome and towers of St Stephen's Basilica *(see pp116–17).*

0 metres	300
0 yards	300

Hungarian Academy of Sciences

Elizabeth Bridge, constructed in 1897–1903, was at that time the longest suspension bridge in the world. Destroyed in 1945, it was rebuilt in its current form by Pál Sávolya.

The bridgehead of Chain Bridge is guarded by two vast stone lions sculpted by János Marschalkó. According to an anecdote János was heartbroken because he forgot to give the lions any tongues, so he drowned himself in the river. In fact the lions do have tongues, but they are not easily visible.

Piers, from which passenger cruises operate daily in summer, are spaced frequently along the Danube in central Budapest.

Elizabeth Bridge to Lágymányosi Bridge

LIKE PARIS, BUDAPEST has fully exploited the opportunities given by its river. The most important and beautiful buildings of Buda and Pest crowd along the banks of the Danube. These include the Royal Palace, churches, historic palaces and houses, and Hungary's Parliament.

VÖRÖSMARTY TÉR M

FERENCI TÉRE

ERZSÉBET HÍD

SZABADS

Royal Palace
From the Danube the lower sections of the defensive walls, with fragments dating from the Middle Ages, can be seen. The enormous mass of the Habsburg Royal Palace was built within these (see pp70–71).

Inner City Parish Church
This church was built in the 12th century on the ruins of Roman Contra Aquincum's walls. The spot was, from early times, an important place for crossing the river (see pp124–5).

Gellért Hotel and Baths Complex
The architects of this hotel maximized its river façade to make it as imposing as possible (see pp90–91).

Technical University
The campus of Hungary's largest educational institution occupies almost the entire space between Liberty Bridge and Petőfi Bridge (see p157).

An embankment walk extends along the length of the Danube on the Pest side. It is a favourite place to meet or to go for a stroll and is lined by up-market hotels and restaurants.

Little Princess (1989) was so liked by Charles, Prince of Wales, on his visit here that he invited its designer, László Marton, to exhibit some of his works in London.

K Á L V I N
T É R
Ⓜ

Liberty Bridge was built between 1894–9 by Hungarian engineer János Feketeházy. Opened by Emperor Franz Joseph, it initially took his name. All its original features were retained when it was rebuilt after World War II: on top of the bridge there are legendary Hungarian *turul* birds and royal crests.

University of Economics
Formerly a customs' headquarters, this building has an elegant façade decorated with ten allegorical figures. These are the work of German sculptor August Sommer (see p138).

P E T Ő F I   H Í D

L Á G Y M Á N Y O S I
H Í D

Lágymányosi Bridge, Budapest's most modern and southernmost bridge, is pictured here under construction. Opened in 1996, it is designed to carry traffic on a ring road bypassing the city centre.

BUDAPEST AREA BY AREA

CASTLE DISTRICT

Bas-relief on the Eugene of Savoy monument

THE HILL TOWN of Buda grew up around its castle and Mátyás Church from the 13th century onwards. At 60 m (197 ft) above the Danube, the hill's good strategic position and natural resources made it a prize site for its earliest inhabitants. In the 13th century, a large settlement arose when, after a Tartar invasion, King Béla IV decided to build his own defensive castle and establish his capital here. The reign of King Mátyás Corvinus in the 15th century was an important period in the evolution of Buda, but it suffered neglect under Turkish rule during the next century and was then destroyed by Christian troops. The town was reborn, however, and assumed an important role during the 18th and 19th centuries under the Habsburgs. By the end of World War II, the Old Town had been almost utterly destroyed and the Royal Palace burnt to the ground. Since the war the Royal Palace and Old Town have been reconstructed, restoring the original allure of this part of the city.

SIGHTS AT A GLANCE

Churches
Buda Lutheran Church ⑰
Church of St Mary Magdalene ⑳
Mátyás Church pp82–3 ⑪

Museums and Galleries
Budapest History Museum ①
Golden Eagle Pharmacy Museum ⑨
Hungarian National Gallery pp74–7 ④
Ludwig Museum Budapest - Museum of Contemporary Art ⑤

Museum of Commerce and Catering ⑱
Museum of Military History ㉑
Széchenyi National Library ②

Historic Streets and Squares
András Hess Square ⑭
Holy Trinity Square ⑩
Lords' Street ㉒
Mihály Táncsics Street ⑮
Parade Square ⑧
Parliament Street ⑲
Vienna Gate Square ⑯

Palaces, Historic Buildings and Monuments
Fishermen's Bastion ⑫
Hilton Hotel ⑬
Mátyás Fountain ③
National Dance Theatre ⑦
Sándor Palace ⑥

GETTING THERE
Castle Hill and the Old Town are largely pedestrianized, but there are a couple of car parks where cars and coaches can park for a fee, allowing visitors to walk to the area. Bus 16 runs from Clark Ádám tér to Dísz tér, and a funicular railway (Sikló) connects Clark Ádám tér to Szent György tér. There is also a minibus (Várbusz) that arrives at this square from Moszkva tér to the north.

---

0 metres   400
0 yards   400

KEY

▮ Street-by-Street map *See pp70–71*

▮ Street-by-Street map *See pp78–9*

P Parking

ℹ Tourist information

◁ **Fountain on Tárnok utca in the Old Town**

Street-by-Street: The Royal Palace

THE ROYAL PALACE has borne many incarnations during its long life. Even now it is not known exactly where King Béla IV began building his castle, though it is thought to be nearer the site of Mátyás Church *(see pp82–3)*. The Holy Roman Emperor Sigismund of Luxembourg built a Gothic palace on the present site, from which today's castle began to evolve. In the 18th century, the Habsburgs built their monumental palace here. The current form dates from the rebuilding of the 19th-century palace after its destruction in February 1945. During this work, remains of the 15th-century Gothic palace were uncovered. Hungarian archeologists decided to reveal the recovered defensive walls and royal chambers in the reconstruction.

An ornamental gateway, dating from 1903, leads from the Habsburg Steps to the Royal Palace. Nearby, a bronze sculpture of the mythical *turul* bird guards the palace. This statue marks the millennium anniversary of the Magyar conquest in 896.

★ Mátyás Fountain
In the northwest courtyard of the Royal Palace stands the Mátyás Fountain. It was designed by Alajos Stróbl in 1904 and depicts King Mátyás Corvinus and his beloved Ilonka ❸

Lion Gate, leading to a rear courtyard of the Royal Palace, gets its name from the four lions that watch over it. These sculptures were designed by János Fadrusz in 1901.

TIMELINE

1255 First written document, a letter by King Béla IV, refers to building a fortified castle	**c.1400** Sigismund of Luxembourg builds an ambitious Gothic palace on this site	**1541** After capturing Buda, the Turks use the Royal Palace to stable horses and store gunpowder	**1719** The building of a small palace begins on the ruins of the old palace, to a design by Hölbling and Fortunato de Prati	**1881** Miklós Ybl *(see p119)* begins programme to rebuild and expand the Royal Palace

1200	1400	1600	1800

c.1356 Louis I builds a royal castle on the southern slopes of Castle Hill	**1686** The assault by Christian soldiers leaves the palace completely razed to the ground	**1849** Royal Palace is destroyed again, during an unsuccessful attack by Hungarian insurgents	Turul *bird*
1458 A Renaissance palace evolves under King Mátyás	**1749** Maria Theresa builds a vast palace comprising 203 chambers		

The dome of the Royal Palace
was rebuilt in the Neo-Classical
style after the Neo-Baroque
dome, designed by Alajos
Hauszmann, was de-
stroyed in the razing
of the palace in
World War II.

LOCATOR MAP
See Street Finder, maps 1, 3 & 9

| 0 metres | 50 |
| 0 yards | 50 |

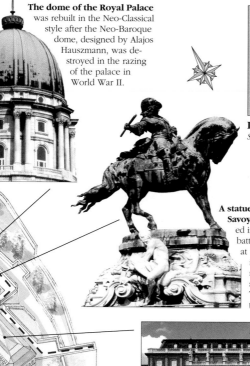

**A statue of Prince Eugene of
Savoy**, by József Róna, was unveiled in 1900. It commemorates the
battle of Zenta in 1697, victory
at which was a turning point
in the Turkish war. The bas-
reliefs on the base depict
scenes from the battle. Two
Turkish prisoners cower by
the feet of the prince.

★ Hungarian National Gallery
*Artworks depicting Hungary's turbulent
history are displayed here. Periods of both
foreign domination and patriotic home rule
are brought to life through the gallery's
extensive collection* ❹

KEY

- - - Suggested route

BUILDING THE ROYAL PALACE

In the 15th century, a Gothic Royal Palace
was built on the site, but it was rebuilt in
the Renaissance style by King Mátyás in
1458. After the Turkish occupation it was
razed and reborn on a smaller scale. Maria
Theresa further developed the palace and
it was rebuilt again after World War II to
a design originally completed in 1905.

■ 15th century　□ 1749
■ 1719　　　　□ 1905

STAR SIGHTS

★ Mátyás Fountain

★ Hungarian
National Gallery

Renaissance majolica floor from the 15th century, uncovered during excavations on Castle Hill and displayed at the Budapest History Museum

Budapest History Museum **❶**
BUDAPESTI TÖRTÉNETI MÚZEUM

Szent György tér 2. **Map** 3 C1 (9 B4).
☎ 225 78 09. 🚌 5, 16, 78, Várbusz.
🕐 Mar–mid-May, mid-Sep–Oct: 10am–6pm Mon, Wed–Sun; mid-May–mid-Sep: 10am–6pm daily; Nov–Feb: 10am–4pm Mon, Wed–Sun. 📷 ♿

SINCE THE UNIFICATION of Budapest in 1873, historic artifacts relating to Hungary's capital have been collected. Many are now on show at the Budapest History Museum (also called the Castle Museum).

During the rebuilding that followed the destruction suffered in World War II, chambers dating from the Middle Ages were uncovered in the south wing (wing E) of the Royal Palace. They provide an insight into the character of a much earlier castle within today's Habsburg reconstruction.

These chambers, including a tiny prison cell and a chapel, were recreated in the basement of the palace. They now house an exhibition, the Royal Palace in Medieval Buda, which displays authentic weapons, seals, tiles and other early artifacts.

On the ground floor, Budapest in the Middle Ages illustrates the evolution of the town from its Roman origins to a 13th-century Hungarian settlement. The reconstructed defensive walls, gardens and keep on this level are further attractions. Also on this floor are the Gothic Statues from the Royal Palace, dating from the 14th and 15th centuries. These were uncovered by chance in the major excavations of 1974. On the first floor, Budapest in Modern Times traces the history of the city from 1686 to the present.

Széchenyi National Library **❷**
NEMZETI SZÉCHENYI KÖNYVTÁR

Szent György tér 6. **Map** 3 C1 (9 B4).
☎ 224 38 45. 🚌 5, 16, 78, Várbusz.
🕐 Sep–Jul: 1am–9pm Mon, 9am–9pm Tue–Fri, 9am–5pm Sat.

A MAGNIFICENT COLLECTION of books has been housed, since 1985, in wing F of the Royal Palace, built in 1890–1902 by Alajos Hauszmann and Miklós Ybl (see p119).

***Corviniani* illuminated manuscript in the Széchenyi National Library**

Previously, the library was part of the Hungarian National Museum (see pp130–33).

Among the library's most precious treasures is the *Corviniani*, a collection of ancient books and manuscripts that originally belonged to King Mátyás Corvinus (see p24–5). His collection was one of the largest Renaissance libraries in Europe. Also of importance are the earliest surviving records in the Hungarian language, dating from the early 13th century.

The library was established by Count Ferenc Széchenyi in 1802. He endowed it with 15,000 books and 2,000 manuscripts. The collection now comprises five million items; everything that has been published in Hungary, in the Hungarian language or that refers to Hungary is here.

Crest on the Mátyás Fountain in a courtyard at the Royal Palace

Mátyás Fountain **❸**
MÁTYÁS KÚT

Royal Palace. **Map** 1 C5 (9 B3).
🚌 5, 16, 78, Várbusz.

THE ORNATE FOUNTAIN in the northwest courtyard of the Royal Palace (situated between wings A and C) was designed by Alajos Stróbl in 1904. The statue is dedicated to the great Renaissance king, Mátyás, about whom there are many popular legends and fables.

The Romantic design of the bronze sculptures takes its theme from a 19th-century ballad by the poet Mihály Vörösmarty. According to the tale, King Mátyás, while on a hunting expedition, meets a beautiful peasant girl, Ilonka, who falls in love with him.

This representation shows King Mátyás disguised as hunter, standing proudly with his kill. He is accompanied by his chief hunter and several hunting dogs in the central part of the fountain. Beneath the left-hand columns sits Galeotto Marzio, an Italian court poet, and the figure of the young Ilonka is beneath the columns on the right.

In keeping with the romantic reputation of King Mátyás, a new tradition has grown up concerning this statue. The belief is that anyone wishing to revisit Budapest should throw some coins into the fountain to ensure their safe return.

Hungarian National Gallery ❹

MAGYAR NEMZETI GALÉRIA

See pp 74–7.

Ludwig Museum Budapest - Museum of Contemporary Art ❺

LUDWIG MÚZEUM BUDAPEST - KOTÁRS MŰVÉSZETI MÚZEUM

Disz tér 17. **Map** 3 C1 (9 B4). 〖 375 91 75. 🚌 5, 16, 78, Várbusz. ⏰ 10am–6pm Tue–Sun (until 8pm Thu). 📷 ♿

SINCE 1991, WING A of the Royal Palace has been the home of both the Museum of Contemporary History and the Ludwig Collection.

The former was previously the Museum of the Hungarian Workers' Movement. It now has exhibitions on the recent

The western elevation of the Neo-Classical Sándor Palace

social history of Hungary, and includes documents and exhibits dating from the early 20th century to the present day.

The Ludwig Collection is located on the second floor and displays a collection of 150 modern works of art. These were donated, originally loaned, by German patrons Peter and Irene Ludwig in 1989. There is a permanent exhibition showing work by Hungarian artists from the 1960s onwards and another that includes works by artists such as Pablo Picasso.

Sándor Palace ❻

SÁNDOR PALOTA

Szent György tér 1–3. **Map** 1 C5 (9 A3). 🚌 5, 16, 78, Várbusz. ⬤ *to the public.*

BY THE TOP OF the cog-wheel railway stands the grand Neo-Classical mansion, Sándor Palace. It was commissioned in 1806 by Count Vincent Sándor from architects Mihály Pollack and Johann Aman.

The bas-reliefs that decorate the palace are the work of Richárd Török, Miklós Melocco and Tamás Körössényi. The decoration on the western ele-

vation depicts Greek gods on Mount Olympus. The southern elevation shows Count Sándor being knighted and the northern elevation features a 1934 sculpture of Saint George by Zsigmond Kisfaludi Stróbl.

Sándor Palace functioned as the prime minister's official residence from 1867 to 1944, when it was severely damaged in World War II. It was restored, and is now the residence of the President of Hungary.

National Dance Theatre ❼

NEMZETI TÁNCSZÍNHÁZ

Szinház utca 1–3. **Map** 1 C5 (9 A3). 〖 318 60 66. 🚌 5, 16, 78, Várbusz. ⏰ 1–6pm Mon–Sun.

AN UNLIKELY assortment of institutions have stood on the site now occupied by the Castle Theatre. The church of St John the Evangelist, founded by King Béla IV, stood here in the 13th century. This church was then used as a mosque under Ottoman rule, and in 1686 was demolished by the Christian armies that retook the city. In 1725 the Carmelite order built a Baroque church in its place, and it is this building that was first converted into a theatre in 1786, during the reign of Emperor Joseph II.

Farkas Kempelen, a famous Hungarian designer, undertook the conversion of the church, adding a Rococo façade and seats for 1,200 spectators. The first plays were in German and it was not until 1790 that any work was staged in Hungarian. Beethoven's concert of 1800 is commemorated by a plaque.

The building suffered considerable damage in World War II and was restored in 1978. It now houses the National Dance Theatre.

Imre Bukta's *Pig Killing* (1993) on display in the Ludwig Collection

Hungarian National Gallery ❹

ESTABLISHED IN 1957, the Hungarian National Gallery houses a comprehensive collection of Hungarian art from medieval times to the 20th century. Gathered by various groups and institutions since 1839, these works had previously been exhibited at the Hungarian National Museum *(see pp130–33)* and the Museum of Fine Arts *(see pp146–9)*. The collection was moved to the Royal Palace (wings B, C and D) in 1975. There are now six permanent exhibitions, presenting the most valuable and critically acclaimed Hungarian art in the world.

Sisters by Erzsébet Schaár

St Anne Altarpiece
(c.1520)
Elaborately decorated, this folding altarpiece from Kisszeben is one of the Gothic highlights in the gallery.

Madonna of Toporc
(c. 1420)
This is a captivating example of medieval wood sculpture in the Gothic style. It was originally crafted for a church in Spiz (now part of Slovakia).

First floor

Madonna of Bártfa
(1465–70)
This painting of a Madonna and Child is from a church in Bártfa (now in Slovakia). It is thought to have been painted in Cracow, Poland.

★ The Visitation *(1506)*
This painting by Master MS is a delightful example of late Gothic Hungarian art. It is a fragment of a folding altarpiece from a church in Selmecbánya in modern-day Slovakia.

Ground floor

Main entrance

KEY

☐	Stone sculptures and artifacts
☐	Gothic works
☐	Late Gothic altarpieces
☐	Renaissance and Baroque works
☐	19th-century works
☐	Early 20th-century works
☐	Temporary exhibitions

STAR EXHIBITS
★ The Visitation
★ Picnic in May

Luischen (1884)
One of the earliest works by the sculptor Alajos Stróbl is this marble bust of Luischen on display on the first floor.

Second floor

VISITORS' CHECKLIST

B, C and D wings in the Royal Palace. **Map** 3 C1 (9 B4).
375 75 33. 5, 16, 78, Várbusz. 10am–6pm Tue–Sun.
to arrange for an English-speaking guide contact ext 616.
W www.mng.hu

Woman Bathing (1901)
This painting by Károly Lotz, better known for his frescoes, is the best example of Neo-Classical painting in Hungary. It reflects his fascination for the work of the French painter, Ingres.

GALLERY GUIDE
Early stone and Gothic exhibits are on the ground floor. Late Gothic, Renaissance and Baroque works and 19th-century works share the first floor. Works from the 20th century are on the second floor, and temporary exhibits are displayed on the top floor.

Third floor

Churning Woman (1872–73)
This painting is by Mihály Munkácsy, Hungary's most internationally celebrated artist. The tiredness of the woman's features with her worn hands show the reality of a life of poverty.

★ **Picnic in May** (1873)
The captivating colours of this landscape scene were painted by Pál Szinyei Merse. He was influenced by two works of Edouard Manet and Claude Monet, both entitled Le Déjeuner sur l'Herbe.

Exploring the Hungarian National Gallery

Secession poster

The works are displayed in six permanent exhibitions and give a thorough insight into Hungarian art from the early Middle Ages to the present day. Although one-and-a-half centuries of Turkish occupation and wartime destruction interrupted the development of Hungarian art, the birth of national pride in the 19th century allowed a new indigenous style to develop. Among the most interesting are the Hungarian paintings of the late 19th century, when a greater diversity of styles came to the fore.

The Habsburg Crypt, with the sarcophagus of Palatine Archduke Joseph

characterized, as its name suggests, by the sentimental and gentle imagery of the Madonna playing with the Christ child.

The Annunciation, a magnificent late Gothic work by Master GH, is, in fact, only the main section of an altar; the other pieces are now in Esztergom *(see p164).*

RENAISSANCE AND BAROQUE WORKS

The exhibition begins with a still life by Jakab Bogdány (1660–1724) and portraits by Ádám Mányoki (1673–1757) *(see p28),* who actually settled outside Hungary. As a result of the powerful influence of the Habsburgs during this period *(see pp28–9),* Baroque art was overwhelmingly dominated by Austrian artists. Painters such as Joseph Dorfmeister and Franz Anton Maulbertsch and sculptors Georg Raphael Donner and Philipp Jakob Straub were the acknowledged masters. Jan Kupetzky's portraits are also exemplary models of this era.

The sculptures by Donner and the sacred paintings of Dorfmeister conclude this section of the gallery.

THE LAPIDARIUM

On the ground floor, to the left of the main entrance, is a display of stone objects discovered during the reconstruction of the Royal Palace *(see p70).* Called the Lapidarium, it includes sculptures and fragments of architectural features, such as balustrades and windows, that decorated the royal chambers during the Angevin and Jagiełło eras *(see p18).* The most valuable exhibit, however, is a sculpture of King Béla III's head, which dates from around 1200.

Also in this first section are two marble bas-reliefs of King Matthias and his wife Beatrice, by an unknown Renaissance master from Lombardy.

The second section exhibits late Gothic and Renaissance artifacts from other palaces in Hungary. There are pillars and balustrades from the palace at Visegrád and bas-reliefs from a chapel in Esztergom.

King's head sculpted from red marble

GOTHIC WORKS

A collection of painted panels, sculptures and fragments of altar decoration is opposite the Lapidarium. Note, however, the image of the *Madonna of Bártfy,* which is a rare complete example from the Gothic period.

The sculptures of the "Beautiful Madonnas" are executed in the Soft Style. This style is

LATE GOTHIC ALTARPIECES

One of the star exhibits of this collection is the imposing late Gothic altarpiece. Arranged in the Great Throne Room, the majority of these vast altarpieces date from the 15th and early 16th centuries.

The Great Throne Room, displaying the collection of folding altarpieces

Architecturally these altarpieces are pure Gothic, while adorned with sculptures and paintings revealing a Renaissance influence. This is evident in the altars of St Anne and St John the Baptist from a church in Kisszeben (now Sabinov in Slovakia), which date from 1510–16. The most recent altarpiece dates from 1643 and is from the church of Our Lady Mary in Csíkmenaság.

Lebanese Cedar by Tivadar Kosztka Csontváry (1907)

Bertalan Székely's *Women of Eger* (1867), depicting the Turkish wars

19TH-CENTURY WORKS

THE WONDERFUL collection of works from this period reflects the rise of fine art in Hungary in the 19th century.

Historicist art developed during this period. Among those distinguishing themselves in particular were Gyula Benczúr and Bertalan Székely, who produced the epic works *The Return of Buda in 1686* (1896) and *Women of Eger* (1867) respectively. The latter depicts the women of the town defending the Castle of Eger against the Turks.

Viktor Madarász's work *The Mourning of László Hunyadi* (1859) refers to the execution of László Hunyadi by the Habsburgs in 1457. It alludes, too, to the execution of many Hungarians after the crushing of the uprising against Austria in 1849 (*see pp30–31*).

European developments in fine art can also be seen in Hungarian painting from the late-19th century. The influence of Impressionism, for example, is best seen in Pál Szinyei Merse's *Picnic in May* (1873).

Hungarian Realism is expressed in the work of László Paál and Mihály Munkácsy, the latter being widely regarded as the country's greatest artist. Paintings by Munkácsy which deserve particular attention are *The Yawning Traveller* (1869), *Woman Carrying Brushwood* (1870), *Dusty Road* (1874), and the still life *Flowers* (1881).

It is also worth spending a few moments seeing the paintings of the Neo-Classical artists. The work of Károly Lotz, who is perhaps better known for his frescoes that can be seen on walls and ceilings around Budapest, is exhibited here.

20TH-CENTURY WORKS

EXAMPLES OF WORK from the Secession era through to Expressionism and Surrealism, and even contemporary art are exhibited here. They provide a comprehensive review of 20th-century Hungarian art.

The work of József Rippl-Rónai, who studied in France, shows the influence of the Secession style in *The Palace in Körtvélyes* and *Woman with a Birdcage*. But one of the most engaging artists from the early-20th century is Károly Ferenczy whose *The Painter* (1923) exemplifies the serene qualities of his work.

Tivadar Kosztka Csontváry is an artist whose work did not follow any conventional style but was greatly admired, even by Pablo Picasso. Two paintings in particular capture his abstract interpretation of the world: the *Ruins of the Greek Amphitheatre in Taormina* (1905) and the well-known *Lebanese Cedar* (1907).

The Eight, a group of artists who set up the first Hungarian avant-garde school, were active between the two world wars. Notable examples of their work are *Young Girl with a Bow* by Béla Czóbel, *Woman Playing a Doublebass* by Róbert Berény, *The Oarsmen* by Ödön Marffy, *Walking by the Water Tower* by István Farkas and *Riders at the Edge* by Károly Kernstok.

The best works of Hungarian Expressionism can be seen in the paintings *Along the Tracks*, *For Bread* and *Generations*, by Gyula Derkovits.

Among the sculptures on display, the most interesting are *Raising Oneself* and *The Sower*, by Ferenc Medgyessy, and *Standing Girl*, by Béni Ferenczy. The exhibition is completed by a section on contemporary artists.

The Painter by Károly Ferenczy (1923), a typically peaceful work

Street-by-Street: the Old Town

Bas-reliefs on a house on Fortuna utca

BUDA'S OLD TOWN has been a barometer of Hungary's changing fortunes. It developed, to the north of the Royal Palace, from the 13th century. Under kings such as Sigismund, it flourished, and wealthy German merchants set up shops in Lords' Street (Úri utca) to supply the court. The area was later destroyed by the Turks and again by their evictors. It was most recently rebuilt after World War II, but genuine relics can be hunted out in its cobbled streets and squares.

Mihály Táncsics Street
During the Middle Ages, this street was inhabited by Jews. A museum at No. 26, on the site of an old synagogue, displays finds such as tombstones **⓯**

The State Archive of Historic Documents, located in a Neo-Romanesque building, houses items that were transferred to Buda in 1785 from the former capital of Hungary, Bratislava.

Surviving tower of the Church of St Mary Magdalene

Defensive walls

0 metres 50
0 yards 50

★ Museum of Commerce and Catering
This unusual museum offers visitors a glimpse into catering and the trades connected with it from days gone by. A 19th-century grocer's shop is recreated and period utensils and posters can also be seen **⓲**

KEY

– – – Suggested route

★ Lords' Street
Once the homes of aristocrats and merchants, the houses on this street have medieval foundations. Many have Gothic details and peaceful courtyards **㉒**

★ Mátyás Church
*Although with much
earlier parts, this church
is mainly a Neo-Gothic
reconstruction dating
from 1874–96. A pictur-
esque vestibule on the
church's southern façade
covers an original Gothic
portal dating from the
14th century* ⑪

LOCATOR MAP
See Street Finder, maps 1 & 9

This statue of St Stephen, or
István, the first crowned king of
Hungary *(see pp22–3)*, was
erected in 1906. Its pedestal
includes a bas-relief showing
scenes from the king's life.

Fishermen's Bastion
*Designed by Frigyes Schulek in
1895, this fantastical structure
never had the role of a defensive
building, despite its name. It
serves instead as a viewing terrace. The conical towers are
an allusion to the tribal tents
of the early Magyars* ⑫

Holy Trinity Square
*In 1713, after an epi-
demic of the plague
was overcome, a
column represent-
ing the Holy Trinity
was raised in
this square* ⑩

**Golden Eagle
Pharmacy Museum**
*From the 18th century a phar-
macy called "Under the Golden
Eagle" traded in this medieval
house, now a museum* ⑨

**House of
garian Wines**
s wine-tasting
detailing the
ine-growing
ns of Hungary.

STAR SIGHTS

★ **Mátyás Church**

★ **Museum of
Commerce and
Catering**

★ **Lords' Street**

Batthyány Palace on Parade Square

Parade Square ❽

Dísz tér

Map 1 B5 (9 A3). ▦ Várbusz.

Parade square is named after the military parades held here in the 19th century. At the northern end of the square is the Honvéd Monument, built in 1893 by György Zala. It honours and commemorates those who died during the recapture of Buda from Austria in 1848.

The house at No. 3 was built between 1743–8, by József Giessl. This two-floor Baroque palace was the home of the Batthyány family until 1945. Although the building has been frequently remodelled, the façade has remained intact.

A few houses on Parade Square were built incorporating medieval remains. Such houses can be seen at Nos. 4–5 and 11, built by Venerio Ceresola. The former has seat niches dating from the 13th century.

Golden Eagle Pharmacy Museum ❾

Aranysas Patikamúzeum

Tárnok utca 18. **Map** 1 B5 (9 A2). 〖 375 97 72. ▦ 16, Várbusz. ○ Mar–Oct: 10:30am– 5:30pm Tue–Sun; Nov–Feb: 10:30am–3.30pm Tue–Sun. ▨

This pharmacy was opened in 1688 by Ferenc Ignác Bösinger and traded under the name the "Golden Eagle" from 1740. It moved to this originally Gothic building, with its Baroque interior and Neo-Classical façade, in the 18th century.

The museum opened here in 1974. It displays pharmaceutical items from the Renaissance and Baroque eras, including a collection of china instruments.

Holy Trinity Square ❿

Szentháromság tér

Map 1 B4 (9 A3).
▦ Várbusz from Moszkva tér.

This square is the central point of the Old Town. It takes its name from the Baroque Holy Trinity Column, originally sculpted by Philipp Ungleich in 1710–13, and restored in 1967. The column commemorates the dead of two outbreaks of the plague, which struck the inhabitants of Buda in 1691 and 1709.

The pedestal of the column is decorated with bas-reliefs by Anton Hörger. Further up are statues of holy figures and at the summit is a magnificent composition of the figures of the Holy Trinity. The central section of the column is decorated with angelic figures surrounded by clouds.

Buda's Old Town Hall, a large Baroque building with two courtyards, was also built on the square at the beginning of the 18th century. It was designed by the imperial court architect, Venerio Ceresola, whose architectural scheme incorporated the remains of medieval houses. In 1770–74 an east wing was built, and bay windows and a stone balustrade with Rococo urns, by Mátyás Nepauer, were also added. The corner niche, opposite Mátyás Church, houses a small statue by Carlo Adami of Pallas Athene.

At No. 6 is the House of Hungarian Wines with an extensive selection of wines to sample and buy.

Mátyás Church ⓫

Mátyás templom

See pp82–3.

Fishermen's Bastion ⓬

Halászbástya

Szentháromsag tér. **Map** 1 B4 (9 A2). ▦ Várbusz from Moszkva tér.

Frigyes schulek designed this Neo-Romanesque monument to the Guild of Fishermen in 1895. It occupies the site of Buda's old defensive walls and a medieval square where fish was once sold. This building, from which a beautiful view of the Danube and Pest can be seen, is a purely aesthetic addition to Castle Hill. In front of the bastion is a statue of St István, the king who introduced Hungary to Christianity.

Buda's Old Town Hall, its clock tower crowned with an onion-shaped dome, on Holy Trinity Square

Bas-relief depicting King Mátyás on the façade of the Hilton Hotel

Hilton Hotel ⑬

HILTON SZÁLLÓ

Hess András tér 1–2. **Map** 1 B4 (9 A2). **☎** 488 66 00. **☒** Várbusz.

Buﬁ IN 1976, the Hilton Hotel is a rare example of modern architecture in the Old Town. Controversial from the outset, the design by the Hungarian architect Béla Pintér combines the historic remains of the site with contemporary materials and methods.

From 1254 a Dominican church, to which a tower was later added, stood on this site, followed by a late-Baroque Jesuit monastery. The remains of both these buildings are incorporated into the design. For example, the remains of the medieval church, uncovered during excavations in 1902, form part of the Dominican Courtyard, where concerts and operettas are staged during the summer season.

Similarly, the main façade, overlooking the Danube, comprises part of the façade of the Jesuit monastery. To the left of the entrance is St Nicholas's Tower. In 1930, a replica of the 15th-century German bas-relief of King Mátyás, considered to be his most authentic likeness, was added to this tower.

András Hess Square ⑭

HESS ANDRÁS TÉR

Map 1 B4 (9 A2).
☒ Várbusz from Moszkva tér.

THIS SQUARE IS NAMED after the Italian-trained printer who printed the first Hungarian book, *Chronica Hungarorum*, in a printing works at No. 4 in 1473. The house was rebuilt at the end of the 17th century as an amalgamation of three medieval houses, with quadruple seat niches, barrel-vaulted cellars and ornamental gates.

The former inn at No. 3 was named the Red Hedgehog in 1696. This one-floor building has surviving Gothic and Baroque elements.

The square also features a statue by József Damkó

Hedgehog on the façade of No. 3 András Hess Square

of Pope Innocent XI, who was involved in organizing the armies who recaptured Buda from the Turks. It was built to mark the 250th anniversary of the liberation, in 1936.

Mihály Táncsics Street ⑮

TÁNCSICS MIHÁLY UTCA

Map 1 B4 (9 A2). **☒** Várbusz.
Museum of Musical History
☎ 214 6770. **◯** 10am–5pm Tue–Sun. **☒**

STANDING AT NO. 7 is Erdődy Palace, built in 1750–69 for the Erdődy family by Mátyás

Nepauer, the leading architect of the day. It features outstanding Baroque façades on its Danube, courtyard and street sides. Like many houses on this street, it was erected on the ruins of medieval houses.

In 1800, Ludwig van Beethoven, who was then giving concerts in Budapest, resided here for a short period.

The palace now houses the Museum of Musical History and the Béla Bartók archives. A permanent exhibition illustrates musical life in Budapest from the 18th to 20th centuries, and includes the oldest surviving Hungarian musical instruments.

The Royal Mint stood on the site of No. 9 during the Middle Ages, and, in 1810, the Joseph Barracks were built here. These were later used by the Habsburgs to imprison leaders of the 1848–9 uprising, including Mihály Táncsics himself.

An original mural has survived on the façade of the house at No. 16, which dates from around 1700. It depicts Christ and the Virgin Mary surrounded by saints. The bas-reliefs on the gateway are, however, from a Venetian church.

Relics of Buda's Jewish heritage can be found at Nos. 23 and 26. The remains of a 15th-century synagogue stand in the garden of the mansion at No. 23. During archeological excavations, tombs and religious items were also found in the courtyard of No. 26.

The Museum of Musical History on Mihály Táncsics Street

Mátyás Church ⓫

THE PARISH CHURCH of Our Lady Mary was built on this site between the 13th and 15th centuries. Some of the existing architectural style dates from the reign of Sigismund of Luxembourg, but its name refers to King Mátyás Corvinus, who greatly enlarged and embellished the church. Much of the original detail was lost when the Turks converted the church into the Great Mosque in 1541. During the liberation of Buda the church was almost totally destroyed, but was rebuilt in the Baroque style by Franciscan Friars. The church sustained more damage in 1723, and was restored in the Neo-Gothic style by Frigyes Schulek in 1873–96. The crypt houses the Museum of Ecclesiastical Art.

Rose Window
Frigyes Schulek faithfully repro-duced the medieval stained-glass window that was in this position during the early Gothic era.

Béla Tower
This tower is named after the church's founder, King Béla IV. It has retained several of its original Gothic features.

★ Baroque Madonna
According to legend, the original statue was set into a wall of the church during the Turkish occupa-tion. When the church was virtually destroyed in 1686, the Madonna made a miraculous appearance. The Turks took this as an omen of defeat.

Main Portal
Above the arched west entrance is a 19th-century bas-relief of the Madonna and Child, seated between two angels. The work is by Lajos Lantai.

STAR FEATURES

- ★ Baroque Madonna
- ★ Mary Portal
- ★ Tomb of King Béla III and Anne de Châtillon

★ **Tomb of King Béla III and Anne de Châtillon**
The remains of this royal couple were transferred from Székesfehérvár Cathedral to Mátyás Church in 1860. They lie beneath an ornamental stone canopy in the Trinity Chapel.

VISITORS' CHECKLIST

Szentháromság tér 2. **Map** 1 B4 (9
A2). Várbusz. 9am–5pm
Mon–Fri, 9am–1pm Sat, 1–5pm Sun.
7am, 8:30am, 6pm.
Museum 9am–5pm Sun–Fri.

Pulpit
The richly decorated pulpit includes the carved stone figures of the four Fathers of the Church and the four Evangelists.

The roof is decorated with multicoloured glazed tiles.

. The main altar was created by Frigyes Schulek and based on Gothic triptychs.

Stained-Glass Windows
Three arched windows on the south elevation have beautiful 19th-century stained glass. They were designed by Frigyes Schulek, Bertalan Székely and Károly Lotz.

★ **Mary Portal**
This depiction of the Assumption of the Blessed Virgin Mary is the most magnificent example of Gothic stone carving in Hungary. Frigyes Schulek reconstructed the portal using fragments that remained after World War II.

TIMELINE

c.1387 Church redesigned as Gothic hall-church by Sigismund of Luxembourg

1458 Thanksgiving mass following the coronation of Mátyás Corvinus

1541 Turks convert church into a mosque

1686 After liberation of Buda from Turkish rule, church is almost destroyed. New church built with a Baroque interior

Holy figures on the pulpit

1250	1350	1450	1550	1650	1750	1850	1950

1309 Coronation of the Angevin king Charles Robert

1255 Church originally founded by King Béla IV after the Mongol invasion

1526 Cathedral burnt in the first attack by Turks

1470 Mátyás Tower is completed after its collapse in 1384

1896 Frigyes Schulek completes the reconstruction of the church in the Neo-Gothic style

1945 Church is severely damaged by German and Russian armies

1970 Final details are completed in post-war rebuilding programme

Vienna Gate, rebuilt in 1936, commemorating the liberation of Buda

In 1966 the world's first catering museum opened here. Small but charming, this exhibition displays, among other items, the interior of a Buda pâtisserie from 1870 and the bust of Emil Gerbeaud, the founder of Pest's most famous coffee shop, by Alajos Stróbl.

Parliament Street ⓳
ORSZÁGHÁZ UTCA

Map 1 A4 & 1 B4.

THIS STREET was once inhabited by Florentine artisans and craftsmen working on King Mátyás' Royal Palace (see pp70–71) and was known for a time as Italian Street. Its present name comes from the building at No. 28, where the Hungarian parliament met from 1790–1807. This building was designed in the 18th century by the architect Franz Anton Hillebrandt as a convent for the Poor Clares. However, Emperor Joseph II dissolved the order before the building was completed.

Numerous houses on this street have retained attractive Gothic and Baroque features. No. 2, now with a Neo-Classical façade, is the site of the Alabárdos Étterem (see p196), but its history dates back to the late 13th century. In the 15th century, Sigismund of Luxembourg built a Gothic mansion here and some details, such as the colonnade around the courtyard and the murals on the second floor, have survived until the present day. The entrance to No. 9 features the Gothic traceried seat niches popular in Buda at this time.

In front of the Neo-Classical house at No. 21 is a statue of Márton Lendvay (1807–58), a famous Hungarian actor and member of the Hungarian National Theatre.

Vienna Gate Square ⓰
BÉCSI KAPU TÉR

Map 1 B4.
🚌 Várbusz from Moszkva tér.

THE SQUARE TAKES its name from the gate that once led from the walled town of Buda towards Vienna. After being damaged several times, the old gate was demolished in 1896. The current gate, based on a historic design, was erected in 1936 on the 250th anniversary of the liberation of Buda from the Turks.

The square has a number of interesting houses. Those at Nos. 5, 6, 7 and 8 were built on the ruins of medieval dwellings. They are Baroque and Rococo in design and feature sculptures and bas-reliefs. The façade of No. 7 has medallions with the portraits of Classical philosophers and poets; Thomas Mann, the German novelist, lodged here between 1935–6. No. 8, meanwhile, is differentiated by its bay windows, attics and the restored medieval murals on its façade.

On the left-hand side of the square is a vast Neo-Romanesque building with a beautiful multicoloured roof, built in 1913–20 by Samu Pecz. This building houses the National Archive, which holds documents dating from before the battle of Mohács in 1526 and others connected with the Rákóczi and Kossuth uprisings (see pp 25, 31 and 38).

Behind the Vienna Gate Square is a monument built in honour of Mihály Táncsics, the leader of the Autumn Uprising. It was unveiled in 1970.

Buda Lutheran Church ⓱
BUDAVÁRI EVANGÉLIKUS TEMPLOM

Bécsi kapu tér. **Map** 1 B4.
🚌 Várbusz. ♿

FACING THE VIENNA GATE is the Neo-Classical Lutheran church, built in 1896 by Mór Kollina. A plaque commemorates pastor Gábor Sztéhló, who saved 2,000 children during World War II.

At one time, a painting by Bertalan Székely, called Christ Blessing the Bread, adorned the altar, but it was unfortunately destroyed during the war.

Museum of Commerce and Catering ⓲
KERESKEDELMI ÉS VENDÉGLÁTÓIPARI MÚZEUM

Fortuna utca 4. **Map** 1 B4.
📞 375 62 49. 🚌 16, Várbusz.
🕐 10am–5pm Wed–Fri, 10am–6pm Sat–Sun. 📷 ♿

FORMERLY THE Fortuna Inn from 1784–1868, this building was erected on the ruins of three medieval houses in the 17th and 18th centuries. The façade has original Gothic niches and a Baroque gate.

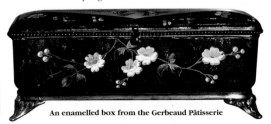

An enamelled box from the Gerbeaud Pâtisserie

The reconstructed Baroque tower of the Church of St Mary Magdalene

Church of St Mary Magdalene ⑳

MÁRIA MAGDOLNA TEMPLOM TORNYA

Kapisztrán tér 6. **Map** 1 A4.
Várbusz.

N OW IN RUINS, this church was built in the mid-13th century. During the Middle Ages, Hungarian Christians worshipped here as Mátyás Church was only for use by the town's German population.

The church did not become a mosque until the second half of the Turkish occupation, but was severely damaged in 1686 during the liberation of Buda. A Baroque church and tower were then built by the Franciscans who took it over.

After World War II, all but the tower and the gate were pulled down. These now stand in a garden, together with the reconstructed Gothic window.

Museum of War History ㉑

HADTÖRTÉNETI MÚZEUM

Kapisztrán tér 2–4. **Map** 1 A4.
356 95 86. Várbusz.
Apr–Sep: 10am–6pm daily;
Oct–Mar: 10am–4pm daily.
by arrangement.

T HE MUSEUM IS LOCATED in a wing of the former Palatine barracks. It houses a wide range of military items relating to the skirmishes and wars that have afflicted Budapest from before the Turkish occupation to the 20th century. Uniforms, flags, weapons, maps and ammunition from as far back as the 11th century give an insight into the long, turbulent history of Budapest.

Of particular interest is the exhibit concerning the 1956 Uprising. Photographs illustrate the 13 days of demonstrations that ended in a Soviet invasion and a huge civilian death toll.

Lords' Street ㉒

ÚRI UTCA

Map 1 A4, 1 B4 and 1 B5 (9 A2).
Várbusz. **Telephone Museum**
201 81 88. Apr–Oct: 10am–6pm daily; Nov–Mar 10am–4pm daily. **Labyrinth** 212 02 07.
9:30am–7:30pm daily.

T HE BUILDINGS IN Lords' Street were destroyed first in 1686 and again in 1944. Reconstruction in 1950–60 restored much of their original medieval character. Almost all have some remnant of a Gothic gateway or hall, while the façade is Baroque or Neo-Classical.

An excellent example of a Gothic façade can be seen on Hölbling House at No. 31. Enough of its original features survived the various wars and renovations to enable architects to reconstruct the façade in considerable detail. The first-floor window is a particularly splendid Gothic feature. The houses opposite are also examples of this restoration work.

The building at No. 53 was rebuilt between 1701–22 as a Franciscan monastery, but in 1789 it was restyled for use by Emperor Joseph II. In 1795, Hungarian Jacobites, led by Ignác Martinovics, were imprisoned here; a plaque records this event. A well featuring a copy of a sculpture of Artemis, the Greek goddess of hunting, by Praxiteles, was set in front of the house in 1873.

There are two museums located on Lords' Street. The Telephone Museum, at No. 49, is a former telephone exchange and one of the most fun and interactive museums in the city. At No. 9 is the entrance to the Labyrinth. Visitors to this new attraction can explore a section of the expansive complex of cellars, dungeons, springs and caves that run beneath Castle Hill. Within the Labyrinth is an exhibition focusing on the early period of Hungarian history and on the legends, such as that of the Magic Stag, that are connected with this era.

Lords' Street, which runs the full length of the Old Town

GELLÉRT HILL AND TABÁN

Carving on the altar in the Cave Church

RISING STEEPLY beside the Danube, Gellért Hill is one of the city's most attractive areas. From the top, at a height of 140 m (460 ft), a beautiful view of the whole of Budapest unfolds. The Celtic Eravi, who preceded the Romans, formed their settlement on the hill's northern slope *(see p94)*. Once called simply Old Hill, many superstitions and tales are connected

with it. In 1046, heathen citizens threw a sealed barrel containing Bishop Gellért, who was trying to convert them to Christianity, from the hill to his death. Afterwards, the hill was named after this martyr. Gellért Hill bulges out slightly into the Danube, which narrows at this point. This made the base of the hill a favoured crossing place, and the settlement of Tabán evolved as a result.

KEY

▨	Street-by-Street map *See pp88–9*
🅿	Parking
Ⓜ	Metro
🚓	Police station
✉	Post office
🚌	Bus stop

0 metres   300

0 yards   300

SIGHTS AT A GLANCE

Museums
Semmelweis Museum of Medical History **12**

Churches
Cave Church **2**
Tabán Parish Church **10**

Historic Buildings
Citadel **4**
Golden Stag House **13**

Hotels and Baths
Gellért Hotel and Baths Complex pp90–91 **1**
Rác Baths **9**
Rudas Baths **6**

Districts, Squares and Monuments
Liberation Monument **3**
Miklós Ybl Square **11**
Queen Elizabeth Monument **7**
Statue of St Gellért **5**
Tabán **8**

GETTING THERE
The easiest ways to ascend Gellért Hill are to drive up, or to take bus 27, which makes its way from Móricz Zsigmond körtér right up to the top of the hill. Tram 19 travels to Tabán along the Danube from the tram station at Batthyány tér, while bus 86 stops there on its route from Óbuda. Buses 5, 7, 8, 78, 112 and 116, all originating in Pest, also make stops in Tabán.

◁ **The Statue of St Gellért, dedicated to a murdered 11th-century bishop**

Street-by-Street: Gellért Hill

THE HILL TO THE SOUTH OF CASTLE HILL was long regarded as a notorious spot. In the 11th century, Prince Vata, brother of King István, incited a heathen rebellion here that resulted in the death of Bishop Gellért. During the Middle Ages, witches were even reputed to celebrate their sabbath here. Under the Turks, a small stronghold was first built on the hill to protect Buda. In 1851, the Austrians placed their own bleak and intimidating Citadel at the summit. Not until the end of the 19th century did the popular image of Gellért Hill begin to change, when it became a venue for picnicking parties. In 1967, the area around the Citadel was made into an attractive park.

Queen Elizabeth Monument
Close to the entrance to Elizabeth Bridge stands this statue of Emperor Franz Joseph's wife, who was popular with the Hungarians **7**

★ Statue of St Gellért
Blessing the city with his uplifted cross, the martyred Bishop Gellért is the patron saint of Budapest **5**

HEGYALJA ÚT

Citadel
Once a place to inspire terror, the Citadel now hosts a hotel, restaurant and wine bar, where people can relax and enjoy the view **4**

0 metres   500
0 yards   500

KEY

– – – A suggested route

Liberation Monument
At the foot of the Liberation Monument, towering above the city, are two sculptures, one representing the battle with evil **3**

STAR SIGHTS

★ Statue of St Gellért

★ Cave Church

The observation terraces on Gellért Hill provide those who climb up to them with a beautiful panorama over the southern part of Buda and the whole of Pest.

LOCATOR MAP
See Street Finder, maps 3, 4 & 9

★ **Cave Church**
This church was established in 1926 in a holy grotto. Under the Communists, the Pauline order of monks was forced to abandon the church, but it was reopened in 1989 ❷

Gellért Hotel and Baths Complex
One of a number of bath complexes built at the beginning of the 20th century, this magnificent spa hotel was erected here to exploit the natural hot springs ❶

Rudas Baths
These famous Turkish baths, which date from the 16th century, have a characteristic Ottoman cupola ❻

SZENT GELLÉRT RAKPART

THE RESERVOIR

In 1978, a reservoir for drinking water was established close to the Uránia Observatory on Gellért Hill. The surface of the reservoir is covered over and provides a point from which to observe the Royal Palace (*see pp70–71*) to the north. A sculpture by Márta Lessenyei decorates the structure.

Sculpture by Márta Lessenyei on Gellért Hill's reservoir

Gellért Hotel and Baths Complex ❶

Stained-glass window by Bózó Stanisits

Bᴇᴛᴡᴇᴇɴ 1912–18, this hotel and spa was built in the modernist Secession style *(see pp54–7)* at the foot of Gellért Hill. The earliest reference to the existence of healing waters at this spot dates from the 13th century, during the reign of King András II and in the Middle Ages a hospital stood on the site. Baths built here by the Ottomans were referred to by the renowned Turkish travel writer of the day, Evliya Çelebi. The architects of the hotel were Ármin Hegedűs, Artúr Sebestyén and Izidor Sterk. Destroyed in 1945, it was rebuilt and modernized after World War II. The hotel has several restaurants and cafés. The baths include an institute of water therapy, set within Secession interiors, but with modern facilities.

Outdoor Wave Pool
An early swimming pool with a wave mechanism, built in 1927, is situated at the back of the complex, looking towards Gellért Hill behind.

★ Baths
Two separate baths, one for men and one for women, are identically arranged. In each there are three plunge pools, with water at different temperatures, a sauna and a steam bath.

Balconies
The balconies fronting the hotel's rooms have fanciful Secession balustrades that are decorated with lyre and bird motifs.

★ Entrance Hall
The interiors of the hotel, like the baths, have kept their original Secession decor, with elaborate mosaics, stained-glass windows and statues.

Sun Terraces
Situated in the sunniest spot, these terraces are a popular place for drying off in the summer.

VISITORS' CHECKLIST

Szent Gellért tér. **Map** 4 E3.
466 61 66. 7, 7A, 86.
18, 19, 47, 49.
Baths Entrance on Kelenhegyi út. 6am–6pm Mon–Fri, 6am–4pm Sat & Sun.

Hot pool with medicinal spa water

Eastern-Style Towers
The architects who designed the hotel gave its towers and turrets a characteristically oriental, cylindrical form.

Main Staircase
The landings of the main staircase have stained-glass windows by Bózó Stanisits, added in 1933. They illustrate an ancient Hungarian legend about a magic stag, recorded in the poetry of János Arany.

Restaurant Terrace
From this first-floor terrace, diners can appreciate a fine view of Budapest. On the ground and first floors of the hotel there are a total of four cafés and restaurants.

★ Main Façade
Behind the hotel's imposing façade are attractive recreational facilities and a health spa that is also open to non-guests. The entrance to the baths is around to the right from the main entrance, on Kelenhegyi út.

STAR FEATURES

★ Entrance Hall

★ Baths

★ Main Façade

Gellért Hotel and Baths Complex ❶
GELLÉRT SZÁLLÓ ÉS FÜRDŐ

See pp90–91.

Cave Church ❷
SZIKLATEMPLOM

Gellért rakpart 1a. **Map** 4 E3. 🚋 7, 7A, 86. 🚊 18, 19, 47, 49.

O**N THE SOUTHERN** slope of Gellért Hill, the entrance to this grotto church is a short walk from the Gellért Hotel and Baths Complex. Based on the shrine at Lourdes, the church, designed by Kálmán Lux, was established in 1926.

The church was intended for the Pauline order of monks, which was founded in the 13th century by Eusebius of Esztergom. In 1934, 150 years after Joseph II had dissolved the order in Hungary, 15 friars arrived back in the city from exile in Poland. However, their residence lasted only until the late 1950s, when the Communist authorities suspended the activities of the church, accusing the monks of treasonable acts, and sealed the entrance to the grotto.

The church and adjoining monastery were reopened on 27 August 1989, when a papal blessing was conferred on its beautiful new granite altar, designed by Győző Sikot. To the left within the grotto is a copy of the *Black Madonna of Czestochowa* and a depiction of a Polish eagle. Visitors will also see a painting of St Kolbe, a Polish monk who gave his life to protect other inmates at Auschwitz concentration camp. A memorial plaque lists the names of the camps where Polish soldiers were interned during World War II, together with the towns and schools where Polish refugees were sheltered in those years.

The monastery can be reached through the Chapel of St István inside the church. While in this chapel it is worth pausing to look at Béli Ferenc's exquisite wooden sculptures. At the entrance to the church stands a statue of St István.

Liberation Monument ❸
FELSZABADULÁSI EMLÉKMŰ

Map 4 D3. 🚋 27.

P**OSITIONED HIGH** on Gellért Hill, this imposing monument towers over the rest of the city. It was designed by the outstanding Hungarian sculptor Zsigmond Kisfaludi Stróbl and set up here to commemorate the liberation of Budapest by the Russian army in 1945 (*see p34*). The monument was originally intended to honour the memory of István, son of the Hungarian Regent Miklós Horthy, who disappeared in 1943 on the eastern front. However, after the liberation of the city by Russian troops, Marshal Kliment Woroszyłow spotted it in the sculptor's workshop and reassigned it to this purpose.

The central figure on the monument is a woman holding

The Liberation Monument, standing at the top of Gellért Hill

aloft a palm leaf. Standing on its pedestal, this reaches a height of 14 m (46 ft). At the base of the monument there are two allegorical compositions, representing progress and the battle with evil.

The arrival of the Russians in Budapest was a liberation but also the beginning of Soviet rule. After Communism's fall, a figure of a Russian soldier was removed from the monument to Statue Park (*see p160*).

Citadel ❹
CITADELLA

Map 4 D3. 🚋 27. ⭘ *daily.*
🏨 **Hotel Citadella** 📞 466 57 94.
Citadella Discotheque 📞 209 32 71. ⭘ *10pm–4am daily.* **Restaurant** 📞 386 48 02. ⭘ *11am–11pm daily.*

A**FTER THE SUPPRESSION** of the uprising of 1848–9 (*see pp30–31*), the Habsburgs decided to build a fortification on this strategically important site. Constructed in 1850–54, the Citadel housed 60 cannons, which could, in theory, fire on the city at any time. In reality, from its very inception the Citadel did not fulfil any real military requirements, but served rather as a means of intimidating the population.

The Citadel is some 220 m (720 ft) long by 60 m (200 ft) wide, and has walls 4 m (12 ft) high. After peace was agreed with the Habsburgs, Hungarian society continually demanded the destruction of the Citadel, but it was not until 1897 that the Austrian soldiers left their barracks here. A section of its

Entrance to the Cave Church, run by the Pauline order of monks

entrance gateway was then symbolically ripped out.

After much discussion in the early 1960s, the Citadel was converted into a leisure complex. A restaurant *(see p196)*, hotel *(see p182)* and even a nightclub now attract customers up Gellért Hill. From the old defensive walls of the Citadel there is a spectacular panorama of the city.

Statue of St Gellért ❺
SZENT GELLÉRT EMLÉKMŰ

Map 4 E3. 🚍 *27*.

IN 1904 A VAST monument was established on the spot where Bishop Gellért was supposedly murdered in the 11th century. According to the tale, the bishop was thrown into the Danube in a barrel, by a mob opposed to the adoption of Christianity. St Gellért holds a cross in his outstretched hand and a Hungarian convert to Christianity is depicted kneeling at his feet.

The statue was designed by Gyula Jankovits, while the semi-circular collonade behind it is by Imre Francsek. A water source that bubbles up here was used to create the fountain. Overlooking the Elizabeth Bridge, the monument can be seen from virtually every part of the city. It is an especially impressive spectacle at night, when it is illuminated.

The main plunge pool at the Rudas Baths, covered by a Turkish cupola

Rudas Baths ❻
RUDAS GYÓGYFÜRDŐ

Döbrentei tér 9. **Map** 4 D2 (9 C5). 📞 *375 83 73.* **Spa Baths (men only)** ◯ *6am–6pm Mon–Fri, 6am–noon Sat–Sun.* **Swimming pool** ◯ *6am–5pm Mon–Fri, 6am–noon Sat–Sun.*

DATING ORIGINALLY from 1550, these baths were greatly extended in 1566 by Sokoli Mustafa, an Ottoman pasha. The main part of the baths dates from this period. In this section there are an octagonal plunge pool and four small corner pools with water of varying temperatures. An Ottoman cupola provides the roof over the baths.

In more recent years the baths have been extensively modernized and in 1952 a covered swimming pool was added to the complex.

While the swimming pool is mixed, the warm, healing spa water (principally used to remedy rheumatic illnesses) is reserved exclusively for men.

Queen Elizabeth Monument ❼
ERZSÉBET KIRÁLYNÉ SZOBRA

Döbrentei tér. **Map** 4 D2 (9 C5).

THIS MONUMENT TO Queen Elizabeth, wife of Habsburg Emperor Franz Joseph, was created by György Zala.

The statue was erected in its present location in 1986. It stands close to the Elizabeth Bridge *(see p63)*, which was also named after the empress, who showed great friendship to the Hungarians. The statue stood on the opposite side of the river from 1932 until 1947, when the Communists ordered it to be taken down.

The Gellért Monument, a landmark of Budapest overlooking the Elizabeth Bridge

Tabán ❽

Map 3 C1, C2, C3 (9B5). ▦ 18, 19.
▦ 5, 78, 112.

THE TABÁN now consists of a pleasant park and a few historic buildings, but was once very different. In the early 20th century this district, nestling in between Castle Hill and Gellért Hill, was a slum which was cleared as part of a programme to improve the city. Only a few buildings, including Tabán Parish Church, escaped the demolition.

Natural conditions ensured that this was one of the first places in the area where people chose to live. The Celtic Eravi were the first to make a settlement here, while the Romans later built a watchtower from which they could observe people using a nearby crossing point over the river. The first reference to bathing in thermal waters in Tabán dates from the 15th century. The Turks took advantage of this natural asset and built two magnificent baths here, the Rác Baths and the Rudas Baths *(see p93)*, around which a blossoming town was established. Apart from the baths, virtually everything was destroyed in the recapture of Buda in 1686 *(see p26)*.

In the late 17th century, a large number of Serbs, referred to in Hungarian as Rácami, moved into the Tabán after fleeing from the Turks. They were joined by Greeks and Gypsies. Many of the inhabitants of the Tabán at this stage were tanners or made their living on the river. On the hillside above grapevines were cultivated. By the early 20th century, though picturesque, the district was still without proper sanitation. The old, decaying Tabán, with its numerous bars and gambling dens, was demolished and the present green space established in its place.

Gardens with terraces, *decorative stairways and arcades designed by Miklós Ybl were established here to connect the Royal Palace (see pp70–71) with the banks of the Danube.*

A statue of Miklós Ybl, the 19th-century architect, was erected here in 1894. It was designed by Ede Mayer.

Several Ottoman tombstones *stand here. They are the remnants of a cemetery in which the Turks who died defending Buda in 1686 were buried.*

Golden Stag House

0 metres   150

0 yards   150

Rác Baths �ⓐ

RÁC GYÓGYFÜRDŐ

Hadnagy utca 8–10. **Map** 4 D2 (9 B5).
📞 375 83 73. 🚌 18, 19.
🕐 6:30am–6pm Mon, Wed, Fri
(women); 6:30am–6pm Tue, Thu,
Sat (men). 🖼 🚫 except by special
permission.

TAKING THEIR name from the
Serbian, or Rác, people
who once lived here, the baths
date back to the Turkish era
(see pp26–7). This is not clear
from the outside, as the baths
were redeveloped in 1869 to
a design by Miklós Ybl. Inside,
however, original Ottoman
features include an octagonal
pool and cupola. Many locals
take the waters for their
believed therapeutic benefits.

The façade of the Rác Baths

Tabán Parish Church 🔟

TABÁNI PLÉBÁNIATEMPLOM

Attila út 11. **Map** 4 D1 (9 C5). 📞 375
54 91. 🚌 18, 19.

A TEMPLE IS thought to have
stood on this site even in
the reign of Prince Árpád. In
the Middle Ages a church was
built here, which was converted into a mosque by the
Turks and subsequently destroyed. In 1728–36, after the
Habsburgs had taken control
of the city, a second church
was erected to a design by
Keresztély Obergruber. Mátyás
Nepauer added the tower in
the mid-18th century. In 1881
the façade was extended and
the tower crowned by a Neo-
Baroque dome.
   Inside the church, on the
right-hand side under the
choir gallery, is a copy of a

**Tabán Parish Church, with its
Neo-Baroque domed tower**

12th-century carving entitled
Christ of Tabán; the original
is now in the collection of the
Budapest History Museum
(see p72). The altar, pulpit and
several paintings adorning the
walls of the church all date
from the 19th century.

Miklós Ybl Square 🇦🇲

YBL MIKLÓS TÉR

Map 4 D1 (9 C4). 🚌 19.

I T IS NO COINCIDENCE that the
important architect Miklós
Ybl *(see p119)* is commemorated by a statue in this square,
close to many of his buildings.
Among Ybl's most monumen-
tal projects were the State
Opera House *(see pp118–19)*,
St Stephen's Basilica *(see
pp116–17)* and also a large-
scale rebuilding of the Royal
Palace *(see pp70–71)*.
   The Várkert Kiosk, on the
square, was also built by Ybl.
Initially it pumped water up
to the Royal Palace, but in
1903 it was converted into a
café. Since 1992 the building
has contained the Casino-
Valentine Restaurant *(see p196)*.

Semmelweis Museum of Medical History 🇦🇲

SEMMELWEIS ORVOSTÖRTÉNETI MÚZEUM

Apród utca 1–3. **Map** 4 D1 (9 B4).
📞 375 35 33. 🚌 18, 19.
🕐 10:30am–5:30pm Tue–Sun.
🖼 🎥 🚫

T HIS MUSEUM is located in the
18th-century house where
Dr Ignáz Semmelweis was
born in 1818. He is renowned
for his discovery of an
antiseptic-based treatment for
puerperal fever, a fatal condition common among women
who had recently given birth.
   The history of medicine from
ancient Egypt onwards is portrayed in the museum, which
includes a replica 19th-century
pharmacy. Semmelweis's
surgery can also be seen with
its original furniture. In the
courtyard is a monument called
Motherhood by Miklós Borsos.

Golden Stag House 🇦🇲

SZARVAS HÁZ

Szarvas tér 1. **Map** 3 C1 (9 B4).
📞 375 64 51. 🚌 19.

S TANDING AT the foot of
Castle Hill is this distinctive early 19th-century house.
It received its name from the
inn that opened here called
"Under the Golden Stag" –
above the entrance you will
see a bas-relief depicting a
golden stag pursued by two
hunting dogs. The building
still accommodates a restaurant of that name, Aranyszarvas
(see p196), which specializes
in game dishes. There is also
a separate wine bar located
in the cellar.

Bas-relief above the entrance to Golden Stag House

NORTH OF THE CASTLE

BETWEEN CASTLE HILL and the western bank of the Danube, extending north from the Chain Bridge towards Margit körút, is the area known as Víziváros or Water Town. This area gained its name in the Middle Ages due to constant flooding. It was originally an area inhabited by artisans and fishermen who, consequently, remained poorer than their neighbours on Castle Hill. Today,

Decoration on the Millachera well

the church towers of Víziváros create a wonderful vista along the western bank of the Danube.

In the Middle Ages and during the 150 years of Turkish occupation this area north of Castle Hill was fortified by a system of walls. A short section of these walls still exists by No. 66 Margit körút, and is commemorated by a plaque. The tomb of Gül Baba, a Turkish dervish, is in the north of the area. It is one of the few surviving Ottoman monuments.

SIGHTS AT A GLANCE

Churches
Calvinist Church ❸
Capuchin Church ❷
St Anne's Church pp102–3 ❹
St Elizabeth's Church ❻

Historic Buildings and Monuments
Tomb of Gül Baba ❽
Tunnel ❶

Squares
Batthyány Square ❺

Baths
Király Baths ❼
Lukács Baths ❾

GETTING THERE
This area is well served by public transport. Buses 4, 16, 86 and 105 run to Clark Ádám tér (next to the Chain Bridge). Tram 19, metro line M2 (red) and the HÉV suburban train converge at Batthyany tér. The tram and HÉV run parallel with the Danube, the tram from the south, the HÉV from the north. The M2 metro links the area with Pest to the east.

0 metres 300
0 yards 300

KEY

	Street-by-Street map *See pp98–9*
P	Parking
🚉	Train station
M	Metro station
⊠	Post office
⛴	River boat boarding point
🚓	Police station

◁ **The Calvinist Church, viewed from the Danube, beautifully illuminated at night**

Street-by-Street: Víziváros

Fő UTCA, the main street of Víziváros (Water Town), runs the length of the neighbourhood. Numerous cafés and restaurants, spectacular Baroque monuments, and a promenade along the Danube give this area a charming atmosphere. A fine array of churches, in an interesting assortment of architectural styles, reflect the history of the area as far back as the Middle Ages. From the Danube promenade the panorama of Pest opposite, with Parliament *(see pp108–9)* in the foreground, can best be viewed.

★ St Elizabeth's Church
The Baroque pulpit in this church was carved by the Franciscans, for whom the church was built in the mid-18th century ❻

The Hikisch House was built on top of medieval walls. The façade, dating from 1795, features bas-reliefs of cherubs carrying out different tasks. Other reliefs depict allegories of the four seasons.

The White Cross Inn, one of Budapest's earliest inns, was established in 1770. Its asymmetrical façade was created by joining two houses together. Among those reputed to have stayed here are Emperor Joseph II and also Casanova.

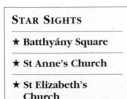

0 metres   100

0 yards   100

★ Batthyány Square
A monument to Ferenc Kölcsey (1790–1838) overlooks this square. He was a literary critic and political commentator of the early 19th century, and also wrote the prayer Lord, Bless Hungary, *which is used as the lyrics for the Hungarian national anthem* ❺

STAR SIGHTS

★ Batthyány Square

★ St Anne's Church

★ St Elizabeth's Church

KEY

- - - Suggested route

★ St Anne's Church
Characteristic of the late Baroque period, the interior of this church is quite stunning. The main portal is decorated with allegorical sculptures of Faith, Hope and Charity ④

LOCATOR MAP
See Street Finder, maps 1 & 9

Calvinist Church
The roof of this church, built in 1893–6, is covered with colourful ceramic tiles from the Zsolnay factory (see p56). They are a strong focal point in the panorama of Buda ③

A Monument to Samu Pecz stands beside one of his most important buildings, the Calvinist Church. Pecz was a follower of the Neo-Gothic movement and constructed many other important buildings in the city.

Capuchin Church
In its original medieval form, this church underwent conversion into a mosque at the hands of the Turks. Many Gothic elements have survived, however. Its present structure dates from 1854–6 ②

To Clark Ádám tér and the Chain Bridge

Kapisztory House, at No. 20 Fő utca, was built in 1811 for the Greek merchant, Joseph Kapisztory. Its unusual turretted cylindrical window is an attractive feature of this street.

The imposing entrance to the Tunnel on Clark Ádám tér

Tunnel ❶

ALAGÚT

Clark Ádám tér. **Map** 1 C5 (9 B3).
🚌 16, 86.

THE SCOTTISH ENGINEER Adam Clark settled in Hungary after completing the Chain Bridge *(see p62)*. One of his later projects, in 1853–7, was building the Tunnel that runs right through Castle Hill, from Clark Ádám tér to Krisztinaváros. The Tunnel is 350 m (1,150 ft) long, 9 m (30 ft) wide and 11 m (36 ft) in height.

The entrance on Clark Ádám tér is flanked by two pairs of Doric columns. This square is the city's official centre because of the location here of the Zero Kilometre Stone, from which all distances from Budapest are calculated.

The Tunnel's western entrance was originally ornamented with Egyptian motifs. However, it was rebuilt without these details after it was damaged in World War II.

Capuchin Church ❷

KAPUCINUS TEMPLOM

Fő utca 32. **Map** 1 C4 (9 B2). 📞 201 47 25. ☙ by arrangement.

THE ORIGINS OF this church date from the 14th century, when the mother of Louis I, Queen Elizabeth, decided to establish a church here. Fragments of walls on the northern façade survive from this time.

During the Turkish occupation *(see pp26–7)*, the church was converted into a mosque. Features from this period, such

as the window openings and and the doorway on the southern façade, have remained despite the fighting of 1686.

Between 1703–15 the church was rebuilt, following a Baroque design created by one of the Capuchin Fathers.

In 1856 the church was again restyled, by Ferenc Reitter and Pál Zsumrák, who linked differently styled façades harmoniously together. The statue of St Elizabeth on the mid-19th-century Romantic façade also dates from 1856.

The altar of the Capuchin Church

Calvinist Church ❸

REFORMÁTUS TEMPLOM

Szilágyi Dezső tér 3. **Map** 1 C4 (9 B2). 📞 201 37 25.

ONE OF BUDAPEST'S more unusual churches, the Calvinist Church was built by Samu Pecz between 1893–6 on the site of a former medieval market. It is one of the major examples of his work.

Despite the use of modern tiles on the roof, the church is

Neo-Gothic in style. It is also interesting to note that Pecz used this traditional design of medieval Catholic churches for a Calvinist church, which has very different liturgical and ecclesiastical needs.

St Anne's Church ❹

SZENT ANNA TEMPLOM

See pp102–3.

Batthyány Square ❺

BATTHYÁNY TÉR

Map 1 C3 (9 B1). Ⓜ *Batthyány tér.*

BATTHYÁNY SQUARE is one of the most interesting squares on the Danube's western bank. Beautiful views of Parliament and Pest on the opposite bank unfold from here.

In 1905 the square was renamed after Count Lajos Batthyány, the prime minister during the Hungarian uprising of 1848–9 *(see pp30–31)*, who was shot by the Austrian army.

The square features buildings in many different styles. The Hikisch House, at No. 3, dating from the late 18th century, is late Baroque. It is notable for the bas-reliefs on its façade depicting the four seasons. The White Cross Inn, at No. 4, also late Baroque, features Rococo decoration. On the western side of the square is the first covered market in Buda, dating from 1902. Though damaged in World War II, it is now fully restored.

The Hikisch House, with bas-reliefs representing the four seasons

St Elizabeth's Church ⓺

ERZSÉBET APÁCÁK TEMPLOMA

Fő utca 41–43. **Map** 1 C3 (9 B1).
█ 201 80 91. Ⓜ Batthyány tér.

IN 1731–57 A CHURCH was built for the Franciscan order on the ruins of a former mosque, to a design by Hans Jakab. In 1785, after he had dissolved the Franciscan order, Emperor Joseph II gave the church to St Elizabeth's Convent.

The Baroque interior is adorned with late 19th-century frescoes, including one of St Florian protecting Christians from a fire in 1810. Their resonance is due to their recent restoration. The original pulpit and pews, carved by the friars, have remained intact.

In the early 19th century, a hospital and hostel were built adjacent to the church. These were run by the Elizabeth Sisters.

Király Baths ⓻

KIRÁLY GYÓGYFÜRDŐ

Fő utca 84. **Map** 1 C2.
█ 201 43 92. Ⓜ Batthyány tér.
◯ 7am–5pm Mon, Wed, Fri (women); 9am–8pm Tue, Thu, Sat (men).

THE OTTOMAN Király Baths are one of the city's four remaining Turkish baths (see p50–53). Built from 1566–70, with 19th-century neo-classical additions, they retain many original features, the most beautiful being the central cupola hall with its octagonal pool. From here radiate out the smaller pools of different temperatures, the steam rooms and saunas.

At the end of Fő utca, in the square that bears his name is the monument to the Polish general József Bem. The hero of the 1848–9 uprisings, he is depicted with his arm in a sling. It was in this state, in the front line of the Battle of Pisk, that he inspired the Hungarian troops to attack the bridge and achieve victory over the Habsburg armies. Memorable words, which he uttered during the battle, are engraved on the base of the monument.

Tiles on the Tomb of Gül Baba

Tomb of Gül Baba ⓼

GÜL BABA TÜRBÉJE

Mecset utca 14. **Map** 1 B1.
▦ 91. ◯ May–Oct: 10am–6pm Tue–Sun; Nov–Apr: 10am–6pm Mon–Sun.

GÜL BABA WAS a Muslim dervish and member of the Bektashi order, who died in 1541, just after the capture of Buda. He was one of the few Turks who was respected and revered by the people of Hungary. His remains now lie in a tomb built between 1543 and 1598.

According to legend, it was Gül Baba who introduced roses to Budapest. From this came both the name of this area, Rózsadomb, meaning Rose Hill, and Gül Baba's own name, which in English means Father of Roses. Fittingly, the tomb of Gül Baba is surrounded by a lovely rose garden.

A 400-year-old dome covers the octagonal tomb. Inside, the sarcophagus is draped in green cloth with gold citations from the Koran. Pictures, religious items and beautiful rugs also adorn the tomb.

Lukács Baths ⓽

LUKÁCS GYÓGYFÜRDŐ

Frankel Leo út 25–9. **Map** 1 C1.
█ 326 16 95. ◯ 6am–7pm daily.
▦ 17.

THIS FAMOUS SPA is named after St Luke. Although the Neo-Classical complex was established in 1894, the baths are one of a number still operating in the city (see pp50–53) that date back to the period of Turkish rule.

Set in peaceful surroundings, the complex comprises the 16th-century Komjády (Császár) thermal baths and two outdoor swimming pools. Natural hot springs keep these pools heated all year round, allowing locals and tourists to bathe in comfort even in winter.

It is also worth entering the overgrown courtyard to see a statue of St Luke, dating from 1760, and the plaques inscribed with thanks by bathers from around the world who benefited from the healing waters.

Lukács Baths, with beautiful old plane trees growing outside

St Anne's Church ❹

BUDAPEST IS HOME to many churches, but the twin-towered parish church of Víziváros is one of its most beautiful Baroque examples. Initially a Jesuit church, the architect who first designed it is unknown. Building was begun in 1740 by Kristóf Hámon and completed after his death by Mátyás Nepauer. In 1763 an earthquake seriously damaged the building and the dissolution of the Jesuit order ten years later further delayed the completion of the church. Thus it remained unconsecrated until 1805. The rectory now houses the Angelika café.

Crucifix on the St Cross altar

The twin towers are crowned by magnificent Baroque spires.

Façade
Buda's coat of arms appears in the centre of the tympanum. The symbol of the Trinity is above this, between two kneeling angels.

★ Pulpit
This magnificent, late Baroque pulpit was created by Károly Bebó in 1773. It features gilded details and angels that embody theological virtues. The reliefs were added at a later date.

Main entrance

Organ
The organ case from a former Carmelite church on Castle Hill was transferred to St Anne's Church in the late 18th century, after the dissolution of the order by Emperor Joseph II.

★ Painted Ceiling
The painted ceiling in the cupola of the chancel depicts the Holy Trinity. It was painted in 1771 by Gergely Vogl. There are also Neo-Baroque frescoes in the nave dating from 1938.

VISITORS' CHECKLIST

Batthyány tér 7. **Map** 1 C3 (9 B1).
📞 201 34 04. Ⓜ *Batthyány tér.*
⭕ *only for services.* ✝ *daily.*
Angelika café 📞 *212 37 84.*
⭕ *10am–10pm daily.*

★ High Altar
The sculptures depict Mary, as a child, being brought into the Temple of Jerusalem by St Anne, her mother. Completed in 1773, it is regarded as one of the most beautiful works of Károly Bebó.

Church Pew
The choir pews are decorated with intricately carved wooden panels which feature figurative scenes.

Baptismal Font
Concealed behind a pillar, this baptismal font has a carved pedestal and a simply, but beautifully, decorated cover.

Side Altar
This late Baroque altar of St Francis the Saviour, like the altar of St Cross on the opposite side of the church, is the work of Antal Eberhardt and dates from 1768. The picture in the centre was, however, executed by Franz Wagenschön.

STAR FEATURES

★ **Painted Ceiling**

★ **High Altar**

★ **Pulpit**

AROUND PARLIAMENT

Towards the end of the 18th and throughout the 19th century Pest underwent a series of huge changes. In 1838 a flood destroyed most of the rural dwellings that had occupied the area until that time. The unification of Budapest in 1873 and the 1,000-year anniversary, in 1896, of the Magyar conquest also boosted the city's development. The medieval walls that originally

An ornate lantern on the Parliament

marked Pest's limits were crossed as the area was gradually urbanized. This period produced a number of the most important buildings in Hungary, including St Stephen's Basilica, Parliament and the Hungarian Academy of Sciences, which were built in a variety of revivalist styles. Many Neo-Classical residences were also built, particularly on Nádor utca, Akadémia utca and Október 6 utca.

SIGHTS AT A GLANCE

Historic Buildings and Palaces
Central European University **6**
Drechsler Palace **12**
Gresham Palace **8**
Hungarian Academy of Sciences **9**
Ministry of Agriculture **3**
Parliament pp108–9 **1**
Post Office Savings Bank **5**
Radisson Béke Hotel **13**

Museums
Ethnographical Museum **2**

Squares
Liberty Square **4**
Roosevelt Square **7**

Theatres
Budapest Operetta Theatre **14**
State Opera House pp118–19 **11**

Churches
St Stephen's Basilica pp116–17 **10**

GETTING THERE
The M2 metro line (red) runs to Kossuth Lajos tér and the M3 metro line (blue) runs to Arany János utca. Tram 2 runs north along the Danube and terminates past Parliament at Margaret Bridge. Trolley buses 70 and 78 also serve this area.

KEY

Street-by-Street map *See pp106–7*

Street-by-Street map *See pp112–13*

P   Parking

M   Metro station

⊠   Post office

🚓   Police station

ℹ   Tourist information

0 metres   500
0 yards   500

◁ Neo-Gothic spires, flying buttresses and stained-glass windows on Hungary's Parliament

Street-by-Street: Kossuth Square

Brigadier Woroniecki

THIS SQUARE expresses well the pomp and pride with which Pest was developed during the 19th and early 20th centuries. Parliament dominates the square on the Danube side, but equally imposing are the Ministry of Agriculture and the Ethnographical Museum on the opposite side. Several monuments commemorate nationalist leaders and provide a visual record of Hungary's recent political history.

★ **Ethnographical Museum**
Among 170,000 exhibits amassed in the museum's collection is a captivating collection of folk costumes representing the various nationalities and ethnic groups in Hungary ❷

★ **Parliament**
This building has become the recognized symbol of democracy in Hungary, despite the dome being crowned by a red star during the Communist period ❶

Attila József was a radical poet whose work sensitively explored the human condition. In 1937 he committed suicide, aged 32. This statue by László Marton dates from 1980.

B A L A S S I   B Á L I N T   U .

LAJOS KOSSUTH (1802–94)

The popularity of Lajos Kossuth among the Hungarian people is immense. He led the 1848–9 uprising against Austrian rule *(see pp30–31)*, and was one of the most outstanding political figures in Hungary. He was a member of the first democratic government during the uprising, and briefly became its leader before being exiled after the revolt was quashed in 1849.

Stained-glass window depicting Lajos Kossuth

0 metres   150

0 yards   150

Ferenc II Rákóczi, the prince of Transylvania, led one of the earliest revolts for independence against the Habsburgs in 1703–11. This bronze equestrian monument can be seen in front of Parliament. It was completed by János Pásztor in 1937.

LOCATOR MAP
See Street Finder, maps 4 & 7

Ministry of Agriculture
A massive Corinthian colonnade, supporting an entablature, lends this Neo-Classical building a dignified character ❸

This monument to Imre Nagy symbolizes the insurgent prime minister's 1956 defection from the side of Communism to the side of the people – a protest that cost him his life.

The Hungarian TV headquarters were designed in the Neo-Classical style by Ignác Alpár. Constructed in 1905, the building originally housed the Stock Exchange.

VECSEY UTCA

RIBALDI UTCA

UTCA

Plaque commemorating Brigadier Woroniecki, hero of the uprising of 1948–9

KEY

– – – Suggested route

STAR SIGHTS

★ **Parliament**

★ **Ethnographical Museum**

Parliament ❶

Hungary's Parliament is the country's largest building and has become a symbol of Budapest. A competition was held to choose its design, the winner being Imre Steindl's rich Neo-Gothic masterpiece built between 1884–1902. Based on the Houses of Parliament in London, completed by Charles Barry in 1835 – 6, it is 268 m (880 ft) long and 96 m (315 ft) high, and comprises 691 rooms.

One of the pair of lions at the main entrance

Aerial View
The magnificent dome marks the central point of the Parliament building. Although the façade is elaborately Neo-Gothic, the ground plan follows Baroque conventions.

★ **Domed Hall**
Adorning the massive pillars that support Parliament's central dome are figures of some of the rulers of Hungary.

Danube façade

★ **National Assembly Hall**
Formerly the upper house, this hall is now where the National Assembly convenes. Two paintings by Zsigmond Vajada hang on either side of the Speaker's lectern. These were especially commissioned for the building.

South wing

Gables
Almost every corner of the Parliament building features gables with pinnacles based on Gothic sculptures.

Lobby
Lobbies, the venues for political discussions, are to be found along the corridors beneath stained-glass windows.

Dome
The ceiling of the 96-m (315-ft) high dome is covered in an intricate design of Neo-Gothic gilding combined with heraldic decoration.

VISITORS' CHECKLIST

Kossuth Lajos tér. **Map** 2 D3 (9 C1). 441 49 04. 2, 2A. Kossuth tér. 70, 78. guided tours only. English: times vary; phone for information.

Gobelin Hall
This hall is deco-rated with a Gobelin tapestry illustrating Prince Árpád, with seven Magyar leaders under his command, signing a peace treaty and blood oath.

North wing

Congress Hall
This vast hall is virtually a mirror image of the National Assembly Hall. Both halls have public galleries running around a horseshoe-shaped interior.

...e Royal Insignia, ...cluding the ...ronation Mantle ...e p132), are kept in ...e Domed Hall.

The main entrance on Kossuth Lajos tér

STAR FEATURES

★ **National Assembly Hall**

★ **Domed Hall**

Main Staircase
The best contemporary artists were invited to decorate the interior. The sumptuous main staircase features ceiling frescoes by Károly Lotz and sculptures by György Kiss.

The magnificent hall of the Ethnographical Museum

Parliament ●

ORSZÁGHÁZ

See pp108–9.

Ethnographical Museum ●

NÉPRAJZI MÚZEUM

Kossuth Lajos tér 12. **Map** 2 D3 (9 C1). **C** 473 24 00. **M** Kossuth Lajos tér. **O** 10am–6pm daily. 🎨 📷 ▯

THIS BUILDING, designed by Alajos Hauszmann and constructed between 1893–6, was built as the Palace of Justice and, until 1945, served as the Supreme Court.

The building's design links elements of Renaissance, Baroque and Classicism. The façade is dominated by a vast portico crowned by two towers. It also features a gable crowned by the figure of the Roman goddess of justice in a chariot drawn by three horses, by Károly Senyei. The grand hall inside the main entrance features a marvellous staircase and frescoes by Károly Lotz.

The building was first used as a museum in 1957, housing the Hungarian National Gallery (see pp74–7), which was later transferred to the Royal Palace. The Ethnographical Museum has been here since 1973.

The museum's collection was established in 1872 in the Department of Ethnography at the Hungarian National Museum (see pp130–33). There are now around 170,000 exhibits, although the majority are not currently on display. The collection includes artifacts reflecting the rural folk culture of Hungary from the prehistoric era to the 20th century. A map from 1909 shows the settlement of the various communities who came to Hungary. Ethnic items relating to these communities, as well as primitive objects from North and South America, Africa, Asia and Australia, can also be seen.

The museum has two very informative permanent displays: Traditional Culture of the Hungarian Nation, on the first floor, and From Primeval Communities to Civilization, on the second floor.

Ministry of Agriculture ●

FÖLDMŰVELÉSÜGYI MINISZTÉRIUM

Kossuth Lajos tér 11. **Map** 2 D3 (9 C1). **M** Kossuth Lajos tér.

ON THE SOUTHEAST side of Kossuth Square is this huge building, bordered by streets on all its four sides. It was built for the Ministry of Agriculture by Gyula Bukovics at the end of the 19th century.

The façade is designed in a manner typical of late Historicism, drawing heavily on Neo-Classical motifs. The columns of the colonnade are echoed in the fenestration above the well-proportioned pedimented windows.

On the wall to the right of the building two commemorative plaques can be seen. The first is dedicated to the commanding officer of the Polish Legion, who was also a hero of the 1948–9 uprising (see p30–31). Brigadier M Woroniecki, who was renowned for his bravery, was shot down on this spot by the Austrians in October 1849.

The second plaque honours Endre Ságvári, a Hungarian hero of the resistance movement, who died in the fighting against the Fascists in 1944.

The two sculptures in front of the building are by Árpád Somogyi. The *Reaper Lad* dates from 1956 and the *Female Agronomist* from 1954.

Liberty Square ●

SZABADSÁG TÉR

Map 2 E4 (10 D1). **M** Kossuth Lajos tér, Arany János utca.

AFTER THE enormous Neuge bäude Barracks were demolished in 1886, Liberty Square was laid out in its place. The barracks, built for the Austrian troops, once dominated the southern part of Lipótváros (Leopold Town). It was here that Hungary's first independent prime minister, Count Lajos Batthyány was executed on 6 October 1849. Since 1926, an eternal flame (see p31) has been burning at the corner of Aulich utca, Hold utca and Báthory utca to honour all those executed during the uprising.

Two particularly impressive buildings by Ignác Alpár are on opposite sides of the square. The former Stock Exchange, now the Hungarian TV headquarters (Magyar Televízió székháza), dates from 1905 and shows the influence of the Secession style. The Hungarian National Bank (Magyar Nemzeti Bank) is decorated in a pastiche of Historicist styles and also dates from 1905.

Bas-reliefs on the former the Stock Exchange

Beautiful Secession interior of the Post Office Savings Bank

An obelisk by Károly Antal stands at the northern end of the square commemorating the Red Army soldiers who died during the siege of Budapest in 1944–5. A second statue is to the US general Harry Hill Bandholtz. He led the allied forces that thwarted the Romanian troops looting the Hungarian National Museum.

Post Office Savings Bank ❺
POSTATAKARÉK PÉNZTÁR

Hold utca 4. **Map** 2 E4 (10 D1).
Ⓜ *Kossuth Lajos tér.*

A MASTERPIECE BY Ödön Lechner, the former Post Office Savings Bank was built between 1900– 1901. Chiefly a Secession architect, Lechner *(see p56)* combined the curvilinear motifs of that style with motifs from Hungarian folk art to produce a unique visual style for his work.

Approaching the Post Office Savings Bank, one can see glimpses of the details that have made this building one of Pest's most unusual sights. The construction methods, interior design and exterior detailing of the building are remarkable. Lechner commissioned the tiles used in the design, including the vibrant roof tiles, from the Zsolnay factory *(see p56)*. The façades are decorated with floral tendrils and icons taken from nature. The bees climbing up the gable walls represent the bank's activity and the pinnacles, which look like hives, represent the accumulation of savings. These features were intended to be accessible to the people who banked here.

The building is not officially open to the public, but it is possible to see the Cashiers' Hall during office hours.

Central European University ❻
KÖZÉP-EURÓPAI EGYETEM

Nádor utca 9. **Map** 2 E5 (10 D2).
Ⓒ *327 30 00.* Ⓜ *Kossuth Lajos tér.*

THIS NEO-CLASSICAL palace can be found on Nádor utca, in the direction of Roosevelt Square. It was built in 1826 by Mihály Pollack for Prince Antal Festetics. Since 1993 it has housed the Central European University.

Founded by the American millionaire George Soros, who was born in Budapest, this international educational establishment is open to students from central and eastern Europe and the former USSR.

The university offers postgraduate courses in subjects ranging from history and law to political and environmental sciences. In Budapest, the Soros Foundation finances numerous other ventures and it has branches in all the central European countries.

THE AMERICAN EMBASSY

This beautiful house, at No. 12 Liberty Square, was designed by Aladár Kálmán and Gyula Ullmann and built between 1899–1901. The façade is decorated with bas-reliefs featuring motifs typical of the Secession style.

By the entrance to the embassy is a plaque with an image of the Catholic Primate, Cardinal Joseph Mindszenty, who was part of the movement seeking to liberate

Plaque commemorating Joseph Mindszenty

Hungary from the Communists after World War II. He was imprisoned by the regime in 1949 and was mistreated for many years. Released during the 1956 uprising, he asked for political asylum in the embassy. He lived here for 15 years in internal exile until, in 1971, the Vatican finally convinced him to leave Hungary.

Street-by-Street: Roosevelt Square

IN 1867, A CERMONIAL MOUND was made of earth from all over the country to celebrate the coronation of Franz Joseph as king of Hungary. Today, the historic earth has been dug into the ground where Roosevelt Square now stands. At the head of the Chain Bridge on the eastern bank of the Danube, it features many of Pest's most beautiful buildings, such as the Hungarian Academy of Sciences, to the north of the square, and Gresham Palace, to the east. The square was named after American president Franklin D Roosevelt in 1947.

No. 1 Akadémia utca was built in the Neo-Classical style by Mátyás Zitterbarth the younger, in 1835. A plaque shows that in November 1848 General József Bem *(see p101)* stayed here when it was the Prince Stephen Hotel.

★ **Gresham Palace**
This 1907 building is one of the most expressive examples of Secession architecture in Budapest ⑧

★ **Hungarian Academy of Sciences**
The debating hall of the Hungarian Academy of Sciences is decorated with sculptures by Miklós Izsó and ceiling paintings by Károly Lotz ⑨

House designed by József Hild in 1836

The Chain Bridge *(see p62)* was built between 1839–49 and was the city's first permanent river crossing. It was destroyed by the German forces in World War II and was reopened in 1949, 100 years after it was first finished.

AKADEMIA UTCA

NADOR UTCA

ROOSEVELT TÉR

The Pichler House is an unusual building. It was completed by Ferenc Wieser between 1853–7 in the style of a Venetian Gothic palace.

LOCATOR MAP
See Street Finder, maps 2, 9 & 10

★ St Stephen's Basilica
The interior of this church was decorated by leading Hungarian artists, such as Alajos Stróbl and Károly Lotz. It was seriously damaged in World War II, and renovation began in the 1980s **10**

NAGY KORONA U

SAS UTCA

SZENT ISTVÁN TÉR

YI UTCA

OLÖBER 6 UTCA

No. 7 Nádor utca is a Neo-Classical building completed in 1830. It has a modest but well-balanced façade accented by pilasters with decorative capitals, and the large first-floor windows are crowned with elegant arches.

| 0 metres | 100 |
| 0 yards | 100 |

KEY

– – – Suggested route

No. 8 József Attila utca, an impressive five-floor office building, was erected in 1898 by Artúr Meinig. It is an attractive example of the use of the Secession style *(see pp54 – 7)*.

STAR SIGHTS

★ **Gresham Palace**

★ **Hungarian Academy of Sciences**

★ **St Stephen's Basilica**

Monument to Ferenc Deák, dating from 1887, in Roosevelt Square

Roosevelt Square ❼
ROOSEVELT TÉR

Map 2 D5 (9 C3). ▦ 16. 🚊 2.

PREVIOUSLY, Roosevelt Square was known by several different names – Franz Joseph Square and Unloading Square among others – but it received its current title in 1947. It is located at the head of the Pest side of the Chain Bridge, and is home to many beautiful and important buildings.

At the beginning of the 20th century the square was lined with various hotels, the Diana Baths and the Lloyd Palace designed by József Hild. The only building from the previous century still standing today is the Hungarian Academy of Sciences. The other buildings were demolished and replaced by the Gresham Palace and the Bank of Hungary, on the corner of Attila József utca. Two large modern hotels, the Atrium Hyatt (see p183) and the Inter-Continental (see p183), stand on the southern side of the square.

There is a statue to Baron József Eötvös (1813–71), a reformer of public education, in front of the Inter-Continental. Situated in the centre of the square are monuments to two politicians who espoused quite different ideologies: Count István Széchenyi (1791–1860), the leading social and political reformer of his age, and Ferenc Deák (1803–76), who was instrumental in the Compromise of 1867, which resulted in the Dual Monarchy (see p32).

Gresham Palace ❽
GRESHAM PALOTA

Roosevelt tér 5–6. Map 2 D5 (9 C3).
【 411 90 00. ▦ 16. 🚊 2.

THIS SECESSION PALACE aroused both controversy and praise from the moment it was built. One of Budapest's most distinctive pieces of architecture, it was commissioned by the London-based Gresham Life Assurance Company from Zsigmond Quittner and the brothers József and László Vágó, and completed in 1907.

This enormous edifice enjoys an imposing location directly opposite the Chain Bridge. The crumbling façade features characteristic Secession motifs (see pp54–7), such as curvilinear forms and organic themes. The ornately carved window surrounds appear as though they are projecting from the walls, blending seamlessly with the architecture. The bust by Ede Telcs, at the top of the façade, is of Sir Thomas Gresham. He was the founder of the Royal Exchange in London and of Gresham's Law: "bad money drives out good".

On the ground floor of the palace there is a T-shaped arcade, covered by a multi-coloured glazed roof, which is occupied by shops and a restaurant. The entrance to the arcade is marked by a beautiful wrought-iron gate with peacock motifs. Still the original gate, it is widely regarded as one of the most splendid examples of design

Bust of Sir Thomas Gresham on the façade of the Gresham Palace

from the Secession era. Two plaques inside the entrance list the directors of the London and Hungarian offices. Inside the building, the second floor of the Kossuth stairway has a stained-glass window by Miksa Róth, featuring a portrait of Lajos Kossuth (see p106).

In 2003 the palace opened as a Four Seasons Hotel, the second in Central Europe, and the first in Hungary.

Miklós Izsó's sculptures inside the Hungarian Academy of Sciences

Hungarian Academy of Sciences ❾
MAGYAR TUDOMÁNYOS AKADÉMIA

Roosevelt tér 9. Map 2 D4 (9 C2).
【 411 61 00. ▦ 16.

BUILT BETWEEN 1862–4, this Neo-Renaissance building was designed by the architect Friedrich August Stüler.

The statues adorning the façade represent six disciplines of knowledge – law, history, mathematics, sciences, philosophy and linguistics – and are the works of Emil Wolf and Miklós Izsó. On the Danube side are allegories of poetry, astronomy and archeology, and on the corners of the building are statues of renowned thinkers including Isaac Newton, René Descartes and Miklós Révay. The beautiful interior features more statues by Miklós Izsó, and the library, on the ground floor, has a priceless collection of academic books.

The Neo-Renaissance façade of the Drechsler Palace

St Stephen's Basilica ⑩

SZENT ISTVÁN BAZILIKA

See pp116–17.

State Opera House ⑪

MAGYAR ÁLLAMI OPERAHÁZ

See pp118–19.

Drechsler Palace ⑫

DRECHSLER PALOTA

Andrássy út 25. **Map** 2 F4 (10 E2).
M *Opera.*

NOW A 5-STAR hotel, and formerly the State Ballet Institute, the Drechsler Palace was originally built as Neo-Renaissance apartments for the Hungarian Railways Pension Fund in 1883. It was designed by Gyula Pártos and Ödön Lechner to harmonize with the façade of the State Opera House *(see pp118– 19)*.
　Its name derives from the Drechsler Café, which occupied the ground floor of this building towards the end of the 19th and in the early 20th century.

Radisson Béke Hotel ⑬

BÉKE RADISSON HOTEL

Teréz körút 43. **Map** 2 F3.
C *301 16 00.* **M** *Oktogon.*

THIS IS ONE OF the most elegant of Budapest's historic hotels. It was built in 1896 as an apartment building, and in 1912 was restyled by

Béla Malmai as the Hotel Brittania. A mosaic, created by György Szondi, was added to the façade at this time.
　In 1978 the hotel was taken over by the Radisson group, which restored the rich interiors. Notable features are the stained-glass windows in the Szondi Restaurant, by Jenő Haranghy, which illustrate the works of Richard Wagner. The Romeo and Juliet conference room and the Shakespeare Restaurant are named after the murals that decorate them. The Zsolnay Café serves cake and coffee on porcelain from the Pécs factory *(see p56)*.

Budapest Operetta Theatre ⑭

BUDAPESTI OPERETT SZÍNHÁZ

Nagymező utca 17. **Map** 2 F4 (10 F1).
C *472 20 30.* 🚋 *4, 5, 6.*

BUDAPEST HAS a good reputation for musical entertainment, and its operetta scene *(see p208)* is over 100 years old. Operettas were first staged on this site in the Orfeum Theatre, designed in the Neo-Baroque style by the Viennese architects Fellner and Helmer, in 1898. The project was financed by the impressario Károly Singer-Somossy.
　In 1922, the American entrepreneur Ben Blumenthal redeveloped the building and opened the Capital Operetta Theatre, which then specialized in the genre. After 1936, this theatre became the only venue for operetta in Budapest.
　The repertoire of the theatre includes the works of both international and Hungarian composers of this genre, including Imre Kálmán, Ferenc Lehár and Pál Ábrahám, who wrote *The Csárdás Princess.*

Entrance to the Budapest Operetta Theatre on Nagymező utca

St Stephen's Basilica ⑩

St István's coronation

Dedicated to st stephen, or István, the first Hungarian Christian king *(see p22)*, this church was designed by József Hild in the Neo-Classical style, using a Greek cross floor plan. Construction began in 1851 and was taken over in 1867 by Miklós Ybl *(see p119)*, who added the Neo-Renaissance dome after the original one collapsed in 1868. József Kauser completed the church in 1905. It received the title of Basilica Minor in 1938, the 900th anniversary of St István's death.

St Matthew
St Matthew is one of the four Evangelists represented in the niches on the exterior of the dome. They are all the work of the sculptor Leó Feszler.

Dome
Reaching 96 m (315 ft), the dome is visible from all over Budapest.

Observation point

Tower
A bell, weighing 9,144 kg (9 tons) is housed in this tower. It was funded by German Catholics to compensate for the original bell, which was looted by the Nazis in 1944.

Main Portal
The massive door is decorated with carvings depicting the heads of the 12 Apostles.

Mosaics
The dome is decorated with mosaics designed by Károly Lotz.

VISITORS' CHECKLIST

Szent István tér. **Map** 2 E4 (10 D2).
317 28 59. **M** Deák Ferenc tér. **Treasury** 9am–5pm daily (winter: 10am–4pm). daily.

★ **Main Altar**
In the centre of the altar there is a marble statue of St István by Alajos Stróbl. Scenes from the king's life are depicted behind the altar.

★ **Holy Right Hand**
Hungary's most unusual relic is the mummified forearm of King István. It is kept in the Chapel of the Holy Right Hand.

Figures of the 12 Apostles, by Leó Feszler, crown the exterior colonnade at the back of the church.

St Gellért and St Emeryka
This portrayal of St Gellért and his pupil, St Emeryka, is the work of Alajos Stróbl.

★ **Paintng by Gyula Benczúr**
This image shows King István, left without an heir, dedicating Hungary to the Virgin Mary, who became Patrona Hungariae, the country's patron.

STAR FEATURES

★ **Main Altar**

★ **Holy Right Hand**

★ **Painting by Gyula Benczúr**

State Opera House ⓫

OPENED IN September 1884, the State Opera House in Budapest was built to rival those of Paris, Vienna and Dresden. Its beautiful architecture and interiors were the life's work of the great Hungarian architect, Miklós Ybl. The interior also features ornamentation by Hungarian artists, including Alajos Stróbl and Károly Lotz. During its lifetime, the State Opera House has seen some influential music directors, including, Ferenc Erkel, composer of the Hungarian opera *Bánk Bán*, Gustav Mahler and Otto Klemperer.

Decorative lamp with putti

Façade
The decoration of the symmetrical façade follows a musical theme. In niches on either side of the main entrance there are figures of two of Hungary's most prominent composers, Ferenc Erkel and Franz Liszt (see p144). Both were sculpted by Alajos Stróbl.

Murals
The vaulted ceiling of the foyer is covered in magnificent murals by Bertalan Székely and Mór Than. They depict the nine Muses.

★ Foyer
The foyer, with its marble columns, gilded vaulted ceiling, murals and chandeliers, gives the State Opera House a feeling of opulence and grandeur.

Main entrance
Wrought-iron lamps illuminate the wide stone staircase and the main entrance.

★ Main Staircase
Going to the opera was a great social occasion in the 19th century. A vast, sweeping staircase was an important element of the opera house as it allowed ladies to show off their new gowns.

Chandelier

The main hall is decorated with a bronze chandelier that weighs 3,050 kg (3 tons). It illuminates a magnificent fresco, by Károly Lotz, of the Greek gods on Olympus.

VISITORS' CHECKLIST

Andrássy út 22. **Map** 2 F4 (10 E2). 📞 *331 25 50*. Ⓜ *Opera*. 📷 🚫 ♿ 🎫 *obligatory*. 🚪 Ⓦ www.opera.hu

Central Stage

This proscenium arch stage employed the most modern technology of the time. It featured a revolving stage and metal hydraulic machinery.

The side entrance has a loggia that reflects the design of the main entrance.

★ Royal Box

The royal box is located centrally in the three-storey circle. It is decorated with sculptures symbolizing the four operatic voices – soprano, alto, tenor and bass.

MIKLÓS YBL (1814 – 91)

The most prominent Hungarian architect of the second half of the 19th century, Miklós Ybl had an enormous influence on the development of Budapest. He was a practitioner of Historicism, and tended to use Neo-Renaissance forms. The State Opera House and the dome of St Stephen's Basilica are examples of his work. Ybl also built apartment buildings and palaces for the aristocracy in this style. A statue of the architect stands on the western bank of the Danube, in Miklós Ybl Square *(see p95)*.

Bust of Miklós Ybl

STAR FEATURES

★ Foyer

★ Royal Box

★ Main Staircase

CENTRAL PEST

AT THE END OF the 17th century much of Pest was in ruins and few residents remained. Within the next few decades, however, new residential districts were established, which are today's mid-town suburbs. In the 19th century, redevelopment schemes introduced grand houses and apartment blocks, some with shops

Bas-relief on the façade of the City Council Chamber

and cafés, as well as secular and municipal buildings. Perhaps the most prominent example of this work is the Hungarian National Museum. At this time Pest surpassed Buda as a centre for trade and industry. This was partly due to the area's Jewish community, who played an active role in its development.

SIGHTS AT A GLANCE

Churches
Calvinist Church ㉒
Chapel of St Roch ⑱
Franciscan Church ㉛
Great Synagogue ⑰
Inner City Parish Church pp124–5 ①
Lutheran Church ⑪
Serbian Church ㉖
Servite Church ⑩
University Church ㉘

Museums
Hungarian National Museum pp130–33 ⑳
Museum of Applied Arts pp136–7 ㉓

Historic Buildings and Monuments
City Council Chamber ㉕
Danube Fountain ⑫
Ervin Szabó Library ㉑
Franz Liszt Academy of Music ⑭
Károlyi Palace ㉙
Klotild Palaces ⑥
Lóránd Eötvös University ㉗
Municipal Council Offices ⑧
New Theatre ⑬
New York Palace ⑮
Pest County Hall ⑦
Turkish Bank ⑨
University Library ㉚
University of Economics ㉔

Streets and Squares
Jewish Quarter ⑯
József Nádor Square ③
Mihály Pollack Square ⑲
Mihály Vörösmarty Square ④
Váci Street ⑤
Vigadó Square ②

KEY

	Street-by-Street map *See pp122–3*
M	Metro station
P	Parking
i	Tourist Information
⊠	Post Office

0 metres 400
0 yards 400

◁ **The well of Danaid, who was condemned to carry water to a leaking barrel, in Szomory Dezső tér**

Street-by-Street: Around Váci Street

THE NOTHERN SECTION of Váci Street has been Budapest's
fashionable area for walking, meeting in cafés and
shopping in elegant boutiques since the early 19th century. Its attractive promenade is an enjoyable place for
an evening stroll, when it is stylishly illuminated.

Gerbeaud Cukrászda
is one of the best
patisseries in town
(see p201).

Servite Church
*Holy figures adorn the
19th-century façade
of this Baroque
church* **10**

**Vigadó
concert
hall**

Mihály Vörösmarty Square
*A Carrara marble monument
to the poet Mihály Vörösmarty
stands in this square. It was
created by Ede Telcs and symbolizes the Hungarian nation
united in the poets's words:
"Your homeland, Hungary,
serve unwaveringly"* **4**

Thonet House was built in
1888–90 by Ödön Lechner
(see p56) and Gyula Pártos.
It stands today in its original
form, featuring Zsolnay
ceramics from Pécs.

**Remains
of Contra
Aquincum**
(see p21)

Péterffy Palace, now the Százéves
Étterem *(see p198)*, is Pest's only
Baroque house. It was built by
András Meyerhoffer in 1755 for the
magistrate, János Péterffy. Above
the gateway there is a beautiful balcony supported by atlantes.

0 metres	50
0 yards	50

★ Váci Street
Budapest's most elegant promenade and shopping area is lined with fashion boutiques, cafés, fountains and statues. Off the street there are old courtyards and shopping arcades **5**

LOCATOR MAP
See Street Finder, maps 2, 7, 8, 10

Párizsi Udvar *(see p205)* is found on the corner of Kígyó utca and Petőfi Sándor utca. The arcade, which features shops, bookshops and a café, is decorated with beautiful wrought-iron work.

★ Klotild Palaces
This beautifully decorated block is one of two buildings, which together form a magnificent gateway to the Elizabeth Bridge **6**

KEY

‒ ‒ ‒ Suggested route

★ Inner City Parish Church
This white limestone and red marble tabernacle, in the church, dates from the early 16th century **1**

STAR SIGHTS
★ Inner City Parish Church
★ Váci Street
★ Klotild Palaces

Inner City Parish Church ❶

THIS CHURCH IS THE oldest building in Pest. It was first established during the reign of St István, the first king of Hungary *(see pp22–3)*, on the burial site of the martyred St Gellért. In the 14th century, a large Gothic church was built, which was used as a mosque under the Turks. Damaged by the Great Fire of 1723, the church was partly rebuilt in the Baroque style by György Pauer in 1725–39. The interior also features Neo-Classical elements by János Hild, as well as some 20th-century works.

The south tower includes one of the surviving walls of the Romanesque church.

★ **Pulpit**
This Neo-Gothic pulpit is beautifully carved from wood. It was produced in 1808 by Fülöp Ungradt.

Main Portal
The late Baroque portal is crowned by a sculpture of the Holy Trinity, inlaid with gold.

A fragment of a wall from the Romanesque church is visible in the lower section of the façade.

Nave
The interior of the church reflects the Gothic and Baroque periods in which it was built. The nave, in the western section of the church, is Baroque in design.

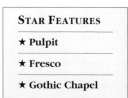

STAR FEATURES
★ **Pulpit**
★ **Fresco**
★ **Gothic Chapel**

★ Fresco
This fragment of a 15th-century Italianate fresco depicts the crucifixion of Christ. It was transferred from the cloister to its current location in the choir.

VISITORS' CHECKLIST

Március 15 tér 2. **Map** 4 E1 (10 D5). **☎** 318 31 08. **M** Ferenciek tere. **○** for services. **✝** daily.

Reconstructed Gothic tabernacle

Main Altar
The original altar was destroyed in World War II, and the current one, by Károly Antal and Pál C Molnár, dates from 1948.

Turkish Prayer Niche
One of the few remnants of the Turkish occupation (see pp26–7) is this mihrab, *or prayer niche, indicating the direction of Mecca.*

★ Gothic Chapel
This vaulted chapel is entered through a painted archway. It features recreated tracery windows.

Crest of Pest
The crest of Pest adorns the pedestal of a Renaissance tabernacle, which was commissioned by Pest's city council in 1507. It is the work of a 16th-century Italian artist.

HISTORICAL FLOORPLAN OF THE CHURCH

Nothing remains of the first church: the oldest sections date from the 12th-century Romanesque church.

KEY

- ▨ Romanesque church
- ☐ Gothic church
- ☐ Baroque church

The opulent façade of the Vigadó concert hall, decorated with figures and busts of statesmen, leaders and other prominent Hungarians

Inner City Parish Church ❶

BELVÁROSI PLÉBÁNIA TEMPLOM

See pp124–5.

Vigadó Square ❷

VIGADÓ TÉR

Map 4 D1 (10 D4). 🚋 2.

THE VIGADÓ concert hall (closed until 2006) dominates the square with its mix of eclectic forms. It was built by Frigyes Feszl in 1859–64 to replace a predecessor destroyed by fire during the uprising of 1848–9 (see pp30–31). The façade includes features such as folk motifs, dancers on columns and busts of former monarchs, rulers and other Hungarian personalities. An old Hungarian coat of arms is also visible in the centre.

The Budapest Marriott Hotel (see p183), located on one side of the square, was designed by József Finta in 1969. It was one of the first modern hotels to be built in Budapest.

On the Danube promenade there is a statue of a childlike figure on the railings. Entitled *Little Princess (see p65)*, it is the 1989 work of László Marton. The square also has craft stalls, cafés and restaurants.

József Nádor Square ❸

JÓZSEF NÁDOR TÉR

Map 2 E5 (10 D3). Ⓜ Vörösmarty tér.

ARCHDUKE JÓZSEF, after whom this square is named, was appointed as the emperor's Palatine for Hungary in 1796 at the age of 20. He ruled the country for 51 years until his death in 1847. One of the few Habsburgs sympathetic to the Hungarian people, he was instrumental in the development of Budapest and, in 1808, he initiated the Embellishment Commission (see p30).

A statue of Archduke József, by Johann Halbig, stands in the middle of the square. It was erected in 1869.

Some of the houses on the square are worth individual mention. The Neo-Classical Gross Palace at No. 1 (see p48) was built in 1824 by József Hild. Once a café, it now houses a bank. The building at Nos. 5–6, which overlooks the

Sculpture in Vigadó Square

southern end of the square, dates from 1859 and was built by Hugó Máltás. At No. 11 is a shop run by the Herend company (see p205). Its factory in southwest Hungary has produced world-renowned porcelain for almost 200 years.

Mihály Vörösmarty Square

VÖRÖSMARTY MIHÁLY TÉR ❹

Map 2 E5 (10 D3). Ⓜ Vörösmarty tér.

IN THE MIDDLE of the square stands a monument depicting the poet Mihály Vörösmarty (1800–55). Unveiled in 1908, it is the work of Ede Telcs. Behind the monument, on the eastern side of the square, is the Luxus department store (see p205). It is located in a three-floor corner building dating from 1911 and designed by Kálmán Giergl and Flóris Korb.

On the northern side of the square there is a renowned pâtisserie, opened by Henrik Kugler in 1858. It was taken over by the Swiss *patissière* Emil Gerbeaud, who was responsible for the richly decorated interior which survives to this day.

Terrace of the Gerbeaud pâtisserie, on Mihály Vörösmarty Square

A tempting selection of coffee, cakes, pastries and desserts are on offer. In summer, these can be taken on a terrace overlooking the square.

Thonet House, decorated with Zsolnay tiles, at No. 11 Váci Street

Váci Street ❺
VÁCI UTCA

Map 4 E1–F2 (10 E5).
Ⓜ Ferenciek tere.

Once two separate streets, which were joined at the beginning of the 18th century, Váci Street still has two distinct characters. Today, part of the southern section is open to traffic, while the northern end is pedestrianized and has long been a popular commercial centre. Most of the buildings lining the street date from the 19th and early 20th centuries. More recently, however, modern department stores, banks and shopping arcades have sprung up among the older original buildings.

Philantia, a Secession style florist's shop opened in 1905, now occupies part of the Neo-Classical block at No. 9, built in 1840 by József Hild. No. 9 also houses the Pest Theatre, where classic plays by Anton Chekhov, among others, are staged. The building was once occupied by the Inn of the Seven Electors, which had a large ballroom-cum-concert hall. It was here that a 12-year-old Franz Liszt performed.

Thonet House, at No. 11, is most notable for the Zsolnay tiles (see p56) from Pécs, which decorate its façade.

No. 13 is the oldest building on Váci Street and was built in 1805. In contrast, the post-modern Fontana department store (see p205) at No. 16, was built in 1984. Outside the store there is a bronze fountain with a figure of Hermes, dating from the mid-19th century.

The Nádor Hotel once stood at No. 20 and featured a statue of Archduke Palatine József in front of the entrance. Today the Taverna Hotel (see p183), designed by József Finta and opened in 1987, stands here.

In a side street off Váci Street, at No. 13 Régiposta utca, is a building from the Modernist period. An unusual sight in Pest, this Bauhaus-influenced building dates from 1937 and is by Lajos Kozma.

Klotild Palaces ❻
KLOTILD PALOTÁK

Szabadsajtó utca. **Map** 4 E1 (10 E5).
Ⓜ Ferenciek tere.

Flanking Szabadsajtó utca, on the approach to the Elizabeth Bridge, stand two massive apartment blocks built in 1902. The buildings were commissioned by the daughter-in-law of Palatine József, Archduchess Klotild, after whom they were named.

They were designed by Flóris Korb and Kálmán Giergl in the Historicist style, with

One of the twin Klotild Palaces, from 1902, by the approach to the Elizabeth Bridge (see p63)

elements of Rococo decoration. Once all rented apartments, now only the upper floors remain residential. The ground floor is occupied by shops, a café and the Budapest Gallery with its exhibition space.

Pest County Hall ❼
PEST MEGYEI ÖNKORMÁNYZAT

Városház utca 7. **Map** 4 F1 (10 E4).
Ⓒ 318 01 11. Ⓜ Ferenciek tere.
Ⓞ 8am–4pm Wed.

Built in several stages, this is one of Pest's most beautiful, monumental Neo-Classical civic buildings. It was erected during the 19th century, as part of the plan for the city drawn up by the Embellishment Commission.

A seat of the Council of Pest has existed on this site since the end of the 17th century. By 1811, however, the building included two conference halls, a prison and a prison chapel. In 1829–32, a wing designed by József Hofrichter was added on Semmelweis utca, which was used to accommodate council employees.

In 1838 another redevelopment programme was begun, this time employing designs by Mátyás Zitterbarth Jr, a highly regarded exponent of Neo-Classical architecture. Completed in 1842, it included an impressive façade, which overlooks Városház utca. This features a portico with six Corinthian columns supporting a prominent tympanum.

Pest County Hall was destroyed in the course of World War II. During post-war rebuilding it was enlarged, with the addition of three internal courtyards, the first of which is surrounded by atmospheric cloisters. Due to the excellent acoustics, concerts are often held here during the summer.

Between Pest County Hall and the Municipal Council Offices building (see p128), in the small Kamermayer Károly tér, there is a monument to the first mayor of Budapest. Károly Kamermayer (1829–97) took office in 1873 after the unification of Óbuda, Buda and Pest. The aluminium monument was designed in 1942 by Béla Szabados.

Municipal Council Offices ❽

FŐVÁROSI ÖNKORMÁNYZAT

Városház utca 9–11. **Map** 4 E1 & F1 (10 E4). 🛈 327 10 00. Ⓜ *Ferenciek tere.*

THE LARGEST BAROQUE building in Budapest, this edifice was completed in 1735 to a design by the architect Anton Erhard Martinelli. It originally functioned as a hospital for veterans of the war between the Christian and Turkish armies at the end of the 17th century *(see pp26–7)*.

In 1894 the city authorities bought the building in order to convert it into council offices. Ármin Hegedűs was commissioned to refurbish the building and a new southern wing was built to his design.

Most notable are the bas-reliefs decorating the gates on the Városház utca side of the building. The scenes depicted in the bas-reliefs commemorate a victory of Charles III *(see p19)* and Prince Eugene of Savoy's role in the war against the Turks *(see p71)*. These are thought to be the work of the Viennese sculptor Johann Christoph Mader.

Turkish Bank ❾

TÖRÖK BANKHÁZ

Szervita tér 3. **Map** 4 E1 (10 D4). Ⓜ *Deák Ferenc tér.*

DATING FROM 1906 and designed by Henrik Böhm and Ármin Hegedűs, the building that formerly housed the Turkish Bank is a wonderful example of the Secession style.

The exterior used modern construction methods to create the glass façade, which is set in reinforced concrete. Above the fenestration, in the gable, is a magnificent colourful mosaic by Miksa Róth. Entitled *Glory to Hungary*, it depicts Hungary paying homage to the Virgin Mary, or *Patrona Hungariae (see p117)*. Angels and shepherds surround the Virgin, along with figures of Hungarian political heroes, such as Prince Ferenc Rákóczi *(see p28)*, István Széchenyi *(see pp30–31)* and Lajos Kossuth *(see p106)*.

Glory to Hungary, the mosaic on the façade of the Turkish Bank

Servite Church ❿

SZERVITA TEMPLOM

Szervita tér 7. **Map** 4 E1 (10 D4). Ⓜ *Deák Ferenc tér.*

THIS BAROQUE CHURCH was built between 1725–32 to a design by János Hölbling and György Pauer. In 1871, the façade was rebuilt and the tower was covered with a new roof, designed by József Diescher.

Above the doorway there are figures of St Peregrin and St Anne, and above them sit St Philip and St Augustine. To the right of the entrance there is a bas-relief by János Istók, dating from 1930. It is dedicated to the heroes of the VIIth Wilhelm Hussar Regiment who gave their lives in World War I.

Lutheran Church ⓫

EVANGÉLIKUS TEMPLOM

Deák tér 4. **Map** 2 E5 (10 E3). 🛈 317 34 13. Ⓜ *Deák Ferenc tér.* ♿ **National Lutheran Museum** 🛈 235 02 07. ⏱ *10am–6pm Tue–Sun.* 📷 🎟 *by arrangement.*

MIHÁLY POLLACK designed this Neo-Classical church, built between 1799–1808. A portico, which features a tympanum supported by Doric columns, was added to the façade in 1856 by József Hild.

The church's simplicity is typical of early Neo-Classicism. It also reflects the notion of minimal church decoration, which was upheld by this branch of Protestantism. Above the modest main altar is a copy of Raphael's *Transfiguration* by Franz Sales Lochbihler, made in 1811. Organ recitals are often held in the church, which has excellent acoustics.

Another Neo-Classical building by Mihály Pollack adjoins the church. Constructed as a Lutheran school, it is now the National Lutheran Museum. The museum illustrates the history of the Reformation in Hungary, with the most interesting exhibit being a copy of Martin Luther's last will and testament. The original document, dating from 1542, is held in the Lutheran Archives.

Neo-Classical main altar in the Lutheran Church

The Danube Fountain, built in 1880–83 by Miklós Ybl

Danube Fountain ⑫

DANUBIUS KÚT

Erzsébet tér. **Map** 2 E5 (10 D3).
Ⓜ Deák Ferenc tér.

THIS FOUNTAIN, which once stood in Kálvin tér, was designed and built by Miklós Ybl (see p94) in 1880–83. It is decorated with copies by Dezső Győri of original sculptures, by Béla Brestyánszky and Leó Feszler, which were damaged in World War II.

The figure at the top of the fountain is Danubius, representing the Danube. The three female figures below symbolize Hungary's three principal rivers after the Danube: the Tisza, the Dráva and the Száva.

New Theatre ⑬

ÚJ SZÍNHÁZ

Paulay Ede utca 35. **Map** 2 F4 (10 E2). Ⓒ 269 60 21. Ⓜ Opera.

ORIGINALLY completed in 1909, this building has undergone many transformations. It was designed by Béla Lajta in the Secession style, and, as the home of the cabaret troupe Parisian Mulató, became a shrine to frivolity.

In 1921 it was completely restyled by László Vágó, who turned it into a theatre. After World War II, the theatre gained a glass-and-steel façade, and a children's theatre company was based here.

Between 1988–90 the building was returned to its original form using Lajta's plans. Gilding, stained glass and marble once more adorn this unusual building. Hungary's New Theatre is now in residence.

Franz Liszt Academy of Music ⑭

LISZT FERENC ZENEAKADÉMIA

Liszt Ferenc tér 8. **Map** 7 A1 (10 F2).
Ⓒ 462 46 00. ⓣ 4, 6 to Király utca.

THE ACADEMY is housed in a late Historicist palace, built between 1904–7 by Kálmán Giergl and Flóris Korb. Above the main entrance there is a statue of Franz Liszt, by Alajos Stróbl. The six bas-reliefs above its base are by Ede Telcs, and depict the history of music.

The Secession interiors of this building have remained intact and deserve particular attention. The *Fount of Youth* fresco, in the first floor foyer, is by Aladár Körösfői-Kriesch, who was a member of the Gödöllő school. The academy has two auditoriums. The first seats 1,200 people and features allegories of musical movements. The second seats 400 and is used for chamber music.

New York Palace ⑮

NEW YORK PALOTA

Erzsébet körút 9–11. **Map** 7 B2.
Ⓒ 322 38 49. Ⓜ Blaha Lujza tér.
Café and restaurant Ⓞ 10am–midnight.

BUILT BETWEEN 1891–5 to a design by the architect Alajos Hauszmann, this building was initially the offices of an American insurance firm.

This five-floor edifice displays an eclectic mix of Neo-Baroque and Secession motifs. The decorative sculptures that animate the façade are the work of Károly Senyei.

On the ground floor is a renowned restaurant and café, called the New York Café (see p200). On the walls are paintings by Gusztáv Mannheimer and Károly Lotz. The beautiful, richly gilded Neo-Baroque interior, with its magnificent chandeliers and marble pillars, now attracts tourists, just as it once attracted the literary and artistic circles in its heyday.

Statue of Franz Liszt above the entrance to the Academy of Music

Hungarian National Museum ⑳

Seal from Esztergom

THE HUNGARIAN National Museum is the country's richest source of art and artifacts relating to its own turbulent history. Founded in 1802, the museum owes its existence to Count Ferenc Széchényi, who offered his collection of coins, books and documents to the nation. The museum's constantly expanding collection of art and documents is exhibited in an impressive Neo-Classical edifice built by Mihály Pollack.

Placing the Cornerstone *(1864)*
This painting by Miklós Barabás shows the ceremony that marked the beginning of construction of the Chain Bridge (see p62) in 1842.

Campaign Chest
This carved Baroque campaign chest features the prince regent's decoration and the Hungarian crest. It dates from the insurrection led by Ferenc Rákóczi II (see p28).

★ Armchair
Adorned with multi-coloured fruit and floral ornamentation, this armchair dates from the early 18th century. It is the work of Ferenc II Rákóczi, who learnt carpentry during his exile in Turkey.

★ Coronation Mantle
This textile masterpiece, made of Byzantine silk, was donated to the church in Székesfehérvár by St Stephen in 1031. It became the Coronation Mantle in the 12th century.

Main entrance

KEY

☐	Coronation Mantle
☐	Roman mosaics
▨	Archaeological exhibition
☐	11th–17th-century exhibition
▨	18th–19th-century exhibition
☐	20th-century exhibition

MUSEUM GUIDE
On the first floor is the Coronation Mantle and the archaeological exhibition. The second floor exhibits comprise Hungarian artifacts from 11th–20th centuries. Roman mosaics can be found in the basement.

★ Funeral Crown
This magnificent 13th-century golden crown was found in the ruins of the Dominican Church and Convent on Margaret Island in the Danube (see pp172–3).

VISITORS' CHECKLIST

Múzeum körút 14–16. **Map** 7 A4 (10 F5). ☎ 338 21 22 (327 77 73 for guided tours in English). 🚌 47, 49. Ⓜ Kálvin tér, Astória. 🚃 9, 15. ◯ 10am–6pm Tue–Sun. 🅿 ✔ 🅱 📷 Ⓦ www.hnm.hu

Second floor

Pelisse
This short jacket is typical of Hungarian national costume. It belonged to Gábor Bethlen, a prince of Transylvania, and dates from around 1620.

First floor

Gothic Well
These recon-structed fragments are part of a well from the Royal Palace at Visegrád (see p164). The well dates from the 14th-century rule of the Angevin dynasty.

Golden Stag
This hand-forged Iron Age figure dates from the 6th century BC. It was originally part of a Scythian prince's shield.

STAR EXHIBITS

★ **Armchair**

★ **Coronation Mantle**

★ **Funeral Crown**

Exploring the Museum's Collection

A 13th-century seal

T HE STEPS OF THE Hungarian National Museum were the scene of a major event in Budapest's history. It was from these steps that, in 1848, the poet Sándor Petőfi first read his *National Song*, which sparked the uprising against Habsburg rule *(see p30–31)*. This moment is commemorated each year on 15 March, when the museum is decorated in the national colours and a re-enactment is performed. Items from the museum's rich collection, including works of art and craft, historical documents and photographs, vividly illustrate this and other events from Hungary's varied and fascinating past.

Remarkably, the royal insignia, which includes a sceptre and golden crown, have survived Hungary's dramatic history. Discovered by the American forces during World War II, they were removed and stored in Fort Knox before being returned to Hungary in 1978.

In 2000, these other treasures of the royal insignia were transferred to the Domed Hall of Parliament *(see pp108–9)*, where they can also be visited.

Monument to poet János Arany in front of the Neo-Classical façade

MUSEUM BUILDING

B UILT BETWEEN 1837–47, according to a design by Mihály Pollack, this imposing Neo-Classical building is one of the finest manifestations of that architecural epoch.

The façade is preceded by a monumental portico, which is crowned by a tympanum designed by Raffael Ponti. The composition depicts the figure of Pannonia *(see p20)* among personifications of the arts and sciences.

In the gardens surrounding the museum there are a number of statues of prominent figures from the spheres of literature, science and art. A monument to the poet János Arany, author of the *Toldi Trilogy*, stands in front of the main entrance. This bronze

and limestone work dates from 1893 and is by Alajos Stróbl. The notable features of the interior include the magnificent paintings by Mór Than and Károly Lotz in the main staircase.

CORONATION MANTLE

O NE OF THE most important Hungarian treasures, the Coronation Mantle *(see pp22–3)*, is currently on display in a separate hall of its own in the museum. Made of Byzantine silk, it was originally donated to the church by St Stephen in 1031. The magnificent gown was then refashioned in the 13th century. The now much faded cloth features an intricate embroidered design of fine gold thread and pearls.

ARCHAEOLOGICAL EXHIBITION

T HE ARCHAEOLOGICAL display was opened in 2002 to celebrate the 200th anniversary of the museum's foundation. The visitor is taken through a display of Hungary's heritage, spanning the period between 400 BC and AD 804, from the first inhabitants of the country at Vértesszőlős until the end of the Early Medieval period, immediately preceeding the Hungarian Conquest.

The exhibition presents some of the latest and important archaeological finds, and abounds in authentic recon-structions of the past.

11TH–17TH-CENTURY EXHIBITION

T HE EXHIBITION begins in the Árpád era and features one of the museum's most valuable exhibits, the crown of Constantine IX Monomachus, decorated with enamel work. Also on display in this section are the funeral decorations of

Carved base of a chalice dating from the 15th century

Béla III, Romanesque sacred vessels, weapons and an interesting collection of coins.

The period of Angevin rule *(see p18)* coincided with the birth of the Gothic style, which is represented here by some excellent examples of gold work. The next two halls explore the reign of Sigismund of Luxembourg *(see p24)* and the achievements of János Hunyadi *(see p24)*. On display here are copies of portraits of King Sigismund by Albrecht Dürer and a richly decorated ceremonial saddle. There are also several platinum and gold pieces, illuminated manuscripts and documents. The lifestyle of peasants from this era is illustrated, as well as the history of the royal court.

The reign of Mátyás Corvinus *(see pp24–5)* and the Jagiełło dynasty *(see p18)* marks the decline of the Gothic period and the birth of the Renaissance. Exhibits from this era include a 15th-century glass goblet belonging to King Mátyás, late Gothic pews from a church in Bártfa, armour and weapons, as well as a 16th-century dress belonging to Maria Habsburg.

Magnificent examples of sculpture, art and artifacts from the 16th and 17th centuries follow. Of interest are items that survived the Turkish occupation *(see pp26–7)*, especially the everyday objects and weapons.

A separate hall is dedicated to the Transylvanian dukedom and the important historical role that it played. Exhibited here are vessels and jewellery elaborately crafted in gold, 17th-century costumes, and original ceramics produced by the people of Haban, who settled there in the early 17th century. This last section of the exhibition ends in 1686, at the time of the liberation of Buda by the Christain armies after the Turkish occupation. In this part of the museum there are also portraits of influential Hungarians from the period, and an interesting exhibition of jewellery dating from the 17th century.

Printing press used in 1848 to print nationalist propaganda

Brooch from the 18th-century

18TH–19TH-CENTURY EXHIBITION

THIS PART OF the museum covers Habsburg rule, a period of great civil unrest. The exhibition begins with artifacts connected to the Rákóczi insurrection of 1703–11 *(see pp28–9)*. Weapons, as well as furniture from Ferenc II Rákóczi's palace, are exhibited here. One item of particular interest is the armchair produced by Rákóczi himself. The next hall is dedicated to 18th-century Hungarian art and culture.

The following rooms portray the Hungarian history of the first half of the 19th century. Artworks, including magnificent portraits and historic paintings, such as *Placing the Cornerstone of the Chain Bridge*, are assembled along with important documents and memoirs from that time.

The central section, dedicated to the uprising of 1848–9 *(see pp30–31)*, features a printing press on which were printed leaflets outlining the 12 demands in Hungary's fight for independence from Austria.

The exhibits from the second half of the 19th century include collections of masonic items, official decorations, coins and historic manuscripts. Items relating to the coronation of Franz Joseph in 1867 and the Millennium Celebrations of 1896 are also displayed here.

20TH-CENTURY EXHIBITION

REFLECTING THE technical developments of this century, Hungary's recent history is presented in a documentary style. Photographs, and documents are widely used to illustrate this period. Artifacts relating to World War I and the era of revolution between the wars, and shocking documents from World War II can be found here. The post-war history of Hungary is depicted mainly from a political perspective. Emphasis is placed on significant episodes, such as the uprising of 1956 and the events of 1989, which signalled the end of Communism in Eastern Europe *(see p35)*.

Guild chest
from the 20th century

Jewish Quarter ⑯

ZSIDÓ NEGYED

Király utca, Rumbach Sebestyén utca, Dohány utca & Akácfa utca. **Map** 2 F5 & 7 A2 (10 F3). **M** *Deák Ferenc tér.*

JEWS FIRST CAME to Hungary in the 13th century and settled in Buda and Óbuda. In the 19th century, a larger Jewish community was established outside the Pest city boundary, in a small area of Erzsébetváros.

In 1251, King Béla IV gave the Jews of Buda certain priviliges, including freedom of

Window of the Great Synagogue

HOLOCAUST MEMORIAL

This sculpture of a weeping willow, designed by Imre Varga, was unveiled in 1991 in memory of the 600,000 Hungarian Jews killed by the Nazis in World War II. It was partly funded by the Hungarian-American actor Tony Curtis.

religion. The Jewish community became well integrated into Hungarian society, until in 1941, a series of Nazi anti-Semitic laws were passed and the wearing of the Star of David was made compulsory. In 1944, a ghetto was created in Pest and the deportation of thousands of Jews to camps, including Auschwitz, was implemented. After heavy fighting between the Russian and German armies, the Soviet Red Army liberated the ghetto on 18 January 1945. In total, 600,000 Hungarian Jews were

victims of the Holocaust. This fact is commemorated by a plaque at the Orthodox Synagogue on Rumbach utca.

In the late 19th century, three synagogues were built and many Jewish shops and workshops were established. Kosher establishments, such as the Hanna Étterem *(see p197)* in the courtyard of the Orthodox Synagogue, and the butcher at No. 41 Kazinczy utca, were a common feature. Shops are now being reconstructed to recreate the pre-ghetto character of the Jewish Quarter.

Great Synagogue ⑰

ZSINAGÓGA

Dohány utca 2. **Map** 4 F1 (10 F4). **(** *342 89 49.* **M** *Astoria.* **Jewish Museum** ◯ *May–Oct: 10am–3pm daily; Nov–Apr: 10am–5pm daily.* 🗓 ✔

THIS SYNAGOGUE is the largest in Europe. It was built in a Byzantine-Moorish style by the Viennese architect Ludwig Förster between 1854 – 9. It has three naves and, following orthodox tradition, separate galleries for women. Together the naves and galleries can accommodate up to 3,000 worshippers. Some features, such as the position of the reading platform, reflect elements of Judaic reform. The interior has valuable decorative fittings, particularly those on the Ark of the Law, by Frigyes Feszl. In 1931, a museum was established

within the synagogue, in which a vast collection of historical relics, Judaic devotional items and everday objects, from ancient Rome to

the present day, has been assembled. It includes the book of Chevra Kadisha from 1792. There is also a moving Holocaust Memorial Room.

A large rose window is the façade's main ornamentation. It is located between two richly decorated towers crowned with distinctive onion domes.

The façade is composed of white and red brick and intricately designed ceramic friezes.

A Hebrew inscription from the second book of Moses is situated under the rose window

Chapel of St Roch ⑱
SZENT RÓKUS KÁPOLNA

Gyulai Pál u 2. **Map** 7 A3. 338 35 15. **M** Astoria or Blaha Lujza tér.

PEST TOWN COUNCIL built this chapel in what was then an uninhabited area. It was dedicated to St Roch and St Rozali, who were believed to provide protection against the plague, which afflicted Pest in 1711.

In 1740 the chapel was extended to its present size, and a tower was added in 1797. The façade is decorated with Baroque figures of saints, although the originals were replaced with copies in .1908.

Inside, on the right-hand wall of the chapel's nave, is a painting of the Virgin Mary from 1740. A painting by Jakab Warsch, depicting the Great Flood of 1838, is in the oratory.

Mihály Pollack Square ⑲
POLLACK MIHÁLY TÉR

Map 7 A4 (10 F5). **M** Kálvin tér. **Festetics Palace** 266 52 22. by prior arrangement.

AT THE REAR of the Hungarian National Museum (see pp130–33) is a square named after Mihály Pollack, the architect of several Neo-Classical buildings such as the museum and Sándor Palace (see p73).

In the late 19th century, three palaces were built side by side on this square for the aristocratic elite of Hungary: Prince Festetics, Prince Eszterházy and Count Károlyi. The beautiful façades makes this one of the city's most captivating squares.

Miklós Ybl (see p94) built the French-Renaissance style palace at No. 6 for Lajós Károlyi, in 1863–5. The façade is decorated with sculptures by Károly Schaffer. There is also a covered driveway for carriages. Next door, at No. 8, is a small palace, which was built in 1865 for the Eszterházy family by Alájos Baumgarten. At No. 10 is the palace built for the Festetics family in 1862, again by Miklós Ybl. The interior, especially the Neo-Baroque staircase, is splendid.

Magnificent staircase inside the Festetics Palace on Mihály Pollack Square

Hungarian National Museum ⑳
NEMZETI MÚZEUM

See pp130–33.

Ervin Szabó Library ㉑
SZABÓ ERVIN KÖNYVTÀR

Szabó Ervin tér 1. **Map** 7 A4 (10 F5). 411 50 00. **M** Kálvin tér. 10am–8pm Mon–Fri, 10am– 4pm Sat.

IN 1887, the wealthy industrialist Wenckheim family commissioned the architect Artur Meining to build a Neo-Baroque and Rococo style palace. The result was the former Wenckheim Palace, regarded as one of the most beautiful palaces in Budapest. The magnificent wrought-iron

Spiral staircase in one of the rooms of the Ervin Szabó Library

gates, dating from 1897, are the work of Gyula Jungfer. Also worth particular attention are the richly gilded salons on the first floor, as well as the dome above an oval panel of reliefs.

In 1926, the city council acquired the building and converted it into a public lending library, whose collection focuses on the city itself and the social sciences.

The Ervin Szabó Library was named after the politician and social reformer Ervin Szabó (1877–1918), who was the library's first director. It has over a hundred branches throughout Budapest and some three million books.

Calvinist Church ㉒
REFORMÁTUS TEMPLOM

Kálvin tér 7. **Map** 4 F2. 217 67 69. **M** Kálvin tér.

THIS SINGLE NAVE church was designed by József Hofrichter and built between 1816–30. In 1848 József Hild designed the four-pillared façade and tympanum, and a spire was added in 1859.

Inside the church it is worth seeing the pulpit and choir gallery, designed by Hild in 1831 and 1854 respectively. The stained-glass windows were the work of Miksa Róth. Sacred artifacts from the 17th and 18th centuries are kept in the church treasury.

Museum of Applied Arts ㉓

Opened in 1896 by Emperor Franz Joseph as part of the Millennium Celebrations, this collection is housed not within a Neo-Classical building, but within an outstanding Secession building designed by Gyula Pártos and Ödön Lechner *(see p56)*. The exterior incorporated elements inspired by the Orient as well as the Zsolnay ceramics characteristic of Lechner's work. Damaged in 1945 and again in 1956, the building only recently regained its original magnificence. The collection, founded in 1872, includes many examples of arts and crafts workmanship.

A Lalique pendant

Renaissance Tile
This tile, which dates from around 1530, depicts Queen Anne, wife of Ferdinand I.

Silver Plate
This magnificent Baroque plate depicts the Battle of Vezekény. It was crafted in 1654 in Augsburg by Philip Jacob Drentwett.

Ground floor

Inner Courtyard
This courtyard, covered by a glazed roof, is surrounded by cloisters with arcades designed in an Indian-Oriental style.

MUSEUM GUIDE
The museum is home to various temporary exhibitions on both floors of the building. Examples of the types of items on show are illustrated here. The major exhibitions tend to change each year, whilst the smaller national and foreign displays change monthly. Recent exhibitions have included a wonderful display of glass and an exploration of clocks and time. The library, dating from 1872, is located on the first floor and contains around 50,000 books.

Main entrance

KEY

�	Library
	Temporary exhibitions
	Non-exhibition space

Pendant with Amphitrite and Triton
This elaborate example of gold work is decorated with enamelwork, pearls and precious stones. It was made in around 1600.

VISITORS' CHECKLIST

Üllői út 33–37. **Map** 7 B5.
📞 456 51 00. Ⓜ Ferenc körút.
🕐 10am–6pm Tue–Sun.
📷 🛍 🖥
🌐 www.imm.hu

Tiffany Glassware
Delicate glasses and vases in multicoloured and opalescent glass were the showpieces of this American workshop.

First floor

Secession Vase
This beautiful Zsolnay ceramic vase is decorated with butterflies. Motifs from nature were a favourite theme of artists working in this genre.

Dresser
This is an unusual example of Hungarian Secession craftsmanship (see pp54–7). It was produced in ebony in the workshop of Endré Thék in 1900.

17th-Century Dress
Colourful traditional costumes, such as this richly embroidered dress, are often displayed in temporary exhibitions.

University of Economics ㉔

KÖZGAZDASÁGTUDOMÁNYI EGYETEM

Fővám tér 8. **Map** 4 F3. **C** 216 18 50. 🚋 47, 49.

FACING THE DANUBE, this Neo-Renaissance edifice was designed by Miklós Ybl (*see p94*) and built as the Main Customs Office in 1871–4.

The façade is 170 m (560 ft) long and features a colonnade supporting a balcony. On the balustrade stand ten allegorical figures by August Sommer.

In 1951, this building opened as a university specializing in economics and management. There is a statue of Karl Marx, after whom the university was once named, in the atrium.

Decorative element on the façade of the City Council Chamber

City Council Chamber ㉕

ÚJ VÁROSHÁZA

Váci utca 62–64. **Map** 4 F2 (10 E5). Ⓜ Deák tér. **C** 318 68 46. 🖪

THIS THREE-FLOOR edifice was built between 1870–75 as offices for the newly unified city of Budapest (*see p32*). Its architect, Imre Steindl, was also responsible for designing Parliament (*see pp108–9*).

The building is a mix of styles. The exterior is a Neo-Renaissance design in brick, with grotesques between the

Façade of the University of Economics, designed by Miklós Ybl

windows, while the interior features cast-iron Neo-Gothic motifs. The Great Debating Hall is decorated with mosaics designed by Károly Lotz.

Many antiquarian bookshops and galleries have now opened around here. Fashionable bars, restaurants and cafés, and the recent pedestrianization, make this a very charming area.

Serbian Church ㉖

SZERB TEMPLOM

Szerb utca 2–4. **Map** 4 F2 (10 E5). Ⓜ Kálvin tér.

SERBS SETTLED IN the now largely residential area around the church as early as the 16th century. The end of the 17th century brought a new wave of Serb immigrants, and by the early 19th century Serbs comprised almost 25 per cent of Pest's home-owners.

In 1698, the Serb community replaced an earlier church on the site with this Baroque one. The church gained its final appearance after a rebuilding project that lasted until the mid-18th century, which was probably undertaken by András Meyerhoffer.

The interior of the church is arranged according to Greek Orthodox practice. A section of the nave, which is entered from the vestibule, is reserved for women. This area is divided

Ceramic tile from the Serbian Church

from the men's section by a partition, and the division is further emphasized by the floor, which has been lowered by 30 cm (1 ft). The choir gallery is enclosed by an iconostasis that divides it from the sanctuary. This iconostasis dates from around 1850. The carving is by the Serb sculptor Miahai Janich and the Italian Renaissance-influenced paintings are the work of the Greek artist Károly Sterio.

Lóránd Eötvös University ㉗

EÖTVÖS LÓRÁND TUDOMÁNY EGYETEM KÖZPONTJA

Egyetem tér 1–3. **Map** 4 F2 (10 E5). Ⓜ Ferenciek tere, Kálvin tér.

IN 1635, Cardinal Péter Pázmány, the leader of the Counter-Reformation, established a university in Nagyszombat (now Trnava in Slovakia). It moved to Buda in 1777, nearly a century after the end of the Turkish occupation (*see pp26–7*), during the reign of Maria Theresa. Emperor Joseph II subsequently transferred the university to Pest, to the environs of the Pauline Church, now called the University Church.

It was not until 1889 that the university was endowed with a permanent home. This Neo-Baroque building, now the Law Faculty, was designed by architects including Sándor Baumgarten and Fülöp Herzog. Another wing was later added by Antal Weber.

The university is named after the noted physicist Lóránd Eötvös (1848–1919).

University Church ㉘

EGYETEMI TEMPLOM

Papnövelde utca 9. **Map** 4 F2 (10 E5).
☎ 318 05 55. **Ⓜ** Kálvin tér.

Tympanum adorning the façade of the University Library

THIS SINGLE-NAVE church, with a richly decorated façade, is considered one of the most impressive Baroque churches in the city. It was built for the Pauline Order in 1725–42, and was probably designed by András Meyerhoffer. The tower was added in 1771. The Pauline Order, founded in 1263 by Canon Euzebiusz, was the only religious order to be founded in Hungary.

The magnificent exterior features a tympanum and a row of pilasters that divide the façade. Figures of St Paul and St Anthony flank the emblem of the Pauline Order, which crowns the exterior. The carved-wood interior of the main vestibule is also worth particular mention.

Inside the church a row of side chapels stand behind unusual marble pilasters. In 1776 Johann Bergl painted the vaulted ceiling with frescoes depicting scenes from the life of Mary. Sadly, these frescoes are now in poor condition.

The main altar dates from 1746, and the carved statues behind it are the work of József Hebenstreit. Above it is a copy of the painting *The Black Madonna of Czestochowa*, which is thought to date from 1720. Much of the Baroque interior detail of the church is the work of the Pauline monks, for example the balustrade of the organ loft, the confessionals and the carved pulpit on the right.

Sculptures decorating the pulpit in the University Church

Károlyi Palace ㉙

KÁROLYI PALOTA

Károlyi Mihály utca 16. **Map** 4 F2 (10 E5). **☎** 317 31 43. **Ⓜ** Ferenciek tere, Kálvin tér. **Petőfi Exhibition** ◯ 10am–6pm Tue–Sun. **🖾** 317 36 11.

IN 1696 THERE was a small Baroque palace on this site, which was extended by András Meyerhoffer between 1759–68. Subsequent rebuilding, which gave the palace a Neo-Classical appearance, was undertaken between 1832–41 by Anton Riegl. It is named after Mihály Károlyi, leader of the 1918–19 Hungarian Republic *(see p34)*, who was born here in 1875.

The palace now houses the Hungarian Museum of Literature and the Petőfi Exhibition, which is dedicated to the poet Sándor Petőfi *(see p31)*. Other Hungarian poets remembered here include Atilla József, Endre Ady and Mór Jókai.

University Library ㉚

EGYETEMI KÖNYVTÁR

Ferenciek tere 6. **Map** 4 F1 (10 E5). **☎** 266 58 66. **Ⓜ** Ferenciek tere, Kálvin tér. ◯ 9am–3:30pm Mon–Fri.

THIS NEO-RENAISSANCE edifice, by Antal Szkalniczyky and Henrik Koch, was built from 1873–6. It is distinguished by the dome on the corner tower. The library's two million works include 11 *Corviniani (see p72)* and 160 medieval manuscripts and miniatures. The reading room has sgraffiti by Mór Than and frescoes by Károly Lotz.

Franciscan Church ㉛

BELVÁROSI FERENCES TEMPLOM

Ferenciek tere 9. **Map** 4 F1 (10 E4). **☎** 317 33 22. **Ⓜ** Ferenciek tere.

A FRANCISCAN CHURCH and monastery have stood on this site, beyond the old city walls, since the 13th century. In 1541 the Turks rebuilt the church as the Mosque of Sinan, but after the liberation *(see pp26–7)* the monks regained the building. Between 1727–43 they remodelled the church in the Baroque style, which it still retains today.

The façade features a magnificent portal incorporating the Franciscan emblem, crowned by a figure of Mary being adored by angels. Sculptures of Franciscan saints also embellish the façade.

The interior of the church is decorated with frescoes, dating from 1894–5, by Károly Lotz and paintings by Victor Tardo Kremer, from 1925–6. The jewel of this church is the Baroque main altar with sculptures that date from 1741 and 1851. The side altars and the pulpit date from 1851–2.

AROUND VÁROSLIGET

VÁROSLIGET, OR CITY PARK, was once an area of marshland, which served as a royal hunting ground. Leopold I gave the land to the town of Pest, but it was in the mid-18th century, under Maria Theresa, that the area was drained and planted. Today's park was designed towards the end of the 19th century in the English style, which was the fashion of the

Statue of János Hunyadi

day. Városliget was chosen as the focus of the Millennium Celebrations in 1896 (see p142), which marked the 1,000-year anniversary of the conquest of the Carpathian basin by the Magyars. A massive building programme was undertaken, which included the Museum of Fine Arts, Vajdahunyad Castle and the impressive monument in Heroes' Square.

SIGHTS AT A GLANCE

Museums
Ferenc Hopp Museum of Far Eastern Art **6**
Franz Liszt Museum **2**
Museum of Fine Arts pp146–9 **9**
Palace of Art **8**
Zoltán Kodály Museum **4**

KEY

- Street-by-Street map See pp142–3
- **P** Parking
- **M** Metro station
- Police station
- Post office
- Tram stop
- Train station

Parks and Zoos
Funfair **12**
Zoo **11**

Streets and Monuments
Andrássy Street **1**
Hermina Street **14**
Millennium Monument **7**
Városligeti Avenue **5**

Historic Buildings
Academy of Fine Art **3**
Erkel Theatre **15**
Széchenyi Baths **13**
Vajdahunyad Castle **10**

GETTING THERE
The M1 metro line runs under Andrássy út from Oktogon to Hősök tere, while bus 4 runs along the street above. Trams, buses and the metro operate in the south of the area, around Thököly út.

◁ The picturesque façade of the Renaissance section of Vajdahunyad Castle, in Városliget

Street-by-Street: Around Heroes' Square

HEROES' SQUARE is a relic of a proud era in Hungary's history. It was here that the Millennium Celebrations opened in 1896. A striking example of this national pride is the Millennium Monument. Its colonnades feature statues of renowned Hungarian leaders and politicians, and the grand central column is crowned by a figure of the Archangel Gabriel. Vajdahunyad Castle was built in Városliget, or City Park, adjacent to the square. Probably the most flamboyant expression of the celebrations, it is composed of elements of the finest architectural works found throughout Hungary.

Árpád, leader of the Magyars

★ **Museum of Fine Arts**
This monumental museum building has an eight-pillared portico supporting a tympanum ❾

Entrance to the Zoo

Millennium Monument
Dominating Heroes' Square, this monument includes a figure of Rydwan, the god of war, by György Zala.

Palace of Art
The crest of Hungary decorates the façade of this building. Dating from 1895, it is the country's largest venue for artistic exhibitions ❽

Secession pavilion

THE HUNGARIAN MILLENNIUM CELEBRATIONS

The Millennium Celebrations in 1896 marked a high point in the development of Budapest and in the history of the Austro-Hungarian monarchy. The city underwent modernization on a scale unknown in Europe at that time. Hundreds of houses, palaces and civic buildings were constructed, gas lighting was introduced and continental Europe's first underground transport system was opened.

Archangel Gabriel

0 metres		200
0 yards		200

KEY

- - - Suggested route

★ Széchenyi Baths
This is the largest complex of spa baths in Europe. Its hot springs, discovered in 1876, bubble up from a depth of 970 m (3,180 ft) and are reputed to have considerable healing properties ⓭

LOCATOR MAP
See Street Finder, maps 5 & 6

Városliget

Ják Chapel
This chapel faithfully reproduces the portal of a Benedictine chapel, dating from 1214, which can be found in the area of Ják, near the border with Austria. It is part of the Vajdahunyad Castle complex.

Statue of Anonymous
Completed in 1903 by Miklós Ligeti, this is one of Budapest's most famous monuments.

★ Vajdahunyad Castle
This Baroque section of the castle houses the Museum of Agriculture ⓾

STAR SIGHTS

★ Museum of Fine Arts

★ Vajdahunyad Castle

★ Széchenyi Baths

The former headquarters of the ÁVO at No. 60 Andrássy Street

Andrássy Street **❶**

ANDRÁSSY ÚT

Map 2 F4, 2 F5 (10 E2). **M** *Hősök tere.*

A̲T OKTOGON TÉR, Andrássy Street intersects with the Erzsébet körút and Teréz körút. From here government offices line Andrássy Street, and it loses its commercial character. At No. 60, is the former headquarters of the secret police, the ÁVO, who actively enforced the repressive Stalinist regime of the 1950s. This is now a museum called the House of Terror.

Franz Liszt Museum **❷**

LISZT FERENC EMLÉKMÚZEUM

Vörösmarty út 35. **Map** 5 A5.
C 322 98 04. **M** *Vörösmarty utca.*
🕓 10am–6pm Mon–Fri, 9am–5pm Sat. ▨ ▧ *by arrangement.*

T̲HIS NEO-RENAISSANCE corner house was designed in 1877 by Adolf Lang. Above the windows of the second floor are bas-reliefs depicting famous composers – J S Bach, Wolfgang Amadeus Mozart, Joseph Haydn, Ferenc Erkel,

Ludwig van Beethoven, and Franz Liszt himself. Liszt not only lived in this house, but also established an Academy of Music in the city *(see p129)*.

In 1986, 100 years after Franz Liszt's death, this museum was established in his house. Various items were assembled here, including documents, furniture and two pianos on which he composed and practised his work.

Academy of Fine Art **❸**

KÉPZŐMŰVÉSZETI FŐISKOLA

Andrássy út 69–71. **Map** 5 A5.
C 342 17 38. **M** *Vörösmarty utca.*
Barcsay Gallery 🕓 10am–6pm Mon–Fri, 10am–1pm Sat.

T̲HE ACADEMY OF Fine Art began as a drawing school, later becoming a Higher School of Art. Since 1876, it has occupied these adjacent buildings on Andrássy Street.

The two-floor Neo-Renaissance building at No. 71 was designed in 1875, by Lajos Rauscher. Its façade is decorated with sgrafitti by Robert Scholtz. The Italianate Renaissance exterior of No. 69, designed by Adolf Lang from 1875–7, is distinguished by Corinthian pilasters and a full-length balcony. The entrance hall and first-floor corridor feature frescoes by Károly Lotz. Only the Barcsay Gallery is open to visitors, but the interior can be glimpsed from here.

Sgrafitto by Robert Scholtz

Zoltán Kodály Museum **❹**

KODÁLY ZOLTÁN EMLÉKMÚZEUM

Kodály Körönd 1. **Map** 5 B5.
C 342 84 48. **M** *Kodály Körönd.*
🕓 10am–6pm Thu–Sat, 10am–2pm Sun, 10am–4pm Wed. ▨ ▧

Z̲OLTÁN KODÁLY (1881–1967) was one of the greatest Hungarian composers of the 20th century. His profound knowledge of Hungarian folk music allowed him to use elements of it in his compositions, which reflected the fashion for Impressionism and Neo-Romanticism in music.

This museum was established in 1990 and occupies the house where he lived and worked from 1924 until his death in 1967. A plaque set into one of the walls of the house bears testimony to this fact. The museum consists of three rooms that have been preserved in their original style, and a fourth room that is used for exhibitions. An archive has also been created here, in which the composer's valuable handwritten music scores and a wealth of correspondence are kept.

Worthy of attention are the composer's piano in the salon and a number of folklore ceramics which Kodály collected in the course of his ethnographical studies. Portraits and busts of Kodály by Lajos Petri can also be viewed.

Városligeti Avenue **❺**

VÁROSLIGETI FASOR

Map 5 C5. **M** *Hősök tere.*

T̲HIS BEAUTIFUL street, lined with plane trees, leads from Lövölde tér to Városliget.

At the beginning of the avenue is a Calvinist church built in 1912–13 by Aladár Árkay. This stark edifice is virtually bereft of any architectural features. However, stylized, geometric folk motifs

Original furnishings in the salon in the Franz Liszt Museum

Chinese gate at the Ráth György Museum on Városligeti Avenue

have been used as ornament-ation and harmonize with the interior Secession decoration.

In front of the church is the Ráth György Museum, part of the Ferenc Hopp Museum of Far Eastern Art, displaying artifacts from China and Japan collected in the 19th century.

Further along the avenue is a Lutheran church. It was constructed between 1903–5 to a Neo-Gothic design by Samu Pecz, who also designed the interior detail. Worthy of note is the painting on the high altar, by Gyula Benczúr, enti-tled *The Adoration of the Magi.*

Ferenc Hopp Museum of Far Eastern Art ❻

HOPP FERENC KELET-ÁZSIAI MŰVÉSZETI MÚZEUM

Andrássy út 103. **Map** 5 B4.
📞 *322 84 76.* Ⓜ *Bajza utca.*
🕐 *10am–6pm Tue–Sun.*
For guided tours call 456 51 00.
Rath György Museum 📞 *342 39 16.*
🕐 *10am–6pm Tue–Sun.*

FERENC HOPP (1833–1919), a wealthy merchant and the proprietor of an opthalmic shop, was the first great Hun-garian traveller, amassing a collection of more than 20,000 items from countries such as India, China and Vietnam.

The collection's smaller examples of art and handi-crafts can be seen in his former home, while its garden features large stone sculptures and architectural fragments.

The Chinese and Japanese collection is displayed in the Ráth György Museum at No. 12 Városligeti Avenue.

Millennium Monument ❼

MILLENIUMI EMLÉKMŰ

Map 5 C4. Ⓜ *Hősök tere.*

THIS MONUMENT was designed by György Zala and Albert Schikedanz to commemorate Hungary's Millennium Celebrations in 1896, but was not completed until 1929.

At the centre of the monu-ment is a 36-m (120-ft) high Corinthian column, upon which stands the Archangel Gabriel holding St István's crown and the apostolic cross. These objects signify Hungary's conversion to Christianity under King István *(see p22).* At the base of the column there are equestrian statues of Prince Árpád and six of the conquering Magyar warriors.

A stone tile set in front of the column marks the Tomb of the Unknown Soldier.

The column is embraced by two curved colonnades, feat-uring allegorical compositions at both ends. Personifications of War and Peace are nearest the column, while Knowledge and Glory crown the far end of the right-hand colonnade, and Labour and Prosperity crown the far end of the left. Statues of great Hungarians, including statesmen and monarchs, are arranged within the colonnades.

The right-hand colonnade of the Millennium Monument on Heroes' Square, completed in 1929

Museum of Fine Arts ❾

THE ORIGINS OF the Museum of Fine Arts' comprehensive collection date from 1870, when the state bought a magnificent collection of paintings from the aristocratic Esterházy family. The museum's collection was enriched by donations and acquisitions, and in 1906 it moved to its present location. The building, by Fülöp Herzog and Albert Schickedanz, is Neo-Classical with Italian-Renaissance influences. The tympanum crowning the portico is supported by eight Corinthian columns. It depicts the Battle of the Centaurs and Lapiths, and is copied from the Temple of Zeus at Olympia, Greece.

Grimani jug

First floor

The Water Carrier
(*c. 1810*)
La Aquadora *demonstrates the full range of Francisco de Goya's artistic talent.*

Still Life with Turkey
This work is attributed to Jean-Baptiste-Siméon Chardin, a French painter who emulated the 17th-century Dutch masters' genre painting.

★ **Esterházy Madonna**
(*c. 1508*)
This unfinished picture by Raphael is so named because it became the property of the Esterházy family at the beginning of the 19th century.

Lower ground floor

KEY

- ☐ Egyptian artifacts
- ☐ Classical artifacts
- ☐ Sculpture
- ☐ German art
- ☐ Dutch and Flemish art
- ☐ Italian art
- ☐ Spanish art
- ☐ French and English art
- ☐ Drawings and graphic art
- ☐ 19th- and 20th-century works

St James Conquers the Moors (*1750*)
Giambattista Tiepolo portrayed the miraculous appearance of the saint during a battle at Clavijo in 844.

View of Amsterdam
(c. 1656)
Jacob van Ruisdael was a master of Dutch realist landscape painting. He greatly influenced the development of European landscape painting in the 19th century.

VISITORS' CHECKLIST

Hősök tere. **Map** 5 C3.
469 71 00. Hősök tere.
75, 79. 4, 20, 30, 105.
10am–6pm Tue–Sun.
www.szepmuveszeti.hu

Mother and Child
(1905)
The rare subtlety of this intensely intimate picture, by Pablo Picasso, is achieved using watercolour.

Ground floor

★ St John the Baptist's Sermon *(1566)*
In this wonderful painting, Pieter Bruegel the Elder, a renowned observer of daily life, depicts a preacher addressing a group of peasants from Flanders.

These Women in the Refectory *(1894)*
This pastel sketch by the artist Henri de Toulouse-Lautrec, an observer and protagonist in the Parisian demi-monde, depicts prostitutes in a bar.

MUSEUM GUIDE
Restoration work on the museum began in 1997 and is expected to continue until 2006. As a result, not all the rooms are currently open to the public. The works displayed are being moved as restoration work progresses.

STAR EXHIBITS

★ Esterházy Madonna

★ St John the Baptist's Sermon

Exploring the Museum of Fine Arts

Egyptian head (c. 1200 BC)

THE MUSEUM'S COLLECTION encompasses international art dating from antiquity to the 20th century. As well as Egyptian, Greek and Roman artifacts, the museum houses galleries dedicated to a variety of modern art. Alongside its interesting collection of sculptures, there are priceless drawings and works of graphic art. Over the next few years the museum will be undergoing a process of redevelopment. In spite of this, exhibits will continue to be open to the public throughout the duration of the restoration work. Individual collections will simply be moved to different locations as building work progresses.

Albrecht Dürer's simple yet beautiful *Portrait of a Young Man*

EGYPTIAN ARTIFACTS

EGYPTIAN ARTIFACTS have been exhibited in the museum since 1939. Principally, they are the result of 19th-century excavations that involved Hungarian archaeologists.

The rich collection includes stone sculptures from each historic period, from the Old Kingdom to the Ptolemy dynasty. A nobleman's head of a votive statue dates from the New Kingdom and is a particularly beautiful example.

Also worthy of note is the collection of small bronze figures, which also date mainly from the New Kingdom, together with domestic objects that illustrate everyday life.

CLASSICAL ARTIFACTS

THE COLLECTION of Classical artifacts is rather varied. It encompasses works of Greek, Etruscan, and Roman works.

Detail of a hunting scene on a 3rd-century AD Greek sarcophagus

The collection of Greek vases ranks as one of the best of its kind in Europe. A black-figure amphora by Exekias and a kylix from the studio of the painter Andokides are very fine examples of this work.

Bronze work, which dates from various epochs, including the famous Grimani jug from the 5th century BC, gold jewellery, and marble and terracotta sculptures are all exquisite artifacts from this era.

SCULPTURE

UNDOUBTEDLY the most valuable element of this collection is a small bronze sculpture by Leonardo da Vinci (1452–1519). This is an unusually dynamic representation of King François I of France on his horse. Other superb examples of Italian sculpture, by masters such as Andrea Pisano of the Ronni family, can also be seen.

Leonardo da Vinci's figure of François I

GERMAN ART

AMONG THE most valuable works in the collection are the *Portrait of a Young Man*, by Albrecht Dürer, and the carefully composed painting of *The Dormition of Mary*, by Hans Holbein. The work of such masters as Hans Baldung Grien and Lucas Cranach are worth seeing, as is the collection of German and Austrian Baroque painting, which includes work by Franz Anton Maulbertsch.

DUTCH AND FLEMISH ART

THE MUSEUM's Dutch and Flemish collection features works by the finest masters, including influential landscape artist, Jacob van Ruisdael, with *View of Amsterdam (see p147)*. The subtle *Nativity* by Gerard David and Pieter Bruegel's detailed masterpiece *St John the Baptist's Sermon (see p147)*, depicting Flemish peasants listening to the saint's words, are exemplary exhibits. The museum also boasts canvases attributed to Rembrandt, including *St Joseph's Dream*, portraits by Frans Hals and Jan Vermeer's *Portrait of a Lady*. Not to be missed is the magnificent 17th-century Dutch paintings by artists including Adrian van Ostade, Jacob Ruisdael, Jan Steen and others.

The highlight of the Flemish collection is the 17th-century *Mucius Scaevola before Porsenna* by Peter Rubens and his then assistant, Anthony van Dyck. The latter was responsible for the picture of St John the Evangelist, also on display.

Also important are the paintings of Adam and Eve and *Satyr with Peasants* by Jacob Jordaens, who also worked as an assistant to Rubens.

ITALIAN ART

THIS VALUABLE collection of Italian art, which was the core of the Esterházy family's collection, is often considered the museum's biggest attraction. All the schools of Italian painting, from the 13th to the 18th centuries, are on display here. The Renaissance period is perhaps the best represented.

Of particular note is the captivating *Esterházy Madonna (see p146)*, an unfinished painting by Raphael. Another great work by this outstanding artist is the *Portrait of Pietro Bembo*.

There is no shortage of work by famous 16th-century Venetian artists among the paintings collected here. Important works by Titian, Bonifazio Veronese, Antonio Correggio, Jacopo Tintoretto, Giorgione and Giovanni Boltraffio are all exhibited here. An excellent example of Baroque art is Giambattista Tiepolo's vast late 18th-century painting, *St James Conquers the Moors (see p146)*.

Giovanni Boltraffio's *Madonna and Child* **(c. 1506)**

SPANISH ART

THE MOST IMPORTANT features of this collection are seven paintings by El Greco, including *The Annunciation, Christ in the Garden of Gethsemane* and *The Penance of St Mary Magdalene*, a subtle though fully expressive work.

The dramatic *Martyrdom of St Andrew* by Jusepe de Ribera should not be missed, nor the work of artists such as Diego

El Greco's *The Penance of St Mary Magdalene* **(c. 1576)**

Velázquez, Bartolomé Murillo and Francisco Zurbarán. Francisco de Goya's observations of daily life produced paintings such as *The Water Carrier (see p146)*, which also deserves special attention.

FRENCH AND ENGLISH ART

WORKS BY French and English artists are not as numerous as Italian works, for example, but represent the various styles of the two countries.

French works include the well-composed *Resting on the Journey to Egypt* by Nicolas Poussin, *Villa in the Roman Countryside* by Claude Lorrain, and *Still Life with Turkey*, thought to be by Jean-Baptiste-Siméon Chardin *(see p146)*.

The collection of English paintings includes portraits by artists of the calibre of Joshua Reynolds, William Hogarth and Thomas Gainsborough.

DRAWINGS AND GRAPHIC ART

THE COLLECTION of drawings and graphic art combines the work of old masters, including drawings by Leonard da Vinci, Raphael, Albrecht Dürer and Rembrandt, with pieces from artists of the 19th and 20th centuries. The collection is one of Europe's best.

19TH- AND 20TH-CENTURY WORKS

FRENCH PAINTING makes up the largest constituent of the collection of 19th- and 20th-century art. The visitor can admire works by all the major painters of the time, including Pablo Picasso's *Mother and Child (see p147)*, Henri de Toulouse-Lautrec's *These Women in the Refectory (see p147)*, Gustave Courbet's *Wrestlers*, Edouard Manet's *Woman with a Fan* and Camille Pissarro's *Pont-Neuf*. Paul Gauguin's *Black Pigs*, one of his first Tahitian canvases, is also on display here. To complete the collection, the likes of Eugène Delacroix, Claude Monet, Pierre Bonnard, Pierre Renoir and Paul Cézanne are also represented.

Austrian and German 19th- and 20th-century art is represented with works by Waldmüller, Amerling, Lenbach, Leibl and Menzel.

Paul Cézanne's still life, *Credenza*, **dating from 1874 – 7**

The façade of the Palace of Art, featuring a six-columned portico

Palace of Art ❽

MŰCSARNOK

Hősök tere. **Map** 5 C4.
📞 *363 26 71.* Ⓜ *Hősök tere.*
🕐 *10am–6pm Tue–Sun.* 🖼 ♿ 📷

ON THE SOUTHERN side of
Heroes' Square, opposite
the Museum of Fine Arts *(see
pp146–9)*, is the Palace of Art.
This imposing Neo-Classical
building was designed by
Albert Schickedanz and Fülöp
Herzog in 1895. It is Hungary's
largest exhibition space. Temporary exhibitions of mainly
contemporary painting and
sculpture are held here.

The Palace of Art is fronted
by a vast six-columned portico.
The mosaic, depicting St István
as the patron saint of fine art,
was added to the tympanum
between 1938–41. Behind the
portico is a fresco in three
parts by Lajos Deák Ébner,
illustrating *The Beginning of
Sculpture, The Source of Arts*
and *The Origins of Painting.*

Museum of Fine Arts ❾

SZÉPMŰVÉSZETI MÚZEUM

See pp146–9.

Vajdahunyad Castle ❿

VAJDAHUNYAD VÁRA

Városliget. **Map** 6 D4. 📞 *363 19 73.*
Museum of Agriculture 📞 *343 05
73.* 🕐 *Nov–Feb: 10am–4pm Mon–Fri,
10am–5pm Sat & Sun; Mar–Oct:
10am–5pm Mon–Fri, Sun, 10am–6pm
Sat.* 🖼 ♿ 📷

THIS INCREDIBLE, fairytale-like
building is picturesquely
located among the trees at the
edge of the lake in Városliget.
Not a genuine castle but a
complex of buildings reflecting various architectural styles,
it was designed by Ignác
Alpár for the 1896 Millennium
Celebrations *(see p142).*

Alpár's creation illustrated
the history and evolution of
architecture in Hungary. Originally intended as temporary
exhibition pavilions, the castle
proved so popular with the
public that, between 1904–6,
it was rebuilt to brick to
create a permanent structure.

The pavilions are grouped
in chronological order of style:
Romanesque is followed by
Gothic, Renaissance, Baroque
and so on. The individual styles
were linked together to give
the impression
of a single,
cohesive

design. Each of the pavilions
use authentic details copied
from Hungary's most important historic buildings or are a
looser interpretation of a style
inspired by a specific architect
of that historic period.

The Romanesque complex
features a copy of the portal
from a chapel in Ják *(see p143)*
as well as a monastic cloister
and palace. The details on the
Gothic pavilion have been
taken from castles like those
in Vajdahunyad and Segesvár
(both now in Romania). The
architect Fischer von Erlach
was the inspiration for the
Renaissance and Baroque complex. The façade copies part of
the Bakócz chapel in the cathedral at Esztergom *(see p164).*

The Museum of Agriculture
can be found in the Baroque
section. It has exhibits on
cattle breeding, wine-making,
hunting and fishing.

The entire complex reflects
more than 20 of Hungary's
most renowned buildings. The
medieval period, often considered the most glorious time in
Hungary's history, is given
greatest emphasis, while the
controversial Habsburg era is
pushed into the background.

Zoo ⓫

FŐVÁROSI ÁLLAT-ÉS NÖVÉNYKERT

Állatkerti körút 6–12. **Map** 5 C3.
📞 *363 37 97.* Ⓜ *Széchenyi fürdő.*
🕐 *May–Aug: 9am– 6pm Mon–Thu,
9am–7pm Fri–Sun; Mar–Apr,
Sept–Oct: 9am–5pm daily.* 🖼

BUDAPEST'S ZOO is one of the
city's great attractions. It
was established in 1866 by
the Hungarian Academy of
Sciences *(see p114)*. In 1907 it
was bought by the State and
totally redeveloped,

View across the lake of the Gothic (left) and Renaissance (right) sections of Vajdahunyad Castle between 1909–11, by Károly Kós and Dezső Zrumeczky.

The animals are housed in enclosures most of which strive to mimic their natural habitat. The elephant house, however, by Kórnel Neuschloss-Knüsli, is a fine example of Secession style. Károly Kós, on the other hand, adopted a folk style for the aviary, in which a wide variety of birds fly freely.

Funfair ⑫
VIDÁMPARK

Állatkerti körút 14–16. **Map** 6 D2.
☎ 363 26 60. Ⓜ Széchenyi fürdő.
◯ Apr–Oct: 11am–7pm Mon–Fri, 10am–8pm Sat & Sun; Nov–Mar: noon–6pm Mon–Fri, 10am–6pm Sat & Sun.

IN 1878 THERE was already a carousel here, along with games and theatrical shows.

Today it is a charmingly un-sophisticated amusement park with an assortment of old-fashioned rides. Next door is a smaller funfair for toddlers.

There are numerous kiosks, bars and restaurants serving food, so it is easy to spend the entire day here. The circus is also close by (see p211).

Széchenyi Baths ⑬
SZÉCHENYI STRANDFÜRDŐ

Állatkerti körút 11. **Map** 6 D3.
☎ 363 32 10. Ⓜ Széchenyi fürdő.
◯ 6am–7pm Mon–Fri, 6am–5pm Sat & Sun.

A STATUE STANDS at the main entrance to the Széchenyi Baths depicting geologist Vilmos Zsigmond, who discovered a hot spring here while drilling a well in 1879.

The Széchenyi Baths are the deepest and hottest baths in Budapest – the water reaches the surface at a temperature of $74-5°$ C (180° F). The springs, rich in minerals, are distinguished by their alleged healing properties. They are recommended for treating rheumatism and disorders of the nervous system, joints and muscles.

One of the outdoor pools at the beautiful Széchenyi Baths

The spa, housed in a Neo-Baroque building by Győző Cziegler and Ede Dvorzsák, was constructed in 1909–13.

In 1926, three swimming pools were added. Despite being open-air, the pools are popular all year due to the high temperature of the water.

Hermina Street ⑭
HERMINA ÚT

Map 6 E3, 6 E4 & 6 F4. 🚌 70.
Transport Museum ☎ 273 38 40.
◯ Apr–Oct: 10am–5pm Tue–Fri, 10am–6pm Sat & Sun; Nov–Mar: 10am–4pm Tue–Fri, 10am–5pm Sat & Sun. 🎟 ♿ 📷 by arrangement.

THIS BEAUTIFUL street is worth walking along to experience the romantic atmosphere of the historic, elegant villas in this area. Particularly notable is the unusual Secession building at No. 47, Sipeky Balázs Villa (see p55), built in 1905–6 by architects Ödön Lechner, Marcell Komor and Dezső Jakab. The asymmetric design of the villa's façade includes features such as a domed glass conservatory,

A steam train exhibited at the Transport Museum, just off Hermina Street

an ironwork porch and a tall, narrow side tower. The villa's exterior decoration is inspired by Hungarian folk art.

Hermina Chapel at No. 23, by József Hild, was built in 1842–6 in memory of Palatine József's daughter, Hermina Amália, who died in 1842.

Backing onto Hermina Street, at No. 11 Városligeti körút, is the Transport Museum with exhibits on the evolution of air, sea, road and rail transport. Among the trains, helicopters and aeroplanes are some pre-World War II right-hand-drive cars from when Hungarians still drove on the left.

Poster for a gala ballet performance at the Erkel Theatre

Erkel Theatre ⑮
ERKEL SZÍNHÁZ

Köztársaság ter 30. **Map** 7 C3.
☎ 333 01 08. Ⓜ Keleti pu.

AN ALTERNATIVE venue of the National Opera Company, this is the largest theatre in Hungary, seating 2,500 people. Designed in 1911 by Marcell Komor, Dezső Jakab and Géza Márkus, its current form dates from the 1950s. Concerts and operas are performed here.

FURTHER AFIELD

BUDAPEST IS A SPRAWLING city and several sights on its periphery are well worth a visit. North from the centre of Buda are the fascinating ruins of Aquincum, a town founded by the Romans in approximately AD 100. To the west, the city is skirted by wooded hills, which offer walks around beautiful nature reserves and exciting cave visits. Out

Roman urn from Aquincum

to the east of Pest is Kerepesi Cemetery, where a host of famous Hungarians are buried. To the south of the city is the Nagytétény Palace, one of the most beautiful Baroque palaces in Hungary. The new setting for Socialist-era statues, the Park of Monuments, is not far from the palace. All the sights can be reached easily using public transport.

SIGHTS AT A GLANCE

Museums
Aquincum **25**
Gizi Bajor Theatre Museum **19**

Historic Buildings and Monuments
Geology Institute **4**
Ludovika Academy **9**
Nagytétény Palace **23**
Raoul Wallenberg
   Monument **1**
Statue Park **21**
Technical University **16**
Törley Mausoleum **22**
Wekerle Estate **15**

Parks and Recreation Areas
Buda Hills **24**
Budapest Exhibition Centre **11**
Congress Centre **18**
Eagle Hill Nature Reserve **20**
People's Park **10**
People's Stadium **5**
Szemlő-hegy and Pál-völgy
   Caves **2**
University Botanical
   Gardens **8**

Cemeteries
Jewish Cemetery **14**
Kerepesi Cemetery **6**
Municipal Cemetery **13**

Churches
Cistercian Church of St Imre **17**
Józsefváros Parish Church **7**
Kőbánya Parish Church **12**
Újlak Parish Church **3**

KEY

▦	City centre
▢	Greater Budapest
✈	Airport
🚉	Train station
▬	Motorway
▬	Main road
—	Railway

◁ **View of the ruins of the Roman town of Aquincum, founded in around AD 100**

Raoul Wallenberg Monument ❶

RAOUL WALLENBERG SZOBOR

Szilágyi Erzsébet fasor.
🚎 56.

TUCKED AWAY at the junction of Szilágyi Erzsébet fasor and Nagyajtai utca, is this monument to an heroic but little known figure of World War II. Raoul Wallenberg was a Swedish diplomat who used his position to save over 20,000 Hungarian Jews from the extermination camps. He set up safe houses in the city and obtained fake Swedish documents for them.

Following the liberation of Budapest by the Soviet army, Wallenberg disappeared. It is thought he was arrested by the KGB and sent to a prison camp where he died. The memorial, by sculptor Imre Varga, was erected in 1987.

Szemlő-hegy and Pál-völgy Caves ❷

SZEMLŐ-HEGYI-BARLANG ÉS PÁL-VÖLGYI-CSEPPKŐBARLANG

Szemlő-hegy Cave Pusztaszeri út 35.
📞 325 60 01. 🚌 29. ⏰ 10am–4pm Wed–Mon. 🏷 ♿ 📷
Pál-völgy Cave Szépvölgyi út 162.
📞 325 95 05. 🚌 65. ⏰ 10am–4pm Tue–Sun. 🏷 📷

TO THE NORTH of Budapest lies the Pilis mountain range, formed of limestone and dolomite. Natural geological processes which occur within these mountains have created some picturesque caves, two of which are unusual tourist attractions.

Szemlő-hegy Cave features extraordinary formations called "cave pearls", produced when hot spring waters penetrate its limestone walls. In Pál-völgy Cave strange formations protruding from the rock face resemble animals, including an elephant and a crocodile.

It is a good idea to wear warm clothes when visiting the caves as they are cold and damp. Some claim, however, that the atmosphere in the caves has a therapeutic effect on the respiratory system.

The Baroque interior of Újlak Parish Church, dating from 1756

Újlak Parish Church ❸

ÚJLAKI PLÉBÁNIATEMPLOM

Bécsi út 32.
🚎 17.

BAVARIAN SETTLERS first built a small church here early in the 18th century. The present church, designed by Kristóf Hamon and Mátyás Nepauer, was finished in 1756. Its tower was added some years later.

In the Baroque interior there is a depiction of the Madonna, a gift from the inhabitants of Passau to the church. The main altar, dating from 1798, also includes

a painting entitled *The Visitation*, which was the work of Francis Falkoner.

Not far away, at Zsigmond tér, stands the Holy Trinity Column, built in 1691 as a memorial to the city's earliest plague epidemic. The Baroque monument is the work of two Italian sculptors, Venerio Cresola and Bernard Feretti, and was moved from central Buda to Újlak in 1712.

Geology Institute ❹

FÖLDTANI INTÉZET

Stefánia út 14. **Map** 8 F1. 📞 251 09 99. 🚎 75, 77. **Museum** ⏰ 10am–4pm Thu, Sat & Sun. 🏷

THIS BEAUTIFUL and unusual building, housing the Geology Institute, dates from 1898–9 and was designed by Ödön Lechner *(see p56)*.

Lechner's very individual Secession style, also known as the Hungarian National Style, is on show here including motifs drawn from Hungarian Renaissance architecture.

On the picturesque elevations and gables of the building pale yellow plaster walls form a striking contrast to the brick-work quoins and window frames. Here and there Zsolnay blue glazed ceramic ornaments adorn the walls and harmonize with the blue roof tiles. The central pitched roof is topped by three

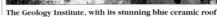

The Geology Institute, with its stunning blue ceramic roof

human figures bent under the weight of a large globe.

Inside the Geology Institute, there is a small museum with rock and mineral exhibits. Lechner's Secession interiors have been carefully preserved in their original condition. The central hall, which is particularly magnificent, can be seen when visiting the museum or on its own with the caretaker's permission.

People's Stadium **5**
NÉPSTADION

Kerepesi út. **Map** 8 F1. **C** 471 41 00 (ext. 4748). 🚇 23, 24, 36.

HUNGARY'S BIGGEST sports stadium was built between 1948–53, to a design by Károly Dávid. The roofless stadium seats 78,000, but is generally at least half empty, only filling to capacity when a major pop group plays here.

The stadium's entrance is at the end of Ifjúság útja, the Road of Youth, a broad avenue lined with Stalinist-era statues. Depicting various sports disciplines, the statues are the work of a number of well-known Hungarian sculptors including Imre Varga and István Tar.

Kerepesi Cemetery **6**
KEREPESI TEMETŐ

Fiumei út 16–20. **Map** 8 E3. 🚇 23, 24, 36.

FOR MORE THAN 150 years since it was established in 1847, the Kerepesi Cemetery has provided the resting place for many of Hungary's most prominent citizens. Fine tombstones mark the graves of some, while others were interred here inside monumental mausoleums.

The mausoleum of the leader of the 1948–9 uprising, Lajos Kossuth (*see p106*) is by Alajos Stróbl, while that of Lajos Batthyány, the first prime minister of Hungary (*see p31*) is the work of Albert Schickedanz.

Ferenc Deák, who formulated the Compromise with Austria (*see p32*), is among the other statesmen buried here.

Also at the cemetery are the graves of poets Endre Ady and Attila József (*see p106*), writers Kálmán Mikszáth Zsigmond Móricz and actors such as Lujza Blaha, whose tomb is particularly beautiful. Sculptors, painters and composers are buried close to great architects, including Alajos Stróbl, Ödön Lechner and Alajos Hauszmann.

Hungarian Communists, including László Rajk (*see p34*), who were sentenced to death in the show trials of 1949, were buried in a separate part of the cemetery. Their funerals inspired a revolutionary spirit which, a few years later, led to the 1956 Uprising (*see p34*).

Józsefváros Parish Church **7**
JÓZSEFVÁROS PLÉBÁNIATEMPLOM

Horváth Mihály tér 7. **Map** 7 C4. **C** 313 61 26. 🚇 83. 🚋 9, 17.

THE BUILDING WORK on this Baroque church began in 1797. It was not completed until 1814, by Fidél Kasselik. At the end of 19th century further additions were made to the structure.

The main altar is by József Hild. A formidable architectural composition, it is based on a triumphal arch. This frames a magnificent painting, *The*

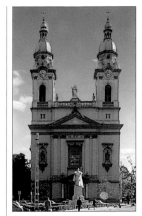

The late Baroque façade of Józsefváros Parish Church

Apotheosis of St Joseph, by Leopold Kupelwieser, an Austrian artist. The church also has two beautiful, late Baroque side altars.

University Botanical Gardens **8**
EGYETEMI BOTANIKUS KERT

Illés utca 25. **Map** 8 D5. **C** 314 05 35. **M** Klinikák. 🕐 9am–4pm Sat–Thu, 9am–12pm Fri. 📷 📷

GARDENS WERE first established on this 3-ha (8-acre) site by the Festetics family. Their modest, early-Neo-Classical villa is now the administration centre for the botanical gardens. It was built in 1802–3, most probably to a design by Mihály Pollack. The smoking room in the villa houses a huge collection of tropical plants. These include the striking *Victoria regia*, which flowers once a year.

The Hungarian author Ferenc Molnár (1878–1952) used the gardens as a setting in his novel, *The Paul Street Boys*, although the lake mentioned in the book no longer exists. Not far away are Pál utca (Paul Street) and Mária utca, the scene of a battle the boys fought. However, the Maria utca of the novel was prior to the invasion of tenement blocks.

The tomb of actress Lujza Blaha at Kerepesi Cemetery

Ludovika Academy ❾
LUDOVIKA AKADÉMIA

Üllői út 82 (off Ludovika tér).
Ⓜ *Klinikák.* 🅲 *267 70 07.*
◯ *10am– 5pm Wed– Mon.* **Natural History Museum** ◯ *10am–6pm Wed– Mon.* 📷 🎫

THE HUGE Ludovika Academy is in district IX, east of the city centre. It was designed in the 1830s by Mihály Pollack, the famous architect of the Hungarian National Museum *(see pp130– 33).* A military academy until 1945, it is an impressive example of Neo-Classical style. Rebuilding work in 1880 left many original features intact, including the main hall and the chapel's interior. Following refurbishment, the academy is now home to the city's new Natural History Museum.

A children's playground in People's Park

People's Park ❿
NÉPLIGET

Ⓜ *Népliget.* **Planetarium** 🅲 *265 07 25.* ◯ *shows: 9:30am, 11am, 1pm, 2:30pm, 4pm Tue–Sun.* 📷 🎫

LANDSCAPED IN THE 1860s, the People's Park, about 5 km (3 miles) southeast of central Pest, is the city's largest park. Its 112 ha (277 acres) consist of large areas of grass and trees interspersed with flowerbeds and children's playgrounds.

At one corner of the park is the popular Planetarium. The paths of the planets, as seen from earth, are projected on to the 23-m (75-ft) dome. Regular evening laser shows with both pop and classical soundtracks also take place here.

Budapest Exhibition Centre ⓫
BUDAPESTI NEMZETKÖZI VÁSÁRKÖZPONT

Albertirsai út 10. 🅲 *263 61 01.*
🚌 *Expo bus from Örs Vezér tér.*

BUDAPEST HAS a long history of trade fairs and exhibitions, which began with the hugely successful Millennium Exhibition of 1896. Budapest Exhibition Centre, also known as HungExpo and built in 1980, is just north of Kőbánya on the city's eastern side. It is the venue for several trade fairs, including the IFABO computer fair *(see p58).* Another popular event is Budapest International Fair, or BNV. Held annually in September, this is a huge shop window for consumer goods from Hungary and other parts of Europe. Visitors to the fair include business people and members of the public.

Kőbánya Parish Church ⓬
KŐBÁNYAI PLÉBÁNIATEMPLOM

Szent László tér. 🚋 *13, 28.*
🚌 *17, 32, 62, 185.* ♿

AN INDUSTRIAL SUBURB on the eastern side of Pest, Kőbánya is the unexpected home of the beautiful Kőbánya Parish Church. Designed by Ödön Lechner *(see p56)* in the 1890s, the church makes magnificent use of the architect's favourite materials, including vibrant roof tiles developed and produced at the now-famous Zsolnay factory in the town of Pécs. Like much of Lechner's work, including the Museum of Applied Arts *(see pp136–7),* the church combines motifs and colours from Hungarian folk art with Neo-Gothic elements. Inside the church, both the altar and the pulpit are superb examples of early 20th-century wood

Gleaming ceramic tiles on the roof of Kőbánya Parish Church

carving. Somehow surviving heavy World War II bombing, a number of Miksa Roth's original stained-glass windows are still in place.

Municipal Cemetery ⓭
RÁKOSKERESZTÚR

See pp158–9.

Jewish Cemetery ⓮
ZSIDÓ TEMETŐ

Kozma út. 🚌 *37.*

NEXT DOOR TO the Municipal Cemetery is the Jewish Cemetery, opened in 1893. The many grand tombs here are a vivid reminder of the vigour and success of Budapest's pre-war Jewish community. At the end of the 19th century, nearly a quarter of the city's inhabitants were Jewish. Tombs to look out for as you stroll among the graves include that of the Wellisch family, designed in 1903 by Arthur Wellisch, and that of Konrád Polnay, which

Schmidl family tomb at the Jewish Cemetry

was designed five years later by Gyula Fodor. Perhaps the most eyecatching of all belongs to the Schmidl family. The startlingly flamboyant tomb, designed in 1903 by architects Ödön Lechner and Béla Lajta, is covered in vivid turquoise ceramic tiles. The central mosaic in green and gold tiles represents the Tree of Life.

Wekerle Estate
WEKERLE TELEP

Kós Károly tér. **M** Határ út, then ▦ 194.

O UT IN DISTRICT XIX, the Wekerle Estate was built between 1909 and 1926, and represents a bold and successful experiment in 20th-century social planning. Named after Prime Minister Sándor Wekerle, the estate was originally known as the Kispest Workers and Clerks Settlement and was built to provide better housing for local workers.

Designed by a group of young architects, students of Ödön Lechner, the buildings have a uniquely Hungarian style. Seeking inspiration from medieval peasant buildings, the architects would visit rural locations, gathering together architectural details in the same way that Béla Bartók and Zoltán Kodály (see p144)

collected folk songs. Other key influences were the English Arts and Crafts movement, and early English new towns such as Hampstead Garden Suburb in London.

Conceived as a self-contained village, the estate enjoys many of its own amenities, including a Catholic church, several schools, a cinema and a police station. Fanning out around Kós Károly tér, 16 types of family house and apartment block are separated by tree-lined streets. Wooden gables and balconies, and sharply pitched, brightly tiled roofs, contribute to the estate's lively and eclectic atmosphere.

Rents on the Wekerle Estate are now high, though the area manages to retain much of its working-class spirit.

Façade of the Technical University, as seen from the Danube

Technical University
BUDAPESTI MŰSZAKI EGYETEM

Műegyetem rakpart 3. **Map** 4 F4. **Ⅽ** 463 11 11. ▤ 4, 6, 18, 19, 47, 49. ▦ 7, 86.

F OUNDED IN 1857, the city's Technical University moved to its present site in 1904. Built on reclaimed marshland, the imposing building overlooks the Danube just south of Gellért Hill (see pp88–9). Extended at the end of World War II, it is now the largest higher education establishment in Hungary. Former students include Imre Steindl, the architect of the Parliament building (see pp108–9), and the richest and most widely known graduate to date, Ernő Rubik, inventor of the Rubik Cube.

Cistercian Church of St Imre
CISZTERCITA SZENT IMRE PLÉBÁNIATEMPLOM

Villányi út 25. **Map** 3 C4. ▤ 61. ▦ 27, 40. ♿

N OT FAR FROM the Technical University is the Cistercian Church of St Imre. The vast Neo-Baroque structure with its double tower was built in 1938 and is typical of the grand and rather sombre architecture in vogue in Budapest during the inter-war years.

Inside the church are relics of St Imre, canonized at the end of the 11th century. Other patron saints of the Cistercian order are depicted above the church's main entrance.

A police station on the early 20th-century Wekerle Estate

Municipal Cemetery ⓭

A NEW, HISTORIC significance was gained by the Municipal Cemetery following the 1956 Uprising *(see p35)*. Here, at Budapest southeastern limits, the leaders and victims of this bloody revolution against the oppressive Stalinist government were secretly buried in mass graves. During the 1970s, the country's democratic opposition began placing flowers on the site, at the far side of the cemetery. In 1990, after the fall of Communism, the revolutionary heroes were given a ceremonial funeral and reburied, and several memorials were set up to them.

View of Plot 300
Until 1989, the state militia guarded access to a thicket which covered the communal graves of the heroes of the 1956 Uprising.

Campanile
A wooden campanile is the type of decoration often found in old Hungarian cemeteries. It stands in front of panels listing the names of over 400 victims of the 1956 Uprising, giving the exact locations of their graves.

Plot 300

PLAN OF THE CEMETERY

In 1886, the city authorities opened a vast, new municipal cemetery in Rákoskeresztúr, on the outskirts of town. It became the largest cemetery in Budapest, occupying 30 sq km (12 sq miles).

Plots 300 and 301

Main entrance

| 0 metres | 500 |
| 0 yards | 500 |

★ **Transylvanian Gate**
The 1956 Uprising Combatants' Association erected the carved Transylvanian Gate which stands at the beginning of one of the paths leading into plot 300. It is inscribed with the words: "Only a Hungarian soul may pass through this gate".

★ Imre Nagy's Grave
A marble slab bears the modest inscription: "Imre Nagy, Prime Minister of Hungary, 1956". Arrested after the uprising, Nagy was interned and shot dead on 16 June 1956 in Budapest, following a bogus political trial.

NAGY, IMRE
MAGYARORSZÁG
MINISZTERELNÖKE
1 9 5 6

VISITORS' CHECKLIST

Kozma utca 8–10, Kőbánya.
210 15 00. 95 from Zalka Máté tér. **Plots 300 and 301** 30 mins walk from the main gate. Fee charged for cars.

Plot 301

Christ the Sorrowful
A figure of Christ the Sorrowful is traditionally placed in a plot containing Protestant graves.

★ Heroes' Monument
This simple monument symbolizes the passage through purgatory. It was created by the leading modern Hungarian sculptor, György Jovánovics.

Protestant Graves
The tradition of Hungarian Protestants is to place a simple wooden post to mark each grave.

STAR SIGHTS

★ **Transylvanian Gate**

★ **Imre Nagy's Grave**

★ **Heroes' Monument**

The main entrance to the Congress Hall in the Congress Centre, a venue for international events and conferences

Congress Centre ⓲

KONGRESSZUSI KÖZPONT

Jagelló út 1–3. **C** 372 54 00.
🚋 61. **◯** for events.

OPENED IN 1975, this large arts complex houses a concert hall, a cinema, conference rooms and several restaurants. It provides a venue for international conferences and events, as well as for the annual Hungarian Film Festival (see p61).

The Congress Centre, with the neighbouring Novotel Budapest Centrum (see p185), was designed by the architect József Finta. The *Tree of Life*, which decorates the main wall of the Congress Hall, is the work of József Király.

Gizi Bajor Theatre Museum ⓳

BAJOR GIZI SZÍNÉSZMÚZEUM

Stromfeld Aurél út 16.
C 356 42 94. **🚋** 105. **◯** Sep–Jun:
2–6pm Thu–Fri, 10am–6pm Sat &
Sun. **🖼 🎦**

THIS MUSEUM was opened in 1952, in a garden villa which once belonged to Gizi Bajor, a leading Hungarian actress of her day. Its exhibits, which include furniture, portraits, theatrical props, fans and velvet gloves, transport visitors to the world of the theatre in the 19th century.

In 1990, the 200th anniversary of theatre in Hungary, the museum's collection was further extended, to include mementos of well-known

contemporary Hungarian actors, after whom some of the museum's rooms are named.

The garden features the busts of several writers and other leading figures in Hungary's cultural history.

Eagle Hill Nature Reserve ⓴

SASHEGY TERMÉSZETVÉDEMI TERÜLET

Tájék utca 26. **C** 319 67 89.
🚌 8, 8A. **◯** Mid-Mar–mid-June &
Sep–mid-Oct: 10am–4pm Sat & Sun.
🎦 compulsory.

A NATURE RESERVE more or less in the centre of a city of two million inhabitants is a remarkable phenomenon.

Access to the summit of this steep, 266-m (872-ft) high hill to the west of Gellért Hill (see pp88–9) is strictly regulated to protect the extremely rare animal and plant species found here. A smart residential quarter, which lies on the lower slope of Eagle Hill, extends almost to the fence of the reserve and the craggy 30-ha wilderness that it encloses.

It is well worth taking a guided walk, particularly in spring or early autumn. Only here is it possible to see *centaurea sadleriana*, a flower resembling a cornflower but much bigger. The reserve is also home to a type of spider not found anywhere else in the world, as well as to extraordinary, colourful butterflies and to *ablebharus kitaibeli*, a rare lizard.

Statue Park ㉑

SZOBOR PARK

Balatoni út & Szabadkai utca.
C 424 75 00. **🚌** 50. **◯** 10am–
dusk daily. **🎦**

IN 1991, BUDAPEST'S City Council decided to gather in one place 41 Communist monuments which had formerly occupied prestigious locations in the city. The park where they can be viewed is now a popular attraction for visitors to the city who are curious about its recent past.

The competition for the design of the park was won by architect Ákos Eleöd and it opened to the public in 1993. Behind a red-brick wall, six rings of monuments are arrayed on the site. Statues of Karl Marx, Friedrich Engels, VI Lenin and Hungarian Communist heroes stand side by side, headed by the leader of the 1919 revolution in Hungary (see p34), Béla Kun. A statue of a Russian soldier removed from the Liberation Monument (see p92) can also be seen in the park.

The park has its own shop which sells books, posters and other paraphenalia connected with the Communist era.

Cubist-style statues of Marx and Engels in the Statue Park

The marble Törley Mausoleum

Törley Mausoleum ㉒

TÖRLEY MAUZOLEUM

Sarló utca 6. ▦ 3.

Until 1880 Budafok had a number of vineyards, but their cultivation was destroyed in that year by a plague of phylloxera (American aphid). It was then that József Törley, who had studied wine-making in Reims, started to produce sparkling wine in Budafok using the French model (see p192). His wines sold well abroad and he quickly expanded his enterprise, storing the wines in the local cellars.

József Törley died in 1900 and was laid to rest in this monumental mausoleum designed by Rezső Vilmos Ray. Constructed of white marble, it is adorned with Eastern motifs and bas-reliefs by József Damkó.

Nagytétény Palace ㉓

NAGYTÉTÉNYI KASTÉLY

Kastélypark utca 9–11. ▯ 226 55 47. ▦ 41. **Nagytétény Palace Museum** ▯ 207 54 62. ◯ Mar–Oct: 10am–6pm Tue–Sun; Nov–Feb: 10am–4pm Tue–Sun.

This is one of the best known Baroque palaces in Hungary. Nagytétény Palace was built in the mid-18th century, incorporating the remains of a 15th-century Gothic building. The work was started by György Száraz and

completed by his son-in-law, József Rudnyánszky, acquiring its final shape in 1766. Based on the typical Baroque layout, it includes a main block and side wings. The coping features the Száraz and Rudnyánszky family crests.

The palace suffered severe damage during World War II, but the original wall paintings and furnishings survived. In 1949, the palace was rebuilt and turned into an interior design museum. Now it is a department of the Museum of Applied Arts (see pp136–7). On display are fine pieces of Hungarian and European furniture from the 15th – 18th centuries, early 19th-century paintings and more functional items, such as tiled stoves.

Standing close to the palace is an 18th-century Baroque church, built on the remains of a medieval church. Original Gothic features incorporated in it include the window openings in its tower and three supports on the outer wall of the presbytery. In 1760, the Austrian artist Johann Gfall created the painting in the dome which features illusory galleries. The altars, pulpit and baptistries also date back to the mid-18th century.

Buda Hills ㉔

BUDAI-HEGYSÉG

Ⓜ Moszkva tér, then cog-wheel railway or chair lift.

To the west of the city centre are the wooded Buda Hills where Budapesters come to walk and relax.

The first station of a cogwheel railway, built in 1874, is on Szilágyi Erzsébet fasor. This runs up Sváb Hill – named after the Germanic Swabians, who settled here under the Habsburgs (see p28) – and then Széchenyi Hill.

From Széchenyi Hill a narrow-gauge railway covers a 12-km (7-mile) route to the Hüvös Valley. As in the days of the Soviet Young Pioneers movement, the railway is entirely staffed by children, apart from the adult train drivers. At the top of János Hill stands the Erzsébet Look-Out Tower, designed by Frigyes Schulek in 1910. A chair lift also connects the summit of János Hill with Zugligeti út and is a good way of making the descent.

Aquincum ㉕

AQUINCUM

See pp162–3.

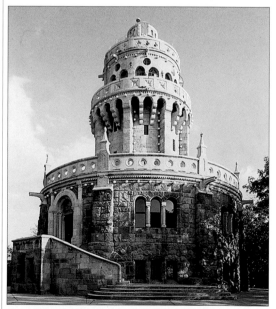

The Erszébet Look-Out Tower at the summit of János Hill

Aquincum ㉕

Roman Column

THE REMAINS OF the Roman town of Aquincum *(see p20–21)* were excavated at the end of the 19th century. Visitors are free to stroll along its streets, viewing the outlines of temples, shops, baths and houses, in what was once the centre of the town. This civilian town was founded at the beginning of the 2nd century AD, a couple of decades after a legionary fortress *(see pp170–71)* was established to its south. In the centre of the site there is a Neo-Classical museum displaying the most valuable Roman archaeological finds. On the other side of the road are the remains of an amphitheatre, where Aquincum's inhabitants once sought entertainment.

View towards the Museum
The area opened to visitors is only a fragment of a much bigger town.

★ Public Baths
The walls of the thermal baths are immaculately preserved. Visiting the baths was a social event for the Romans.

Central Heating System
Archaeologists have here unearthed the Roman version of central heating, an under-floor system in which hot air was circulated under mosaic floors.

★ Macellum
This was the covered market hall. Having shops or stalls positioned around a cool inner courtyard kept the produce fresh and made shopping comfortable all year round (see pp20–21).

STAR SIGHTS

★ **Museum**

★ **Public Baths**

★ **Macellum**

★ Museum
This Neo-Classical Lapidarium is part of the museum, which houses an exhibition of objects found at Aquincum and at other Roman sites nearby. These include weapons and inscribed stone monuments.

VISITORS' CHECKLIST

Szentendrei út 139. ☎ 430 15 63.
🚆 Aquincum. ◯ 9am–5pm
Tue–Sun. 🏛 **Museum**
◯ 10am–5pm Tue–Sun. 📷 ✏
🌐 www.aquincum.hu

Thoroughfare
Paving stones can still be seen on the network of streets that run across the town at right angles.

Double Baths
Built mainly of stone, the baths were once richly decorated. Traces of wall paintings and mosaics can still be seen in some places.

Drain Cover
Aquincum had a water supply system. Carefully crafted drain covers, such as this one, cut into the stone paving slabs, provided the required drainage.

Peristyle House
Surrounded by a colonnade, this courtyard once stood at the centre of a large town house.

Excursions from Budapest

BUDAPEST IS TEN TIMES BIGGER than any other Hungarian city. Sleepy and charming, the towns and villages on these pages are ideal for day or overnight trips. Coaches *(see p226)* and trains *(see p231)* are cheap and reliable. Esztergom, Visegrád and Szentendre to the north of the city can all be reached by boats *(see p227)*, which run throughout the summer along this beautiful stretch of the Danube. More off the beaten track, the towns and villages to the south offer a fascinating glimpse of traditional life.

Esztergom ❶

46 km (28 miles) NW of Budapest.
🚗 *30,000.* 🚊 *from Árpád híd.*
🚉 *from Nyugati pu.* 🚢 *from Vigadó tér (summer only).* 🛈 *Lőrinc utca.*
Cathedral Szent István tér 1.
📞 *(0633) 41 18 95.* ⏱ *Mar–Oct: 6am–6pm; Nov–Apr: 6am– 4pm.*
🔔 **Treasury** ⏱ *Mar–Oct: 9am–4:30pm daily; Nov–Dec: 11am–2:30pm Tue–Sun.* 📷 ⛪ **Castle** Szent István tér 1. 📞 *(0633) 41 59 86.* ⏱ *Apr–Oct: 9am–4:30pm Tue–Sun; Nov–Mar: 10am–3:30pm Tue–Sun.* 📷

ST ISTVÁN, HUNGARY'S first Christian King, was baptized in Esztergom and crowned here on Christmas Day 1000 AD. Almost completely destroyed by the Mongol invasion 250 years later, the city was gradually rebuilt in the 18th and 19th centuries.

Esztergom today is still the country's most sacred city, the seat of the archbishop of Hungary. Dominating the skyline is the huge Catholic **cathedral**, built in the early 19th century. By the southern entrance, built by 16th-century Florentine craftsmen, is the red marble Bakócz burial chapel.

On the northern side is the **treasury** containing a collection of ecclesiastical treasures rescued from the ruins of the 12th-century church that existed on the cathedral site.

Below the cathedral are the remains of the 10th-century **castle**, rebuilt several times. One of its best features is a 12th-century chapel. The picturesque old town is also well worth exploring. At its heart is the town square, which is home to several cafés.

Visegrád ❷

40 km (25 miles) N of Budapest.
🚗 *1,800.* 🚊 *from Árpád híd.*
🚢 *from Vigadó tér (summer only).*
🛈 *Rév utca 15.* 📞 *(0626) 39 81 60.*
Castle 📞 *(0626) 39 81 01.* ⏱ *Apr–Oct: 8:30am–6pm Tue–Sun; Nov–Mar: 10am–3pm Tue–Sun.* 🎦 ⛪
Mátyás Museum & Visegrád Palace
📞 *(0626) 39 80 26.* ⏱ *9am–5pm Tue–Sun.* 🎦 📷 *by arrangement.*

SET ON THE narrowest stretch of the Danube, the village of Visegrád is a popular tourist destination, thanks to its spectacular ruined **castle**.

KEY

▨	City centre
▢	Greater Budapest
═	Motorway
▬	Main road

A 25-minute walk, a bus, or a taxi, will take you up to the castle from Visegrád. Built in the 13th century by King Béla IV, this was once one of the finest royal palaces ever built in Hungary. The massive outer walls are still intact, and offer stunning views over the surrounding countryside.

Halfway down the hill, in the Salamon Tower, is the **Mátyás Museum**, a collection of items excavated from the ruins of the **Visegrád Palace**. Built by King Béla IV at the same time as the castle, the palace was renovated two centuries later, in magnificent Renaissance style, by King Mátyás Corvinus *(see pp24–5)*. Destroyed in the 16th century

Overlooking the Danube, the vast cathedral at Esztergom

after the Turkish invasion, then buried in a mud slide, the ruins were not rediscovered until 1934, when the excavations took place here.

Blagovestenska church in Fő tér, Szentendre's main square

Szentendre ❸

25 km (16 miles) N of Budapest.
🚶 20,000. 🚆 from Batthyány tér. 🚢 from Árpád híd. ⛴ from Vigadó tér (summer only). 🛈 Dumtsa Jenő utca 22. 📞 (0626) 31 79 66. **Belgrade Cathedral** Pátriárka utca 5. 📞 (0626) 31 23 99. 🚹 **Museum of Serbian Art** Pátriárka utca 5. 📞 (0626) 31 23 99. 🕐 May–Sep: 10am–6pm Tue–Sun; Oct–Apr: 10am–4pm Tue–Sun (Jan–Feb: Fri–Sun). 📷 📹 **Margit Kovács Museum** Vastaggyörgy utca 1. 📞 (0626) 31 07 90. 🕐 Nov–Feb: 9am–5pm Tue–Sun; Mar–Oct: 10am–6pm Tue–Sun. 📷 📹 📹 by arrangement.
Hungarian Open Air Museum Sztaravodai u. Pf 63. 📞 (0626) 50 25 11. 🕐 Apr–Nov: 9am–5pm Tue–Sun.

ONLY 25 KM (16 miles) outside Budapest, Szentendre is a town built and inhabited by a succession of Serbian refugees. Most of Szentendre's older buildings date from the 18th-century.

Orthodox religious tradition lies at the heart of the town, which contains many Orthodox churches. The western European façades hide Slavic interiors filled with incense, icons and candlelight. **Blagovestenska Church** on Fő tér, is just one example. Look out for the magnificent iconostasis that separates the sanctuary from the nave. Also of interest is Sunday mass at **Belgrade Cathedral**. Next door is a **Museum of Serbian Art**, full of icons and other religious artifacts.

Since the 1920s, Szentendre has been home to a growing number of artists and the town contains many galleries exhibiting the work of local artists. **Margit Kovács Museum** shows the work of one of Hungary's best-known ceramic artists. Margit Kovács (1902–77) drew inspiration from Hungarian mythology and folk traditions.

To the west of town is the **Hungarian Open Air Museum**, an ethnographical museum, illustrating the different Hungarian regions and their rural architecture and culture.

Vác ❹

40 km (25 miles) N of Budapest.
🚶 36,000. 🚆 from Nyugati pu. 🚌 from Árpád híd. 🛈 Dr Csányi László körút 45. 📞 (0627) 31 61 60.

VÁC HAS STOOD on the eastern bank of the Danube since 1000 AD. Destroyed by war in the late 17th century, the town was rebuilt and today its centre, built around four squares, dates from the early 18th century. At its heart is Marcius 15 tér, where the **Town Hall** and **Fehérek Church** are located. At the northernmost end of the old town, on Köztársaság út, is Hungary's only **Arc de Triomph**. This was built in 1764, after a visit from the Habsburg Empress, Maria Theresa.

Arc de Triomph in Vác, built in honour of Empress Maria Theresa

Interior of Fót's Church of the Immaculate Conception

Fót ❺

25 km (15 miles) NE of Budapest.
🏛 *16,000.* 🚆 *Nyugati pu.* 🚌 *Árpád híd.* ℹ️ *Vörösmarty tér 3.* 📞 *(0627) 53 82 60.* **Károlyi Palace and park** Vörösmarty tér 2. ◯ *by appt.* 📞 *(0627) 35 80 22.* 📷 ♿ *ground floor only.* 🎦 *obligatory.* **Church of the Immaculate Conception** Vörösmarty út 2. 🎦

J UST OUTSIDE Budapest is the small town of Fót. Its main attraction is the **Károlyi Palace**, birthplace of the country's first president, Mihály Károlyi *(see p34).* The palace was built in the 1830s, with a pavilion added on each side a decade later. Also worth a visit is the town's attractive 19th-century **Church of the Immaculate Conception**, with its impressive many-columned nave.

Gödöllő ❻

35km (20 miles) NE of Budapest.
🚆 *Nyugati pu.* **Grassalkovich Mansion** ◯ *Apr–Oct: 9.30am–6pm daily; Nov–Mar: 10am–5pm daily.* 📞 *(0628) 41 01 24.* 📷 ♿ 🎦

G ÖDÖLLŐ IS most famous for its restored Baroque palace, the **Grassalkovich Mansion**. Built in 1741, it was the favourite residence of Queen Elizabeth, wife of Franz Joseph. The permanent exhibition in the Royal Museum incorporates the Ceremonial Hall and reconstructed royal suites, and details the life of the Austro-Hungarian monarchy.

Kecskemét ❼

86km (52 miles) SE of Budapest.
🏛 *110,000.* 🚆 *Nyugati pu.* 🚌 *Népstadion.* ℹ️ Kossuth tér 1. 📞 *(0676) 48 10 65.* **Town Hall** Kossuth tér 1. 📞 *(0676) 48 36 83.* ◯ *7:30am–4pm Mon– Thu, 7:30am–1pm Fri.* 📷 *by appointment.* **Cifra Palace** Rákóczi utca 1. 📞 *(0676) 48 07 76.* ◯ *10am–4:30pm Tue–Sat, 1:30–4:30pm Tue.* 📷 ♿ 🎦

S PREADING OUT in a vast sweep around Budapest is the Great Hungarian Plain, or *Alföld*, which covers nearly half of modern Hungary. For hundreds of years, Kecskemét has been the major market town of the central-southern plain. Distributing and processing the products of the surrounding rich farmland, Kecskemét grew affluent, particularly towards the end of the 19th century. As a result, the town today boasts many gracious squares and splendid 19th and early 20th century buildings. The most famous is Ödön Lechner's massive **Town Hall**. Built between 1893–6, the building is a combination of both Renaissance and Middle-Eastern influences. The flamboyant **Cifra Palace** (Ornamental Palace), built as a casino in 1902, is a uniquely Hungarian variation of the Secession style *(see pp54–7).*

Kecskemét Town Hall, designed by Ödön Lechner

Kiskunfélegyháza ❽

110 km (66 miles) SE of Budapest.
🏛 *40,000.* ℹ️ Kossuth utca 1. 📞 *(0676) 46 32 20.* 🚆 *Nyugati pu.* 🚌 *Népstadion.* **Kiskunsági National Park (office)** Liszt Ferenc utca19. 📞 *(0676) 48 26 11.* ◯ *8am–3pm Mon–Thu, 8am–1pm Fri (park open permanently).* **Kiskun Museum** Dr Holló Lajos utca 9. 📞 *(0676) 46 14 68.* ◯ *late Mar– Oct: 9am–5pm Wed–Sun.* 📷 🎦

M UCH OF THE Great Hungarian Plain, once a vast expanse of marsh and grassland, is now used to grow maize and vines. Small areas, however, have been preserved as national parks. About 10 km (6 miles) to the east of Kiskunfélegyháza is the

Detail of the ornate Town Hall façade at Kiskunfélegyháza

Kiskunsági National Park. Many rare native animals and birds can be seen here, as well as the traditional way of life of the plains herdsman.

The poet and national hero, Sándor Petőfi, was born in Kiskunfélegyháza, and his childhood home is now part of the **Kiskun Museum**. Built in 1912, the **Town Hall** is a masterpiece, combining influences of the Secession style (*see pp54–7*) with motifs from Hungarian folk art.

Ráckeve **9**

43 km (26 miles) SW of Budapest.
🚍 8,500. 🚌 Soroksári út.
🚇 Népstadion.

T HE VILLAGE OF Ráckeve is built on Csepel Island, which extends 54 km (34 miles) south along the middle of the Danube from Budapest. Ráckeve (Rác means Serb in Hungarian) was founded in the 15th century by Serbs from Keve, who fled Serbia after the Turkish invasion (*see pp26–7*).

The oldest building in the village is the **Orthodox church**, built by some of the first of the Serbian refugees. Dating back to 1487, this is the oldest Orthodox church in Hungary. Its walls are covered in well-preserved frescos, the first telling the story of the Nativity and the last showing the Resurrection. The church also boasts a beautiful iconostasis separating the sanctuary from the nave.

Ráckeve's peaceful and convenient situation made it the country home of one of Europe's greatest military strategists, Prince Eugene of Savoy (*see p26*). Credited with the expulsion of the Turks from Hungary at the end of the 17th century, Prince Eugene built himself a country **mansion** on what is now Kossuth Lajos utca. Now used as a hotel, the interior of the house has been modernized, but the elegant façade has been preserved and is well worth a look. The formal gardens can be seen from the river.

Well-preserved frescoes in the Orthodox church at Ráckeve

Martonvásár **10**

30 km (18 miles) SW of Budapest.
🚍 4,900. 🏨 Buda út 13. 📞 (0622) 46 00 16. 🚇 Déli pu. 🚌 Erzsébet tér. **Brunswick Palace** Brunswick utca 2. ◯ 8am–dusk daily (park only). 🖼 **Beethoven Museum** ◯ 10am–noon, 2–6pm Tue–Sun. 🖼 🚻

T HE VILLAGE OF Martonvásár has existed here since medieval times, but its principal tourist attraction is now the **Brunswick Palace**. Towards the end of the 18th century the whole village was bought by the German Brunswick family, and the original palace was built for Anton Brunswick in grand Baroque style. A century later, in 1875, the palace was totally rebuilt, this time in the Neo-Gothic style. Little evidence of the original palace remains today, among the flamboyant turrets and pinnacles. The magnificent parklands, however, are open to the public and are much as they always have been. The estate's church, built in 1775, also remains largely unaltered. The interior of the church is decorated with well-preserved frescoes.

Ludwig van Beethoven was a regular visitor to the original palace. He gave music lessons to the daughters of the house, Thérèse and Josephine, with whom he is said to have fallen in love. Some of the palace rooms have been converted into a small **Beethoven Museum**. Occasional concerts are held in the gardens during the summer months.

The Neo-Gothic Brunswick Palace at Martonvásár

TWO GUIDED WALKS

Anchor at the Vasmacska restaurant

UDAPEST IS A CITY made for exploring on foot. From Turkish bathhouses to Baroque palaces, evidence of the city's long and colourful past is visible at every turn. The following guided walks take you through two fascinating areas: Óbuda to the north of the city centre, once the site of a Roman garrison and now a residential district, and Margaret Island, a park in the middle of the Danube.

Óbuda has yielded a wealth of archaeological discoveries including some of the earliest to be made in Hungary. This walk takes in the ruins of a Roman military camp and amphitheatre, as well as the area's more modern attractions. In contrast, the two-hour walk around the wonderfully car-free Margaret Island includes an exotically landscaped garden and the remains of several historic churches.

A Three-Hour Walk Around Óbuda
(see pp170–71)

Wedding car parked outside Fő tér Palace *(see p171)*

A Two-Hour Walk Around Margaret Island
(see pp172–3)

0 kilometres 2

0 miles 1

KEY

······ Walk route

Statue of a young girl in Margaret Island's landscaped Japanese Garden *(see p173)*

◁ **The courtyard of the exclusive Danubius Grand Hotel on Margaret Island** *(see p173)*

A Three-Hour Walk Around Óbuda

AT FIRST GLANCE ÓBUDA TODAY seems little more than a concrete jungle of tower blocks and flyovers. Behind the grey façade, however, there is a strong local identity and clues to the area's long and colourful past abound. Arriving here in AD 89, the Romans built a garrison in this district shortly before founding the civilian town of Aquincum *(see pp162–3)* to the north. After the departure of Romans in the 5th century AD, successive waves of invaders, including the Magyars *(see pp22–3)* all left their mark on Óbuda (literally "Old Buda"). By the end of the 16th century, Óbuda was a thriving market town, eventually forming part of the city of Budapest in 1873.

A section of Óbuda's impressive Roman amphitheatre ①

The elegant, Neo-Baroque Fő tér Palace with its sentry box ⑪

From the Roman Amphitheatre to the Roman Camp Museum

Begin the walk at the corner of Bécsi utca and Pacsirtamező út, which is dominated by the remains of a very fine Roman amphitheatre ①. The Romans arrived in the region soon after the time of Christ, building this impressive amphitheatre in the middle of the 2nd century AD, by which time Aquincum was the thriving capital of the province of Lower Pannonia *(see pp20–21)*. Originally used by the Roman soldiers from the nearby garrison, it became a fortress in the 9th century for the invading Magyar army. Not much remains of its once huge walls, but the scale of the theatre, which

was designed to seat 14,000, is still awe inspiring. From the amphitheatre, continue along Pacsirtamező út to No. 63, the Roman Camp (Táborváros) Museum ②. In the 1950s, this modern residential district, built on top of a Roman military camp complex, was found to be enormously rich in Roman artifacts. The museum (open Sundays and public holidays) houses Roman finds from the area, including ceramics, glassware and household tools.

Old Óbuda Synagogue to Flórián Tér

Retrace your steps and turn left down Perc utca, up Mókus utca, then Jós utca, turning left into Lajos utca. At No. 163 is the former Óbuda Synagogue ③, now a television studio. Built in the early 1820s to serve the area's growing Jewish community, this is a Neo-Classical building with a six-columned portico. Also on Lajos utca, at No. 168, is Óbuda Parish Church ④. Constructed in 1744–9 on the site of the Roman military camp, the church has survived since then largely unchanged. The

interior includes a magnificently carved pulpit showing the Good Shepherd and Mary Magdalene. Turning left up Óbudai utca, you will pass the house where the popular novelist, bon viveur

The former home of novelist and colourful local figure, Gyula Krúdy ⑤

Roman amphith.

and local character, Gyula Krúdy once lived ⑤. Writing in the early 20th century, much of Krúdy's work looks back at an idealized rural Hungary and is extremely popular in his country. From here, turn right along Tanuló utca and pass the ruins of the 14th-century St

Zichy Palace, built in the 18th century for an aristocratic family ⑩

KEY

• • • Walk route

🚉 HÉV railway station

0 metres   400

0 yards   400

Clare's Nunnery ⑥. Then turn left towards Flórián tér. As you pass Kálvin köz, on the left at No. 2 is the 18th-century Óbuda Calvinist Church ⑦. Next door is the presbytery, built in 1909 to a design by Károly Kós, better known for his work on the Wekerle Estate *(see p157)*. No. 4 is home to a collection of folk crafts. Walk back up to busy Flórián tér, where in 1778 Roman thermal baths were discovered. Hidden in the underpasses beneath the square are the Roman Baths Museum and the Roman Settlement Museum ⑧.

Szentlélek Tér and Fő Tér

Tavasz utca, off to the the right from north of Flórián tér, leads to Szentlélek tér. In the south wing of the Zichy Palace, on Szentlélek tér, is the Vasarely Museum ⑨. The 20th-century artist Victor Vasarely is

remembered as the founder of the Op-Art movement, producing work full of bright colours and optical illusions. The crumbling Zichy Palace ⑩ itself was built for the Zichy family in 1757. Continue north up to Fő tér, one of the few areas of 18th- and 19th-century architecture remaining in Óbuda. On one side of the square stands the Neo-Baroque Fő tér Palace ⑪, its entrance still guarded by an 18th-century sentry box.

Imre Varga Gallery to the Hercules Villa

From Fő tér Palace walk up Laktanya utca, where there is a group of statues, *Women with Umbrellas*, by contemporary sculptor Imre Varga ⑫. At No. 7 Laktanya utca is the Imre Varga Gallery ⑬, where further examples of the sculptor's work can be seen. Finally, make your way up to Szentendrei út and cross it at an underpass. Turn right into Kerék ut (if you miss this, take the next right up Szél utca), then left into Herkules utca then onto Meggyfa utca to finish the walk at No. 21, the ruins of the Hercules Villa ⑭. Once a lavish Roman home, it takes its name from some stunning mosaics *(see p21)*. Near the villa are the remains of the *cella trichora*, an early Christian chapel dating from the fourth century AD.

One of several *Women with Umbrellas* by Imre Varga ⑫

TIPS FOR WALKERS

Starting point: Pacsirtamező út.
Getting there: Bus 60 or tram 17.
Length: 3 km (1.8 miles).
Stops: The Kéhli Restaurant (see p199) on Mókus utca, or the Régi Sipos Étterem (see p199) on Lajos utca for the city's freshest fish.

A Two-Hour Walk Around Margaret Island

H ISTORICALLY INACCESSIBLE in the middle of the Danube, Margaret Island was a retreat for religious contemplation from at least the 11th century onwards. Relics of the island's past include the remains of two monastic churches and also the ruins of the convent home of Princess Margit, daughter of King Béla IV, who gave the island its name. Opened to the public in 1869, Margaret Island is today Budapest's most beautiful park, a car-free haven of greenery in the middle of the city and the ideal location for a peaceful stroll. On the western shore, the Palatinus Strand bathing complex makes use of the mineral-rich hot springs rising on the island.

A relief of Archangel Michael on St Michael's Church ⑨

Centenary Monument to Palatinus Strand

The walk begins amid the peace and greenery of the southern tip of Margaret Island. Proceeding to the north, the first landmark is the Centenary Monument ① *(see p62)*, which stands in front of a sizable fountain. Designed by István Kiss, the monument was made in 1973, to commemorate the centenary of the unification of the towns of Buda, Óbuda and Pest *(see p32)*. At night the fountain is dramatically illuminated. You can also rent four-wheel family bikes here called *Bringóhintó*. Taking a left turn ahead, the Hajós Olympic Pool Complex *(see p53)* ② is soon reached. Built in 1930, the complex was designed by the multi-talented Alfréd Hajós. He won gold medals in swimming

events in the 1896 Olympic Games and was also a member of the Hungarian football team. Continuing northwards, there is a rose garden to the right before the ruins of the early 14th-century Franciscan Church ③ come into view. Constructed in the Gothic style of the time, the church was originally attached to a monastery. Visible in the west wall is the doorway which once led to the organ loft, as well as a spiral staircase and fine arched window. Further on is the busy Palatinus Strand ④ *(see p53)*. In front of the entrance to its pools stands a statue by French sculptor Emile Guilleaume.

Water Tower to St Michael's Church

Clearly visible to the northeast of Palatinus Strand, is the 57-m (187-ft) high Water Tower ⑤. Built in 1911 and now protected by UNESCO, this graceful tower is currently used as an exhibition space for a variety of previously un-exhibited modern crafts and artworks, ranging from puppets to paintings. At the foot of the Water Tower is the Summer Theatre, a large modern amphitheatre seating 3,500 people, which hosts a summer season of operatic performances. To the southeast

Ruins of the 14th-century Franciscan Church ③

The Water Tower

of the Water Tower are the ruins of a 13th-century Dominican Church and Convent ⑥. The latter was once home to Princess Margit, after whom the island is named. King Béla IV *(see p23)* swore that if he succeeded in repelling the Mongol invasion of 1241 that he would offer his daughter to God. He kept his oath, building the church and convent, to which the 9-year-old Princess Margit was sent in 1251. She led a godly and ascetic life and died here at the age of 29. Nearly 300 years later, in 1541, the nuns of the convent fled to Pozsony (now Bratislava, capital of the Slovak Republic) in the face of the Turkish invasion, *(see pp26–7)*, leaving the church and the convent to be destroyed. Severe floods in 1838 led to the discovery of the ruined church and its underground vaults. The tomb of the now-canonized Margit was also excavated here 20 years later. Just to the north of the Dominican Church and Convent, near to the Water Tower, is the beginning of Artists' Avenue ⑦. A collection of contemporary busts of Hungarian writers, painters and musicians lines this promenade leading up to the Grand Hotel Margitsziget. A little way before the hotel is

KEY

•••••• Walk route

0 metres 500
0 yards 500

Stepped pathway through the lush foliage of the Japanese Garden ⑪

Bust of Zsigmond Móricz on Artists' Avenue ⑦

St Michael's Church ⑧. Originally built by members of the Premonstratensian Order, this is the oldest building on the island. In addition, the foundations of an 11th-century chapel have been excavated inside the 12th century church. Destroyed by the invading Turks in 1541, the church was eventually reconstructed in the 1930s, using materials from the original building. In the bell tower hangs a bell which, unusually, survived the Turkish invasion. Probably buried by the monks at the time of the invasion, the bell dates from the early 15th century. It was discovered in 1914 when its walnut-tree hiding place was uprooted during a violent storm.

Grand Hotel Margitsziget to Árpád Bridge
The Grand Hotel Margitsziget ⑨ *(see p185)* was designed in 1872 by Miklós Ybl *(see p119)*. For many years it was the most fashionable hotel in Budapest, known simply as "The Grand". After World War II, the hotel was modernized and called the Danubius Grand, and in the 1970s the luxurious Thermal Hotel Margitsziget ⑩ was built nearby. The two hotels are joined by an underground walkway and offer thermal baths and a variety of spa treatments *(see p52)*. Heading west from the Danubius Thermal Hotel, the final stretch of the walk passes beside the Japanese Garden ⑪. A variety of exotic plants, a rock garden, waterfalls and streams crossed on rustic bridges all add to the garden's atmosphere. The final stopping point on the walk is an unusual musical well, known as the Bodor Well ⑫. The original well was designed and constructed by Transylvanian Péter Bodor in 1820 and stood in the town of Marosvásárhely (modern-day Tirgu Mures, in Romania), which was then part of the Austro-Hungarian Empire. In 1936 this copy was built on Margaret Island. Continuing past the well, at the northern tip of Margaret Island the Árpád Bridge provides another link from the island to the city.

The musical Bodor Well ⑫

TIPS FOR WALKERS

Starting point: Southern end of Margaret Island, reached from Margaret Bridge.
Getting there: Bus 26.
Length: 3.3 km (2 miles).
Stops: There are numerous take-away kiosks and several cafés on Margaret Island, selling drinks, snacks and ice creams in summer. The Danubius Grand Hotel and Danubius Thermal Hotel also have restaurants and cafés.

TRAVELLERS'
NEEDS

WHERE TO STAY

BUDAPEST HAS A broad range of accommodation from top-class hotels, some with spa facilities, and private apartments to campsites and hostels. The larger hotels often belong to well-known groups and meet international standards, but are more expensive. Cheaper accommodation can be found in hostels or bed and breakfasts, or outside the city centre. Travel agents and tourist information offices (*see p179*) will provide information on these options. Of the 200 hotels and pensions we surveyed, over 50 have been selected from across the price catagories and are, in our opinion, the best on offer. Each of these is listed, along with a short description, on pages 180–5 to help you choose the right hotel.

The exterior of the Kempinski Corvinus Hotel (*see p183*)

WHERE TO LOOK

WHEN DECIDING on accommodation, first choose the general location: Buda or Pest, or maybe even the picturesque suburbs further afield. In low-lying Pest, many hotels are literally only a few steps away from most of the major tourist attractions, while visitors staying in hilly Buda can enjoy cool, fresh air and quiet surroundings.

Good value for money can be found by renting a room in one of the small pensions or private hotels in and around Budapest. The more exclusive hotels offer a luxurious stay, but at a much greater price – as much as 40,000 Hungarian forints and above per night.

Most luxury hotels, such as the Hyatt Regency Budapest (*see p181*), are set along the eastern bank of the Danube. Others, such as the Marriott (*see p183*) or the Kempinski

Corvinus (*see p183*) are situated nearer to the centre of Pest, close to the theatres and shops. Those located further out of town are usually an easy journey from the city centre, particularly since hotels are often situated close to metro stations.

Tourinform (*see p179*) is a chain of tourist offices in Budapest that provide information (in Hungarian, English, French, German, Russian and Italian) on accommodation and places to eat, as well as on tourist and cultural events.

Maps can be found on sale here, as well as free booklets and pamphlets. The offices are open daily, even during the winter months. Should visitors need any further information to supplement this guide, this office can offer details of alternative accommodation, from hotels to camp sites. The *Tourist Almanac*, available from most bookshops, is also a useful publication.

Reception desk at the Hilton Hotel (*see p180*) in the Castle District

HOTEL AND PENSION CLASSIFICATION

HOTELS ARE CLASSIFIED in five categories from one to five stars and there are two categories of pension.

At the luxury end of the scale – the five-star and four-star hotels – all rooms have a bathroom, a telephone, a TV, a radio and a refrigerator, and many will be air-conditioned. The majority of these hotels will also offer business and fitness facilities. Three-star hotels have at least one restaurant and one bar, and staff are expected to speak at least one foreign language. Two thirds of the rooms in two-star hotels have their own shower or bath, while rooms in one-star hotels simply have wash-basins with hot and cold running water.

Pensions have a standard minimum room size, and every room has a shower or a bath. The accommodation is clean and simple, and all the necessary services and amenities should be provided by friendly and helpful staff.

The Hyatt Regency (*see p181*), with its suspended model plane

The Radisson Béke Hotel *(see p181)*, featuring György Szondi's mosaic

HOTEL PRICES

ROOM TARIFFS reflect the hotel classification, but it is always wise to double check the price at the time of booking. Accommodation in a centrally located, higher category hotel will be much more expensive than in an out-of-town, lower category hotel. Relatively cheap rooms can be found in pensions and hostels. Hotel prices usually include breakfast, which in hotels with three stars or more typically means a self-service buffet. Pensions also offer good value, substantial meals.

Many luxury hotels, such as the Corinthia Aquincum *(see p185)*, offer substantial weekend reductions in the low season (mid-September to mid-March). During this period a three-night stay would cost the same as one-night stay during the high season.

In spa hotels, such as the Gellért *(see p180)*, which offer hydrotherapy, the fee for using the pools and sauna is included in the room price. However, any treatments, such as massage, will incur an extra charge. Check these details with the hotel in advance.

Prices in Budapest's hotels and pensions are often quoted in Euros.

HIDDEN EXTRAS

BOTH VAT AND resort tax are included in the price of the room (resort tax is charged because Budapest is classed as a health resort), but there are often hidden surcharges that can greatly increase the overall cost of a stay. For example, a number of hotels have currency exchange desks, but these offer a poor rate of exchange. It is better to change money at a bank or *bureau de change* where rates tend to be much more favourable.

Telephone calls, particularly international calls, cost almost twice as much when made from hotel rooms as opposed to public telephones. There are plenty of these in Budapest, although it may be necessary to buy a phone card *(see p222)*.

Most hotels have their own car parks. Some, such as the Inter-Continental *(see p183)*, offer off-street or garage parking, for which a modest fee may be charged.

HOW TO BOOK

THE BUDAPEST tourist season starts in the middle of June and lasts until the beginning of September. During this period, as well as around New Year and the Hungarian Grand Prix weekend *(see p210)*, hotels become fully booked very quickly.

It is advisable to book at least two weeks ahead. Most hotels will accept bookings made by fax and will reply in the same way. Guests should confirm their reservations with a follow-up phone call a few days before arrival.

It is possible to find accommodation if an advance booking has not been made, but rooms in the right location or price range may be harder to come by, especially in the high season. Bookings can be made at Ferihegy 2 airport *(see pp224–5)* and at Nyugati pu, the city's western train station *(see p226–7)*.

Stained-glass window in the Gellért Hotel *(see p180)*

The entrance to the Grand Hotel Margitsziget *(see p185)*, Margaret Island

SERVICE

THE SERVICES and amenities offered by each hotel will vary according to price. As in most other countries, hotel rooms are cleaned regularly, and most higher category hotels offer 24-hour service, including meals that can be brought to the room. This usually incurs an extra charge, but tips are always welcome.

Most reception personnel will speak some foreign languages, most commonly English and German. They are happy to help make sightseeing suggestions.

TRAVELLING WITH CHILDREN

MOST HOTELS welcome children and offer free accommodation to those up to the age of four travelling with their parents. Additional beds can often be provided for older children in the parents' room for a small extra charge. Many hotels also offer a child-minding service.

DISABLED TRAVELLERS

BUDAPEST IS TRYING to make up for the neglect that disabled travellers to the city have suffered. Specialist facilities are gradually being introduced throughout the city. For example, most recently built hotels have facilities enabling disabled guests to have as pleasant and easy a stay as able-bodied people. Such hotels will display information about their facilities for disabled guests. Further information can be obtained from tourist information offices and travel agents.

SELF-CATERING

A FEW HOTELS in Budapest, especially those in the embassy district, such as the Radio Inn *(see p183)*, offer accommodation in suites with kitchenettes. This type of accommodation is particularly good for families as it gives them the option of eating "at home", rather than taking every meal at a restaurant. Another advantage is, of course, the extra space, which allows greater freedom of movement; often hotel suites are equal in size to an apartment.

There are also some specially converted buildings that consist solely of self-catering apartments. The **Charles Apartment House** is a good example of this type of accommodation; the apartments are spacious and well equipped.

HOSTELS

BUDAPEST HAS a few hostels that stay open all year. For visitors on a tight budget, these provide good, if basic, low-cost accommodation. **Travellers' Hostels Universitás** and the **Citadella** *(see p180)*, which is situated in the Citadel *(see pp92–3)* on Gellért Hill, are just some examples. Hostels often provide guests with a choice of staying in a dormitory or a single or double room.

SEASONAL HOSTELS

THE CLOSEST THING to youth hostels that Budapest has are the college halls of residence, which are only available during the summer vacation in July and August. Many students' halls of residence are turned into hostels, adding approximately 4,000 beds to Budapest's accommodation list and providing tourists with a convenient and inexpensive place to stay.

Given their popularity, it is advisable to book a room in advance. This is best done via tourist offices and travel bureaux, rather than contacting individual hostels directly. International Youth Hostels Organisation membership will enable guests to get a discount on room rates.

The interior of the Astoria Hotel *(see p182)*

STAYING IN PRIVATE ROOMS AND APARTMENTS

SOME VISITORS choose to stay in a private home. Accommodation usually consists of a separate bedroom and use of a kitchen and bathroom. The price depends on the facilities and the area, and varies from 1,000–5,000 Hungarian forints per day for a double room and upwards of 500 forints per day for a single room. **Skála Metro** is a reputable agency through which this type of accommodation can be booked.

Renting an apartment is probably the most economical way of having a longer stay in Budapest. As well as using agencies to find private apartments, it is worth checking the *albérlet* (to rent) advertisements in newspapers such as *Expressz* and *Hirdetés*.

CAMPING

CAMPING IS only permitted at designated campsites. There are several of these situated on the outskirts of Budapest. The biggest and most picturesque of them all is **Római Camping**, which is located on the road leading from Óbuda to Szentendre. Campsites are open, in general, from May until the end of October. Some operations, such as the **EXPO**, are open only from 1 July to 31 August, while others are open throughout the year.

The restaurant of the Erzsébet Hotel *(see p182)*, in the city centre

DIRECTORY

INFORMATION

Hungarian National Touist Office (UK)
Embassy of the Republic of Hungary, 46 Eaton Place, London SW1X 8AL.
020 7823 1032.
FAX 020 7823 1459.

Hungarian National Touist Office (US)
150 East 58th Street, 33rd Floor, New York, NY 10155-3398.
212 355 0240.
FAX 212 207 4103.

Tourinform Buda Castle
1016 Budapest, Szentháromság tér. **Map** 1 B4 (9 A2). 488 04 75.
FAX 448 04 74.

Tourinform Liszt Ferenc tér
1061 Budapest, Liszt Ferenc tér 11. **Map** 7 A1.
322 40 98.
FAX 342 93 90.

Tourinform Nyugati Pu
Left wing of main station.
Map 2 F2. 302 85 80.
FAX 302 85 80.

AGENCIES

Express Központi Iroda
1052 Budapest, Semmelweis utca 4.
Map 4 F1 (10 E4).
317 66 34.

Hungarian Youth Hostels Federation
1077 Budapest, Almássy tér 6. **Map** 7 B2.
343 51 67.
FAX 478 04 58.

IBUSZ Travel Agency
1053 Budapest, Ferenciek tere 10. **Map** 4 F1 (10 E4).
485 27 00.
FAX 338 49 87.

SELF-CATERING

Charles Apartment House
1016 Budapest, Hegyalja út 23. **Map** 3 B2 (9 B5).
212 91 69.
FAX 202 29 84.

HOSTELS

Citadella
1118 Budapest, Citadella sétány. **Map** 4 D3.
466 57 94.
FAX 386 05 05.

Martos Hotel
1111 Budapest, Stoczek utca 5–7. 463 36 51.
FAX 463 42 59.

Travellers' Hostel Diáksport
1134 Budapest, Dózsa György út 152. **Map** 5 C4 (8 E1). 413 20 65.
FAX 321 48 51.

SEASONAL HOSTELS

ELTE Kollégium
1118 Budapest, Dayka Gábor utca 4.
319 25 50.
FAX 319 33 38.

Travellers' Hostel Schönherz
1117 Budapest, Irinyi József utca 42. **Map** 4 E5.
340 85 85.
FAX 320 84 25.

Travellers' Hostel Universitás
1111 Budapest, Irinyi József utca 9–11.
Map 4 F5. 340 85 85.
FAX 320 84 25.

Universum Hostel Rózsa
1117 Budapest, Bercsényi utca 28. **Map** 4 E5.
463 42 50. FAX 275 70 46.

PRIVATE ROOMS AND APARTMENTS

Skála Metro
1068 Budapest, Bajcsy-Zsilinszky út 17.
Map 2 E4 (10 D2).
312 36 21.
FAX 312 71 26.

CAMPING

Csillebérc Autós Camping
1121 Budapest, Konkoly Thege út 21.
395 65 27.
FAX 395 73 27.

Haller Camping
1096 Budapest, Haller utca 27.
215 47 75.
FAX 218 79 09.

Metro Tennis Camping
1162 Budapest, Csömöri út 158.
406 55 84.
FAX 405 10 50.

Római Camping
1031 Budapest, Szentendrei út 189.
368 62 60.
FAX 250 04 26.

Choosing a Hotel

THE HOTELS in this guide have been selected for their good value, facilities and location. The list of hotels covers all the areas and price categories with additional information to help you choose a hotel that best meets your needs. Hotels within the same price category are listed alphabetically. For map references see pages 236–245.

	CREDIT CARDS	NUMBER OF ROOMS	RESTAURANT	AIR CONDITIONING	SWIMMING POOL

CASTLE DISTRICT

CARLTON HOTEL BUDAPEST (HUF)(HUF)(HUF)
1011 Budapest, Apor Péter utca 3. **Map** 1 C5. 📞 224 09 99. 🖥 www.carltonhotel.hu
This comfortable hotel is situated beneath the Royal Palace, just off Fő utca and close to Clark Ádám tér *(see p100)*. It has good-sized, if slightly basic, single, double and triple rooms, all with large, bright bathrooms. A hearty buffet breakfast is available. 🔒 1 🎫 TV 🗝 💈 🛋 P 🍽

Credit Cards: AE DC MC V — *Number of Rooms:* 95 — *Air Conditioning:* ●

HILTON (HUF)(HUF)(HUF)(HUF)
1014 Budapest, Hess András tér 1–3. **Map** 1 B4. 📞 488 66 00. 🖥 www.budapest.hilton.com
The Hilton *(see p81)*, one of the most luxurious hotels in Budapest, is located in a building incorporating parts of a Gothic church and Jesuit monastery. In the heart of the Castle District, it offers three restaurants serving Hungarian and international cuisine. High prices, but magnificent views over the Danube and the Pest cityscape. 🔒 1 🎫 24 TV 🗝 💈 🍴 🛋 P 🍽

Credit Cards: AE DC MC V — *Number of Rooms:* 322 — *Restaurant:* ■ — *Air Conditioning:* ●

GELLÉRT HILL AND TABÁN

CITADELLA (HUF)
1118 Budapest, Citadella sétány. **Map** 4 D3. 📞 466 57 94. 🖥 www.citadella.hu
This hostel-style hotel occupies the casements of the Citadel *(see pp92–3)*. It offers inexpensive, neat and clean double and multiple-occupancy rooms. A popular wine bar, restaurant and nightclub are nearby. 🔒 🎫 🗝 P

Number of Rooms: 15

ORION (HUF)(HUF)
1013 Budapest, Döbrentei utca 13. **Map** 4 D1. 📞 356 85 83. FAX 375 54 18.
Hidden in a secluded spot, this pleasant hotel offers clean but plainly decorated rooms, all complete with bathrooms, controlled air conditioning and colour televisions. A small restaurant serves a good range of inexpensive Hungarian and international cuisine. 🔒 1 🎫 24 TV 💈 🍴

Credit Cards: AE DC MC V JCB — *Number of Rooms:* 30 — *Restaurant:* ■ — *Air Conditioning:* ●

FLAMENCO PARKHOTEL (HUF)(HUF)(HUF)
1113 Budapest, Tas vezér utca 7. **Map** 3 C5. 📞 372 20 00.
🖥 www.danubiusgroup.com/flamenco
This hotel is close to Buda's main sights. Built during the 1960s, the interior of the Flamenco Parkhotel depicts Spanish themes. The Solero restaurant and La Bodega wine bar offer Spanish specialities. 🔒 🎫 24 TV 🗝 💈 🛋 P 🍽

Credit Cards: AE DC V — *Number of Rooms:* 358 — *Restaurant:* ■ — *Air Conditioning:* ● — *Swimming Pool:* ■

GELLÉRT (HUF)(HUF)(HUF)(HUF)
1111 Budapest, Szent Gellért tér 1. **Map** 4 D2. 📞 385 22 00.
🖥 www.danubiusgroup.com/gellert
This famous spa hotel *(see pp90–91)* has both indoor and outdoor pools that provide an attractive environment in which to relax. Treatments such as massage are also available. Other facilities include a restaurant, a bar and a beer bar, a nightclub and banqueting halls. 🔒 1 🎫 24 TV 🗝 💈 🛋 P 🍽

Credit Cards: AE DC MC V — *Number of Rooms:* 233 — *Restaurant:* ■ — *Swimming Pool:* ■

NORTH OF THE CASTLE

DUNAPART (HUF)(HUF)(HUF)
1011 Budapest, Szilágyi Dezső tér. **Map** 1 C4 (9 B2). 📞 387 93 61. @ punkosd@alexero.hu
This quirky hotel is located on a boat moored off the western bank of the Danube, close to the Calvinist Church *(see p100)*. Accommodation is in air-conditioned cabins, some with a view of Parliament *(see pp108–9)*. The facilities are good and there is a restaurant, from which diners can enjoy the view of the Chain Bridge and Elizabeth Bridge *(see pp62–3)*. 🔒 1 🎫 TV

Credit Cards: AE DC MC V — *Number of Rooms:* 32 — *Restaurant:* ■ — *Air Conditioning:* ●

MERCURE BUDAPEST BUDA (HUF)(HUF)(HUF)
1013 Budapest, Krisztina körút 41–3. **Map** 1 A4. 📞 488 81 00. 🖥 www.mercure-buda.hu
Built during the 1960s, this hotel is close to the Vérmező park and has a large car park. Some of the rooms have beautiful views overlooking the Castle District. The facilities include a swimming pool, a vegetarian restaurant, a bar and a beer bar. Dogs are welcome. 🔒 1 🎫 TV 🗝 💈 🛋 P

Credit Cards: AE DC V — *Number of Rooms:* 399 — *Restaurant:* ■ — *Air Conditioning:* ● — *Swimming Pool:* ■

Price categories / Info		CREDIT CARDS	NUMBER OF ROOMS	RESTAURANT	AIR CONDITIONING	SWIMMING POOL

Price categories for a standard double room with bathroom per night, including breakfast, and service charges:

(HUF) below 10,000 HUF
(HUF)(HUF) 10,000–20,000 HUF
(HUF)(HUF)(HUF) 20,000–30,000 HUF
(HUF)(HUF)(HUF)(HUF) 30,000–40,000 HUF
(HUF)(HUF)(HUF)(HUF)(HUF) over 40,000 HUF.

CREDIT CARDS
Indicates which credit cards are accepted: AE American Express; DC Diners Club; MC Master Card/Access; V Visa JCB Japanese Credit Bureau.

RESTAURANT
Hotel restaurant or dining room usually open to non-residents unless otherwise stated.

AIR CONDITIONING
All rooms are air conditioned.

SWIMMING POOL
The hotel has an indoor or outdoor swimming pool.

VICTORIA (HUF)(HUF)(HUF) — AE DC MC V JCB — 30 — ● —
1011 Budapest, Bem rakpart 11. **Map** 1 C4 (9 B2). ☎ 457 80 80. W www.victoria.hu
Situated on the western bank of Danube, the Victoria is in easy reach of Buda's main tourist sights. This hotel provides big, comfortable air-conditioned rooms, many with views of the Chain Bridge, the Elizabeth Bridge and Pest. There is no restaurant so breakfast is served in the bar. Facilities include a sauna and an in-house doctor. ⊟ 1 ♯ 24 TV ⚡ ♿ P ▾

AROUND PARLIAMENT

CITY PANZIÓ RING (HUF)(HUF) — AE DC MC V — 39
1137 Budapest, Szent István körút 22. **Map** 7 A1 (10 F1). ☎ 340 54 50. W www.taverna.hu
The City Hotel is within easy reach of Parliament (see pp108–9). All rooms are clean and subtly decorated in neutral shades. There are few facilities and services, and this is reflected in its very reasonable prices. Although there is no restaurant here, there are many places to eat nearby. However, the hotel does have a cheerful breakfast room. ⊟ 1 ♯ TV ⚡ ♿ P

MEDOSZ (HUF)(HUF) — — 67
1061 Budapest, Jókai tér 9. **Map** 7 A1. ☎ 374 30 01. FAX 332 43 16.
This former trade union hostel has been successfully converted into an inexpensive and basic hotel. The modesty of its rooms is more than made up for by its excellent location close to Liszt Ferenc tér and Oktogon tér. ⊟ 1 ♯ TV ⚡ ♿ P

K + K OPERA (HUF)(HUF)(HUF)(HUF) — AE DC MC V — 205 — ■
1065 Budapest, Révay utca 24. **Map** 2 F4 (10 E2). ☎ 269 02 22. W www.kkhotels.com
This hotel belongs to the K + K group and is situated close to the State Opera House (see pp118–19). It offers guests comfortable accommodation in modern, clean and spacious rooms. There is also a café, a pub, a bar and secure car parking facilities for hotel guests. ⊟ 1 TV ⚡ 🍴 ♿ P ▾

RADISSON SAS BÉKE (HUF)(HUF)(HUF)(HUF) — AE DC MC V — 247 — ■ — ● — ■
1067 Budapest, Teréz körút 43. **Map** 2 F3. ☎ 301 16 00. W www.danubiusgroup.com/beke
This old, magnificent hotel (see p115), close to Nyugati pu metro station, has a beautiful mosaic on its façade. The hotel has, in fact, been restored and is now equipped with the latest facilities. The restaurants serve European and Hungarian delicacies, while the first-floor Zsolnay café serves tea and coffee from Zsolany porcelain (see p56). ⊟ 24 TV ⚡ 🍴 ♿ P ▾

ANDRÁSSY HOTEL (HUF)(HUF)(HUF)(HUF)(HUF) — AE DC MC V — 70 — ■ — ●
1063 Budapest, Andrássy út 111. **Map** 2 F4 (10 E2). ☎ 462 21 09. W www.andrassyhotel.com
Elegance and charm meet in the Andrássy Hotel, located on Andrássy Avenue, one of the most prestigious streets in Budapest. Luxury shops, trendy cafés, and historical monuments are only minutes away, while the hotel itself provides beautiful Mediterranean-style rooms. ⊟ 1 ♯ 24 TV ⚡ 🍴 P ▾

HYATT REGENCY BUDAPEST (HUF)(HUF)(HUF)(HUF)(HUF) — AE DC MC V — 344 — ■ — ● — ■
1051 Budapest, Roosevelt tér 2. **Map** 2 D5 (9 C3). ☎ 266 12 34. W www.budapest.hyatt.com
Located close to the Danube, the Atrium Hyatt has views of the Castle District and the Pest cityscape. There are stylish restaurants, serving international and Hungarian cuisine, terrace cafés and a cocktail bar. Souvenir boutiques and the Las Vegas Casino (see p206) are on the ground floor. ⊟ 1 ♯ 24 TV ⚡ 🍴 P ▾

CENTRAL PEST

CITY PANZIÓ MÁTYÁS (HUF)(HUF) — AE DC V — 55
1056 Budapest, Március 15 tér 8. **Map** 4 E1. ☎ 338 47 11. W www.taverna.hu
This small, neat pension offers basic rooms, with showers, at affordable prices. There is no bar or restaurant, but breakfast is available. The City Panzió Mátyás is well located and many of Budapest's attractions are within walking distance or are easily reached on public transport. ⊟ 1 TV ⚡ P

For key to symbols see back flap

	CREDIT CARDS	NUMBER OF ROOMS	RESTAURANT	AIR CONDITIONING	SWIMMING POOL

Price categories for a standard double room with bathroom per night, including breakfast, and service charges:

(HUF) below 10,000 HUF
(HUF)(HUF) 10,000–20,000 HUF
(HUF)(HUF)(HUF) 20,000–30,000 HUF
(HUF)(HUF)(HUF)(HUF) 30,000–40,000 HUF
(HUF)(HUF)(HUF)(HUF)(HUF) over 40,000 HUF.

CREDIT CARDS
Indicates which credit cards are accepted: AE American Express; DC Diners Club; MC Master Card/Access; V Visa JCB Japanese Credit Bureau.

RESTAURANT
Hotel restaurant or dining room usually open to non-residents unless otherwise stated.

AIR CONDITIONING
All rooms are air conditioned.

SWIMMING POOL
The hotel has an indoor or outdoor swimming pool.

EMKE (HUF)(HUF) | AE DC V | 74
1072 Budapest, Akácfa utca 1–3. **Map** 7 B3. 478 30 50. www.pannonia-emke.hu
Situated in the city centre, in a quiet side street close to Blaha Lujza tér, the EMKE offers pleasant rooms, including non-smoking ones. The service is friendly.

KING'S HOTEL KOSHER (HUF)(HUF) | AE | 100
1072 Budapest, Nagy Diófa utca 25–27. **Map** 7 A2 (10 F3). 352 76 75.
@ kingshotel@alexero.hu
Right in the heart of the Jewish Quarter (see p134), this wonderfully restored 19th-century building has been a hotel since 1995. The rooms are modern and plain, but many have small balconies overlooking the quiet residential street. The restaurant offers a tasty range of strictly Kosher meals.

IBIS CENTRUM (HUF)(HUF)(HUF) | AE DC MC V | 126 | | ● |
1092 Budapest, Ráday utca 6. **Map** 7 A5. 215 85 85. www.ibis-centrum.hu
This new hotel is located close to the Hungarian National Museum (see pp130 – 33), Kálvin tér and several restaurants. The comfortable rooms and friendly service ensure a restful stay.

MERCURE BUDAPEST METROPOL (HUF)(HUF)(HUF) | AE DC V JCB | 130 | ■ | ● |
1074 Budapest, Rákóczi út 58. **Map** 7 A3. 462 81 00. www.mercure-metropol.hu
Located in the city centre, close to all amenities and transport links, the Mercure Budapest is a newly renovated hotel housed in a 19th-century building. It offers every modern convenience, including sound-proofing and computer connections in all rooms.

NEMZETI (HUF)(HUF)(HUF) | AE DC MC V JCB | 76 | ■ | ● |
1088 Budapest, József körút 4. **Map** 7 B3. 477 20 00. www.mercure-nemzeti.hu
Built at the end of 19th century, this hotel features a wonderful grand staircase. Its main attraction is the Secession-style restaurant, which offers good food. The rooms are comfortable, and those facing the courtyard are particularly pleasant.

ASTORIA (HUF)(HUF)(HUF)(HUF) | AE DC MC V | 130 | ■ |
1053 Budapest, Kossuth Lajos u. 19–21. **Map** 4 F1 (10 E4). 484 32 00.
www.danubiusgroup.com/astoria
This old hotel, designed in the Secession style (see pp54–7), but with a Neo-Baroque breakfast room, has been refurbished to recreate its original interior. Even if not staying at the hotel, it is worth visiting the café (see p201) to see the beautiful interior.

ERZSÉBET (HUF)(HUF)(HUF) | DC MC JCB | 123 | ■ | ● |
1364 Budapest, Károlyi Mihály utca 11–15. **Map** 4 F1 (10 E5). 328 57 00.
www.danubiusgroup.com/erzsebet
This modern hotel is located close to the shops on Váci utca (Váci Street, see p127). The hotel has a restaurant, café and bar, which have a friendly atmosphere and a high standard of cuisine.

MERCURE BUDAPEST KORONA (HUF)(HUF)(HUF)(HUF) | AE DC MC V | 433 | ■ | | ■ |
1053 Budapest, Kecskeméti utca 14. **Map** 4 F2. 317 41 11.
www.mercure-korona.hu
The Mercure Korona is situated in a small street off Kálvin tér, close to cafés and restaurants. The hotel has a wide range of amenities, including its own swimming pool, gymnasium, sauna and solarium.

TAVERNA (HUF)(HUF)(HUF) | AE DC MC V | 230 | ■ | ● |
1052 Budapest, Váci utca 20. **Map** 4 E1 (10 D4). 485 31 00. www.taverna.hu
Situated on Váci utca (Váci Street, see p127), the Taverna offers all the facilities associated with four-star hotels. The elegant rooms create oases amid the noise and bustle of this busy commercial district.

INTER-CONTINENTAL
(HLF)(HLF)(HLF)(HLF)(HLF)   AE DC V   398
1052 Budapest, Apáczai Csere János utca 12–14. **Map** 2 D5 (9 C3). **[** *327 63 33.*
[W] www.budapest.intercontinental.com
This luxury hotel, situated close to Pest's riverside promenade, offers a magnificent view across the Danube to the Castle District. The facilities include a cocktail bar and a buffet restaurant. The beautifully decorated Viennese Café is located on the first floor.

KEMPINSKI CORVINUS
(HLF)(HLF)(HLF)(HLF)(HLF)   AE DC MC V   369
1051 Budapest, Erzsébet tér 7–8. **Map** 2 E5 (10 D5). **[** *429 37 77.*
[W] www.kempinski-budapest.com
This exclusive hotel often welcomes heads of state and other notable personalities among its guests. The large and luxuriously furnished rooms are enormously relaxing. The hotel has fitness facilities, two restaurants, bars and a pub.

MARRIOTT
(HLF)(HLF)(HLF)(HLF)(HLF)   AE DC MC V   362
1052 Budapest, Apáczai Csere János utca 4. **Map** 4 E1. **[** *266 70 00.* [W] www.marriott.com
The Marriott's excellent facilities include banqueting rooms, three restaurants, a business centre, a sauna and a fitness centre. The rooms are of a high standard and the staff provide an exemplary level of service. It was here, in 1991, that the decision was taken to dissolve the Warsaw Pact and Comecon *(see p35).*

AROUND VÁROSLIGET

LIGET
(HLF)(HLF)   AE DC MC V   139
1068 Budapest, Dózsa György út 106. **Map** 5 C3. **[** *269 53 00.* [W] www.liget.hu
Situated on the edge of the Hősök tere (Heroes' Square, *see pp142–3*), close to the Museum of Fine Arts *(see pp146–9)*, the Liget offers pleasant rooms. Its facilities include a sauna, a solarium and a rent-a-bike scheme.

GOLDEN PARK
(HLF)(HLF)   MC V   170
1087 Budapest, Baross tér 10. **Map** 7 C2 (10 F5). **[** *477 47 77.* [W] www.goldenparkhotel.hu
The Golden Park Hotel is located in the heart of the business centre of Budapest, and has good public transport links to Budapest's major sites. Newly reconstructed and refurbished, it serves a rich buffet-style breakfast and offers comfortable accommodation for individuals and group travellers alike.

RADIO INN
(HLF)(HLF)   MC V   31
1068 Budapest, Benczúr utca 19. Map 5 C4. **[** *342 83 47.* [W] www.radioinn.hu
This pension-style hotel is the official guesthouse of Hungarian National Radio and entertains many visiting personalities. The Radio Inn offers accommodation to tourists in spacious suites with well-equipped kitchens. Although the facilities are fairly basic, the Radio Inn is ideal for families as it is situated in the peaceful embassy quarter and there is a garden.

BENCZÚR
(HLF)(HLF)(HLF)   MC V   93
1068 Budapest, Benczúr utca 35. Map 5 C4. **[** *479 56 50.* [W] www.hotelbenczur.hu
Situated in a quiet street close to Városliget *(see pp142)*, this hotel offers small but comfortable rooms. In addition, there is a good restaurant, as well as a terrace and a garden. Guests are also able to make use of the services of an in-house dentist. Prices are sometimes considerably reduced out of the high season, so it is worth making enquiries.

IBIS BUDAPEST VOLGA
(HLF)(HLF)(HLF)   AE DC MC V JCB   315
1134 Budapest, Dózsa György út 65. Map 5 A1. **[** *329 02 00.* [W] www.ibis-volga.hu
This reasonable hotel complex caters for both tour groups and individuals. It offers functional rooms and good car parking facilities. There are a good range of entertainment options, which include a restaurant, a café, a bar and a nightclub. Medical care can also be obtained here.

GRAND HOTEL HUNGARIA
(HLF)(HLF)(HLF)(HLF)   AE DC MC V JCB   499
1074 Budapest, Rákóczi út 90. **Map** 7 C2. **[** *478 11 00.*
[W] www.danubiusgroup.com/grandhotel-hungaria
Budapest's largest hotel, the Grand Hungaria offers both single and double rooms. All rooms are clean and functional, but since they vary considerably in size it is worthwhile asking to view the room before checking in. The facilities include a café, a restaurant and several bars, as well as a child-minding service.

Price categories for a standard double room with bathroom per night, including breakfast, and service charges:

(HUF) below 10,000 HUF
(HUF)(HUF) 10,000–20,000 HUF
(HUF)(HUF)(HUF) 20,000–30,000 HUF
(HUF)(HUF)(HUF)(HUF) 30, 000–40,000 HUF
(HUF)(HUF)(HUF)(HUF)(HUF) over 40,000 HUF.

CREDIT CARDS
Indicates which credit cards are accepted: AE American Express; DC Diners Club; MC Master Card/Access; V Visa JCB Japanese Credit Bureau.

RESTAURANT
Hotel restaurant or dining room usually open to non-residents unless otherwise stated.

AIR CONDITIONING
All rooms are air conditioned.

SWIMMING POOL
The hotel has an indoor or outdoor swimming pool.

	CREDIT CARDS	NUMBER OF ROOMS	RESTAURANT	AIR CONDITIONING	SWIMMING POOL
FURTHER AFIELD					
AGRO (HUF)(HUF) 1121 Budapest, Normafa út 54. ☎ 375 40 11. ⓦ www.hotelagropanorama.hu This out-of-town hotel, situated on Sváb Hill *(see p161)*, still retains echoes of Budapest's Communist past. However, the Agro's relaxing surroundings and good food are matched by excellent facilities. These include a swimming pool, a bowling alley, tennis courts, a gymnasium and a sauna. There are splendid views, and walking in the Buda Hills *(see p161)* is an enjoyable pastime. ▦ 1 ▦ TV ▦ ▦ Y	AE DC MC V JCB	149	▦		▦
GRIFF (HUF)(HUF) 1113 Budapest, Bartók Béla út 152. ☎ 204 26 66. ⓦ www.hunguesthotels.hu This two-star hotel offers adequate facilities, including colour television in all rooms and a child-minding service. The restaurant regularly features a live Hungarian band. ▦ 1 TV ▦ ▦ ▦ ▦ P	AE MC	108	▦		
IBIS BUDAPEST AERO (HUF)(HUF) 1091 Budapest, Ferde utca 1–3. ☎ 347 97 00. ⓦ www.ibis-aero.hu Situated close to Ferihegy airport, this hotel is particularly convenient for those making only a short stop in Budapest. The rooms are cosy and tastefully decorated, and include some suites for families and rooms for non-smokers. All rooms have balconies. ▦ ▦ TV ▦ ▦ P Y	AE DC MC V JCB	139	▦	●	
MOHÁCSI PANZIÓ (HUF)(HUF) 1022 Budapest, Bimbó út 25a. ☎ 326 77 41. ꜰᴀx 326 7784. This small, pleasant and inexpensive pension is located just off Margit körút, in the Rózsadomb area. The pension offers clean rooms with either a shower or a bath, and all rooms have a television. 1 ▦ TV ▦ P Y		9	▦		
MOLNÁR PANZIÓ (HUF)(HUF) 1124 Budapest, Fodor utca 143. ☎ 395 18 73. ⓦ www.hotel-molnar.hu This mid-range pension is situated in a residential district on the slopes of the Buda Hills (see p161). Its green surroundings add to the homely atmosphere and offer guests complete peace. Family rooms are available. The amenities include a bar, fitness facilities and parking. ▦ 1 ▦ TV ▦ ▦ ▦ P	AE MC V	23	▦		
NORMAFA (HUF)(HUF) 1121 Budapest, Eötvös út 52–54. ☎ 395 65 05. ⓦ www.normafahotel.com Guests have the option of indulging in complete relaxation at the Normafa, or exploring the beautiful scenery on foot. All rooms have terraces, and there is also a swimming pool, a sauna, tennis courts, a restaurant, a café and a beer bar. ▦ 1 ▦ 24 TV ▦ ▦ ▦ P Y	AE MC V	70	▦		▦
OLYMPIA (HUF)(HUF) 1121 Budapest, Eötvös utca 40. ☎ 395 64 52. ꜰᴀx 395 64 43. Built in beautiful surroundings on the slopes of Sváb Hill *(see p161)*, this hotel was originally the Olympic athletes' centre. The air is clean and during the week it is very peaceful. At weekends the area is packed with day-trippers. ▦ 1 ▦ 24 TV ▦ ▦ ▦ P Y	AE DC	166	▦		▦
PANDA (HUF)(HUF) 1026 Budapest, Pasaréti út 133. ☎ 394 19 32. ⓦ www.budapesthotelpanda.com This small hotel is situated in Pasarét, a quiet residential district of Buda. It offers a family atmosphere and a substantial, tasty breakfast. Bus 5 provides quick transport into the centre. ▦ 1 24 TV ▦ ▦ P Y	AE DC MC V JCB	28	▦		
PLATÁNUS (HUF)(HUF) 1087 Budapest, Könyves Kálmán körút 44. ☎ 333 65 05. ⓦ www.hunguesthotels.hu A comfortable, inexpensive hotel situated on the edge of the People's Park *(see p156)* and close to the Népliget metro station. The hotel has clean, functional rooms, and offers good food. Other facilities available include a sauna, a solarium and an in-house doctor. ▦ 1 ▦ 24 TV ▦ ▦ P Y	AE DC MC V JCB	128	▦		

REGE
1021 Budapest, Pálos utca 2. **(** 391 23 00. @ rege@hotel.datanet.hu (HUF)(HUF)
Situated in a high-rise building in the Buda Hills *(see p161)*, this hotel is often patronized by actors. It offers peace and quiet, beautiful views and recreational facilities.

	AE	164	■		■
	DC				
	MC				
	V				

VILLA KORDA
1025 Budapest, Szikla utca 9. **(** 325 91 23. FAX 325 91 27. @ korda@axelero.hu (HUF)(HUF)
This exclusive pension-style hotel was built in a smart residential district on the slopes of Mátyás Hill by the popular Hungarian singer, György Korda. It offers a high standard of service and exclusive company. It is best reached by car due to its location and the steep road that leads to it.

	AE	21	■	●	
	DC				
	MC				
	V				

VADVIRÁG PANZIÓ
1025 Budapest, Nagybányai út 18. **(** 275 02 00. FAX 394 42 92 (HUF)(HUF)
This privately owned pension, located in a quiet and green district of the Buda Hills (see p161), has a homely atmosphere. Its facilities include comfortable rooms with balconies, a dining room, a terrace and a sauna. Close by is where the composer Béla Bartók once lived.

	DC	18			
	MC				
	V				
	JCB				

BUDAPEST
1026 Budapest, Szilágyi Erzsébet fasor 47. **(** 488 98 00. (HUF)(HUF)(HUF)
W www.danubiusgroup.com/budapest
This establishment was built in the late 1960s and was the pride of the local hotel industry for many years. Its location in the Buda Hills *(see p161)* and the magnificent view from the roof terrace remains unrivalled. The facilities include two restaurants and a wine cellar.

	AE	289	■	●	
	DC				
	MC				
	V				
	JCB				

NOVOTEL BUDAPEST CONGRESS
1444 Budapest, Alkotás utca 63–67. **Map** 3 A2. **(** 372 57 00. FAX 466 56 36. (HUF)(HUF)(HUF)
W www.novotel-bud-congress.hu
Situated in the immediate vicinity of the Congress Centre *(see p160)*, the Novotel Budapest Centrum offers modern rooms. The facilities include a swimming pool, a sauna, a bowling alley and a cocktail bar. The hotel also has a large car park. The reception rooms and banqueting halls can accommodate approximately 1,000 people.

	AE	321	■	●	■
	DC				
	MC				
	V				
	JCB				

RUBIN HOTEL & BUSINESS CENTER
1118 Budapest, Dayka Gábor utca 3. **(** 319 32 31. W www.hotelrubin.com (HUF)(HUF)(HUF)
This modern hotel offers various relaxation and sporting facilities, including sauna, swimming pool, tennis courts and bowling alley. It is in a quiet location close to the M1 and M7 motorways. The accommodation range includes some suites with kitchenettes and some maisonettes for families.

	AE	85	■	●	■
	DC				
	MC				
	V				

DANUBIUS GRAND HOTEL MARGITSZIGET
1138 Budapest, Margitsziget. **(** 452 62 00. W www.danubiusgroup.com/grandhotel (HUF)(HUF)(HUF)(HUF)
This hotel on Margaret Island *(see pp172–3)* is linked by a tunnel to the Danubius Thermal Hotel, whose spa facilities guests at the Grand can use. Other attractions include the shaded terrace cafés and restaurants, and the numerous possibilities for taking tranquil walks around the island. A swimming pool and bike hire are also available.

	AE	164	■	●	
	DC				
	V				

THERMAL & CONFERENCE HOTEL HELIA
1133 Budapest, Kárpát utca 62–64. **(** 452 58 00. W www.danubiusgroup.com/helia (HUF)(HUF)(HUF)(HUF)
This is a light and airy hotel located on the bank of Danube, opposite Margaret Island *(see pp172–3)*. From the rooms overlooking the river, guests can watch boats cruising along it. The most modern spa hotel in Budapest, the Thermal Helia offers a full range of health and beauty facilities, including massage, thermal waters and the services of a qualified medical practitioner.

	AE	262	■	●	■
	DC				
	MC				
	V				
	JCB				

CORINTHIA AQUINCUM
1036 Budapest, Árpád fejedelem útja 94. **(** 436 41 00. W www.corinthiahotels.com (HUF)(HUF)(HUF)(HUF)(HUF)
This hotel offers guests everything to pamper themselves or to improve their health. Facilities include an excellent swimming pool, hot- and warm-water spas, a jacuzzi, a sauna, massage and a gymnasium. The hotel also has a resident doctor and staff dedicated exclusively to the needs of disabled guests who come here for treatment. Some rooms have beautiful views of the Danube.

	DC	312	■	●	■
	MC				
	V				
	JCB				

RESTAURANTS, CAFÉS AND BARS

FOLLOWING A VISIT to Budapest, the Nobel Prize-winning Latin American writer Miguel Ángel Asturias said that "the exquisite taste of Hungarian cuisine is a language understood by all". The numerous restaurants, cafés and bars in Budapest give the visitor ample opportunity to sample the delights of this distinctive cuisine. The most typical examples of traditional Hungarian cooking can be seen on pages 190–91, while information on what to drink is given on pages 192–3. A detailed guide to around 60 of the city's best restaurants, covering a selection of price categories, is provided on pages 194–9. This list highlights attractions such as Hungarian specialities and live music. Cafés, wine bars and beer houses can be found on pages 200–201.

WHERE TO LOOK

THERE ARE a great many eating establishments in Budapest and the surrounding suburbs. Good traditional Hungarian dishes can be found within all price ranges in restaurants and inns, but in recent years Budapest has seen the arrival of cuisine from all over the world. Among the ethnic eating options now available are Italian, Greek, Chinese and Thai restaurants. American-style fast food chains are also appearing and are rapidly becoming popular.

The city's main tourist areas are well off for places to eat, but may not offer the best fare or prices. It is often worth looking off the the main roads or away from popular areas to find establishments frequented by local Budapest residents. The restaurants, cafés and bars on Váci utca (Váci Street, *see p127*) are notorious for overcharging, especially at night.

Entrance to Ruszwurm Cukrászda (*see p201*), in the Castle District

TYPES OF RESTAURANTS, CAFÉS AND BARS

BUDAPEST OFFERS a variety of places to eat and a range of prices to suit most budgets. The differences between the types of establishments can be subtle, but they break down roughly into the following types. *Étterem* simply means restaurant – any type of cuisine may be served. A *csárda* comes in various forms. Most are folky restaurants typically offering interesting local specialities. A fisherman's *csárda*, known as a *halászcsárda*, will offer mainly fish dishes and soups. There are two types of inn, a *vendéglő*, which has an informal ambience, and a *kisvendéglő*, (literally a "small inn"), which is similar to a cosy pub. Cafés range from a *kávéház* (coffee house) to a *cukrászda* (patisserie), and types of bars include a *borozó*, a *söröző* and an *eszpresszó* (*see pp200–1*).

Lantern outside the Gerbeaud Cukrászda

WHAT TO ORDER

ORDERING A Hungarian meal may not be as simple as it may first seem. There are many different varieties of Hungarian soups, some of which are a meal in themselves. *Bogrács*, which is often served in a kettle, and bean soups are the heartiest soups and would normally be followed by a light, hot pudding or pancakes. Hungarian fish soup is a particular speciality and owes its red colour to paprika. This should be followed by delicate homemade noodles served with crackling, cheese and cream. There are also many light soups, or small portions of the more substantial soups, which can be eaten as a starter, thus leaving room for the main course.

The archetypal Hungarian main dish is goulash and there are several versions of the basic thick meat stew. Another Hungarian speciality is *pörkölt* (a paprika stew very similar to goulash). This stew is made with lean meat such as veal, poultry or fish, with sour cream added at the end of cooking. Almost all meals are eaten with bread; the white wheat variety is particularly delicious.

Food served in bars or bought from street kiosks is a different matter. More akin to fast food, it is often eaten standing up or on the move. Spicy sausages, liberally seasoned with paprika and garlic are served grilled or boiled. Grilled chicken and various smoked meats are also widely available. Another alternative is the delicious *lángos* (pronounced "langosh"), which is sold at markets. This flat, savoury, yeast cake is served with cram or cheese.

More detailed information on this subject is contained in *What to Eat* in Budapest on pages 190–91.

VEGETARIAN FOOD

VEGETARIAN cuisine *per se* is not found in abundance in Budapest. There are very few vegetarian restaurants, of which one, the Vegetárium, is recommended in this guide *(see p197)*. Ethnic restaurants may offer a wider vegetarian choice.

Nevertheless, meat-free dishes can be found on most Hungarian menus. *Főzelék*, a vegetable dish that normally accompanies steak, sausage or a hamburger, can be ordered on its own or with egg. *Lecsó (see p191)* is another popular vegetable side dish that makes a substantial meal by itself. Other specialities include *túrós csusza*, a pasta dish served with cottage cheese and sour cream. There are also many sweet and savoury varieties of *palacsinta* (pancake).

RESERVING A TABLE

IN HUNGARY it is customary to join other guests at a table, especially during the busy lunch period. To secure a private table, it is advisable to book in advance. This applies equally to Budapest's exclusive restaurants and cheaper establishments.

MENUS AND PRICES

ALL HUNGARIAN restaurants display a menu by the entrance, and, as a rule, this is translated into English or German. The name of the dish is followed by a brief description. The day's "specials" – a set meal consisting of a soup, a main course and a dessert –

A charming outdoor café on Margaret Island

are listed at the head of the menu. Set menus are often very good value and provide an ideal opportunity to sample several Hungarian specialities.

The prices should also be displayed. If they are not, it is wise to go elsewhere or at least see the prices, including any surcharges, before ordering the meal. The introduction of printed and itemized bills has made it more difficult for hidden "extras" to be added to the final bill.

In most Hungarian restaurants the waiters tend to round up the bill, particularly when serving foreign customers. This practice led to a minor scandal in 1997 when several embassies, including the American and British delegations, compiled a blacklist of dishonest restaurants, after receiving numerous complaints, and published it on the Internet. The government closed the offending establishments and the situation has

now improved. Visitors should still be cautious, however. By selecting a restaurant from those listed in this guide *(see pp196–9)*, this problem should be easily avoided.

TIPPING

IN SOME restaurants a service charge is included in the final bill, in others it is customary to tip. If a service charge is added, this should be stated on either the menu or the bill; this could be up to 15 per cent. However, if there is any doubt, it is courteous to leave a tip. In general, an acceptable tip is between 10–15 per cent of the cost of the meal.

CHILDREN

CHILDREN ARE welcomed in all restaurants without exception. If children's portions do not appear on the menu, the chef will prepare suitable dishes to order. These are usually charged at half price. The only exception is dessert, but this can often be shared. However, the desserts in Hungarian restaurants are so delicious that most children will happily eat a whole portion.

USING THE LISTINGS

🍴	fixed-price menu
V	vegetarian dishes
🪑	outdoor eating
🎵	live music
★	highly recommended
💳	credit cards accepted:
AE	American Express
DC	Diners Club
MC	MasterCard
V	VISA
JCB	Japanese Credit Bureau

Price categories for a three-course meal with half a bottle of wine, including service:

HUF under 3,000 HUF
HUF HUF 3,000–4,000 HUF
HUF HUF HUF 4,000–5,000 HUF
HUF HUF HUF HUF 5,000–6,000 HUF
HUF HUF HUF HUF HUF over 6,000 HUF

One of several restaurants to be found on boats on the Danube

Budapest's Best: Restaurants and Cafés

BUDAPEST'S restaurants and cafés are a source of pride. Some of the more famous establishments date back to the 19th century and have become part of the city's history, adding to its character and ambience. As well as traditional Hungarian fare, many different styles of cuisine can be found in Budapest. The following restaurants, taken from the list of over 50 establishments on pages 194–201, give a selection of the best the city can offer.

Carlo's
Good selection of Hungarian dishes and wines with a panoramic view of Parliament (see p195).

North of the Castle

DANUBE

Around Parliament

Castle District

Rivalda Café & Restaurant
Located in the picturesque Castle District, Rivalda offers excellent European cuisine served in a theatrically-inspired interior (see p194).

Pest Buda Vendéglő
Behind this modest entrance, a selection of Hungarian and international culinary delights awaits the visitor (see p194).

Gellért Hill and Tabán

0 metres 500
0 yards 500

Centrál Kávéház és Étterem
Open from early to late, this café offers snacks, meals, coffee and cakes much as it did 100 years ago (see p197).

Gundel Étterem

A house speciality of flambéed pancakes (see p191) *is just one of the many mouthwatering dishes that have given the Gundel its international reputation* (see p198).

New York Kávéház

It is worth enjoying a meal or just a coffee, in order to see inside this magnificent Neo-Baroque restaurant. It has been a focus for Budapest's café society since it opened in 1894. Gypsy musicians play in the evening (see p201).

Around Városliget

Central Pest

Vörös és Fehér

This restaurant offers an outstanding selection of wines that are also available by the glass to accompany mouth-watering dishes ranging from light bites to dinner (see p197).

Vista Café & Restaurant

A huge selection of International and Hungarian dishes are served in this atmospheric venue, where live jazz is often played in the evenings (see p197).

What to Eat in Budapest

HUNGARIAN CUISINE is similar to that of its neighbours, Austria, Slovakia and the Czech Republic. However, it does have one unique characteristic: paprika. This spicy pepper can be found in a many robust Hungarian soups and sauces, and is used as a seasoning for meat and fish dishes. Meat, especially pork and beef, forms the basis of the majority of main course dishes, which are served with potatoes or dumplings. Peppers, which until the mid-19th century were used only as a fever remedy, onions and tomatoes are among the most common vegetable accompaniments.

Hungarian peppers

Libamáj Zsírjában
Goose liver, fried in its own fat, is a Hungarian speciality and is considered a great delicacy.

Hortobágyi Palacsinta
Eaten as a hot starter, these pancakes are filled with paprika-seasoned meat and served in a cream sauce.

Jókai Bableves
This thick bean soup contains smoked gammon, sausage and small dumplings.

Halászlé
Carp filets are the main ingredient of this paprika-seasoned fisherman's soup.

Töltött Paprika
These peppers are stuffed with rice and meat and served in a tomato sauce.

Chips

Grilled pork chop

Grilled sirloin beef

Pickled cabbage, peppers and onions

Borjúpaprikás Galuskával
Pieces of veal in a cream and paprika sauce are served with small flour dumplings.

Fatányéros
This selection of grilled beef and pork is richly garnished with pickles, peppers and chips. It is served in traditional Transylvanian style on a large wooden plate, and each portion is intended for two people. A popular option, fatányéros is available on almost all restaurant menus.

Bélszínszelet Budapest Módra
Sirloin beef steak Budapest-syle is served in a peppery sauce with mushrooms.

Marhapörkölt Tarhonyával
Beef goulash in hot, paprika sauce is often accompanied by soft noodles (tarhonya).

Brassói Aprópecsenye
Pieces of pork, strongly seasoned with garlic and paprika, are stewed and served with fried potatoes.

Bakonyi Sertésborda
A pork chop is served in a creamy mushroom sauce.

Potato

Tomato

Spicy paprika sausage

Onion

Pepper

Borjúbélszín Gundel Módra
A rich mushroom sauce accompanies these medallions of beef.

Lecsó Kolbásszal
Peppers braised in fat with onions and tomatoes is called lecsó, and provides the basis for many Hungarian dishes. Here it is accompanied by spicy sausages, but it can often be ordered on its own as a vegetable dish.

Gundel Palacsinta
Pancakes filled with nut and raisin paste are flambéed and served with chocolate sauce.

Dobos Torta
Delicate slices of sponge cake, layered with a chocolate cream filling, are covered with a golden brown icing.

Rétes
Light French pastry is filled with an apple and raisin, a cherry or a cheese filling, and sprinkled with icing sugar.

What to Drink in Budapest

American-style drinks cabinet

HUNGARY IS FAMOUS for its excellent wines and, although it is not a big country, it has as many as 13 vine-growing regions. These regions produce all the characteristic wine styles, from *pezsgő* (sparkling wine) and light whites that come from Mátra, near Lake Balaton, to dry reds from Villány or Eger, as well as Tokaji, a distinctive sweet dessert wine. Many wines from different vineyards are matured in a maze of underground of cellars in Budafok. They are all widely available in Budapest's many restaurants, wine bars and wine shops. As well as being a prominent wine producer, Hungary also makes beer, *pálinka (*a drink distilled from different orchard fruits), several types of brandy and a bitter herb liqueur called Unicum.

Light Hungarian beers

PÁLINKA

KECSKEMÉT IS the largest region that produces the alcoholic drink *pálinka*, which is distilled from fruit grown in the orchards situated on the Great Hungarian Plain, some 100 km (60 miles) southeast of Budapest. *Pálinka* is a spirit native to Hungary and comes in a variety of flavours including *barack* (apricot) and *cseresznye* (cherry). The best of them, however, is *szilva* (plum) which comes from the Szatmár district and is much favoured by the Hungarians.

Barack pálinka

Pálinka is not the only spirit indigenous to Hungary. Other examples include Törköly, a spirit distilled from rape, which possesses a very delicate flavour, and Vilmos, a brandy made from Williams pears.

SPARKLING WINES

SPARKLING WINE, called *pezsgő* (the Hungarian word for "sparkling"), enjoys a good reputation in Hungary. The classic method of producing these wines was introduced to Hungary from France by József Törley, in 1881. It was Törley *(see p161)* who built

Pezsgő by Törley and Hungaria

the first production plant in Budafok, which continues to produce excellent sparkling wines over 100 years on. Today, Hungary has several other vineyards producing *pezsgő*, mainly concentrated around Budapest, in the Pannonia and Balatonboglár regions. As well as Törley, Hungaria is another good label to look out for.

HUNGARIAN BEERS

IN RECENT YEARS Hungarians have been turning increasingly to beer as their chosen drink as it goes exceptionally well with many traditional, paprika-flavoured Hungarian dishes, goulash among them. There are three remaining authentic Hungarian breweries. These are Arany Ászok, Kőbányai (which was established in the Kőbánya district of Budapest some 150 years ago) and the excellent Dreher. Unfortunately, many other formerly Hungarian breweries have now been taken over by large foreign corporations. However, many of these brands are also well known and all are widely available in Budapest.

HUNGARIAN WINES

THE CHOICE OF good wine available in Hungary has increased dramatically over the past few years. This is thanks to the ever-improving wines being matured in private cellars. The styles currently

One of Budafok's cellars, where wines are aged in barrels

Egri Bikavér, "Bulls' Blood", a full-bodied red wine

A dry white wine from the Badacsony vineyards

SPRITZERS

On hot days, Hungarians enjoy drinking refreshing spritzers. The various types are differentiated by the proportion of white wine to soda water:

Quantity of wine	Quantity of water
Small spritzer *(Kisfröccs)*	
10 cl	10 cl
Large spritzer *(Nagyfröccs)*	
20 cl	10 cl
Long step *(Hosszúlépés)*	
10 cl	20 cl
Janitor *(Házmester)*	
30 cl	20 cl

favoured by the producers include dry white Chardonnay and Reisling, medium-dry Zödszilváni, Hárslevelű and Szürkebarát, medium-sweet Tramini and the aromatic Muskotály, which is produced in Badacsony, Balatonboglár, Csopak and Somló.

Among red wines, the dry Kékfrankos, Burgundi, Oportó, Cabernet and Pinot Noir are popular, as is the medium-dry Merlot, which is produced in Siklós, Sopron, Szekszárd, Tihány and Villány.

Another vine-growing district is Eger, which is famous for its aromatic, robust red Egri Leányka and the dry red Egri Bikavér, or "Bulls' Blood", which is produced from a combination of three grape varieties. Other Hungarian wines take their names from their place of origin or the variety of grape from which they are produced.

TOKAJI

THE DESSERT WINE Tokaji has a very different style. Its bouquet and flavour come from a mould that grows only in the fork of the Bodrog and Tisza rivers and the volcanic soil in which the vines grow.

Tokaji ranges from sweet to dry and is full-bodied and rich. Particularly worth sampling is Aszú, which is made with the addition of over-ripe grapes harvested after the first frost. The proportion of these grapes added to the must (grape juice) determines the wine's body and sweetness. The more of these grapes used, the sweeter and richer the Aszú.

Although cheap varieties of Tokaji do exist, they do not share the quality of the genuine article.

UNICUM

FOR OVER 150 YEARS, a blend of 40 Hungarian herbs has been used to create Unicum. The herbs, which are gathered in three separate areas, are combined to produce this bitter liqueur. Unicum can be drunk either as an apéritif before a meal or afterwards as a digestif with coffee.

The recipe has been held by the Zwack family, and remained a secret, since the reign of King Franz I *(see p19).* Originally, Unicum was prescribed as a remedy for the king by the court physician, who was himself a member of the Zwack family.

Unicum herb liqueur

Sweet Tokaji Szamorodni

Dry Tokaji Szamorodni Száraz

Tokaji Aszú, a renowned golden dessert wine

Pear-flavoured Vilmos liqueur

Sisi, an apricot liqueur

Choosing a Restaurant

T HE RESTAURANTS in this guide have been selected across a wide range of price categories for their good value, exceptional food and interesting locations. The chart below lists the restaurants in Budapest by area; entries are alphabetical within each price category. For map references, see the Street Finder map on pages 234–245.

	CREDIT CARDS	GOOD WINE LIST	HUNGARIAN SPECIALITIES	ATTRACTIVE LOCATION

CASTLE DISTRICT

ÖNKISZOLGÁLÓ ÉTTEREM (HLF)
Hess András tér 4. **Map** 1 B4.
This self-service restaurant has an atmosphere recalling the 1970s. A door in the Fortuna passage leads up to the first floor where really cheap dishes are displayed behind the counter. The menu changes daily. ● *evenings, Sun.* **V**
— Hungarian Specialities ■

PIERROT CAFÉ RESTAURANT (HLF)(HLF)(HLF) — DC MC V JCB
Fortuna utca. 14. **Map** 1 B4. **[** 375 69 71.
This opened as a private café in socialist times. Although redesigned, the elegant interior still has a cosy café atmosphere. Live piano music in the evening and all day at weekends. **V** 🚻 🎵
— Hungarian Specialities ■ — Attractive Location ●

PEST BUDA VENDÉGLŐ (HLF)(HLF)(HLF)(HLF)
Fortuna utca. 3. **Map** 1 B4. **[** 212 58 80.
Small, elegant restaurant with arcaded walls in a listed building. Part of the former underground cave system gives space to a recently opened wine cellar. Not an extensive menu but interesting and excellently prepared dishes. 🚻 🎵
— Good Wine List ● — Hungarian Specialities ■ — Attractive Location ●

ALABÁRDOS ÉTTEREM (HLF)(HLF)(HLF)(HLF)(HLF) — AE DC MC V
Országház utca 2. **Map** 1 B4. **[** 356 08 51.
A truly exclusive place in an outstanding Gothic building. Hungarian specialities of old, pre-paprika times made to please today's taste buds. Evening guitar music adds to the candle-lit medieval atmosphere. ● *Sun.* **V** 🚻 🎵
— Good Wine List ● — Hungarian Specialities ■ — Attractive Location ●

RIVALDA CAFÉ & RESTAURANT (HLF)(HLF)(HLF)(HLF)(HLF)(HLF) — AE MC V JCB
Színház utca. 5–9. **Map** 1 C5. **[** 489 02 36.
Next to the Castle Theatre, thus with a theatre-inspired décor. Contemporary international cuisine with a frequently changing menu to reflect the seasons. Pleasant jazz piano music in the evenings. **V** 🚻 🎵
— Good Wine List ● — Attractive Location ●

GELLÉRT HILL AND TABÁN

TABÁNI KAKAS VENDÉGLŐ (HLF) — AE DC MC V
Attila út 27. **Map** 3 C1. **[** 375 71 65.
Small restaurant with a family atmosphere where poultry dishes are a speciality. Goose and duck can be found in soups and main courses, including the excellent goose breast with bread dumplings and vegetable sauce. 🚻 🎵 ★
— Hungarian Specialities ■

MÁRVÁNYMENYASSZONY ÉTTEREM (HLF)(HLF) — AE DC MC V
Márvány utca 6. **Map** 3 A1. **[** 487 30 90.
An old-style Hungarian restaurant with a fine gipsy band playing every night. Although hidden away, tourists tend to find it. There are several rooms in case you prefer quiet to music. 🎵
— Hungarian Specialities ■

SZEGED ÉTTEREM. (HLF)(HLF)(HLF) — V
Bartók Béla út 1. **Map** 4 E3. **[** 209 16 68.
Next to the Gellért Hotel, a traditional Hungarian restaurant offering a good selection of specialities including several river fish dishes. The *Szegedi halászlé* (Szeged fish soup) is particularly tasty. Lively gipsy band every evening. 🎵
— Hungarian Specialities ■

CITADELLA ÉTTEREM (HLF)(HLF)(HLF)(HLF) — AE DC MC V
Citadella sétány. **Map** 4 D3. **[** 386 48 02.
The casements of the Citadel have been turned into a restaurant consisting of several rooms. A gipsy band plays every night. Traditional Hungarian dishes and a good selection for vegetarians. **V** 🚻 🎵
— Good Wine List ● — Hungarian Specialities ■ — Attractive Location ●

BÚSULÓ JUHÁSZ ÉTTEREM (HLF)(HLF)(HLF)(HLF)(HLF) — AE MC V
Kelenhegyi út 58. **Map** 3 C3. **[** 209 16 49.
Spectacular views from this traditional Hungarian restaurant on the western slopes of Gellért Hill. A wide choice of Hungarian specialities made lighter in the spirit of international gastronomy. Pleasant gipsy music. **V** 🚻 🎵 *except Sun.* 🍴
— Good Wine List ● — Hungarian Specialities ■ — Attractive Location ●

	Credit Cards	Good Wine List	Hungarian Specialities	Attractive Location

Price categories for a three-course meal for one with half a bottle of wine and including service:

(HUF) under 3,000 HUF
(HUF)(HUF) 3,000–4,000 HUF
(HUF)(HUF)(HUF) 4,000–5,000 HUF
(HUF)(HUF)(HUF)(HUF) 5,000–6,000 HUF
(HUF)(HUF)(HUF)(HUF)(HUF) Over 6,000 HUF.

CREDIT CARDS
Indicates which credit cards are accepted: AE American Express; DC Diners Club; MC Master Card/Access; V Visa; JCB Japanese Credit Bureau.

GOOD WINE LIST
Denotes a wide selection of good wines.

HUNGARIAN SPECIALITIES
Typical Hungarian fare is served.

ATTRACTIVE LOCATION
Restaurant can be found in an unusual or historic setting, or has an attractive view.

NORTH OF THE CASTLE

À LA CARTE KISÉTTEREM (HUF)
Iskola utca 29. **Map** 1 C3. (214 00 41.
A small restaurant conveniently situated near Batthyány tér. An unusually wide choice of fish dishes on the respectably long menu. Home-style cooking. Reservation is recommended for both lunch and dinner. **V** ★

SÖRÖZŐ A KIRÁLYI KORONÁHOZ (HUF)
Varsányi Irén utca 33. **Map** 1 B3. (212 25 55.
Small, cosy restaurant with homemade dishes and a good selection of beer. There are a limited number of vegetarian dishes. A favourite with local residents. **V**

CSALOGÁNY ÉTTEREM ÉS KÁVÉZÓ (HUF)(HUF)
Csalogány utca 26. **Map** B3. (487 08 73.
Newly opened restaurant/café with a modern Mediterranean interior. Excellent poultry, fish and meat dishes grilled on lava stones. There is a reasonable selection of vegetarian dishes and salads. Good wines, though not a large selection. **V**

PAKSI HALÁSZCSÁRDA (HUF)(HUF) | | MC V
Margit körút 14. **Map** B1. (212 55 99.
Near Margaret Bridge, this a traditional fishermen's restaurant specializing in the best of Hungarian river fish dishes, such as catfish stew with gnocchi. Gipsy music in the evenings. Reservation recommended for dinner. **V** 🍴 🎵 *except Sun.*

CARLO'S RESTAURANT (HUF)(HUF)(HUF) | AE MC V JCB
Bem rakpart 30. **Map** 1 C3. (488 01 15.
Relaxed restaurant across the river from Parliament offering international and Hungarian cuisine, including the excellently made "Highwayman's soup". There is a weekly changing specials menu, with dishes of home-style cooking. **V** 🍴 🍽 *lunch.*

AROUND PARLIAMENT

BELVÁROSI LUGAS ÉTTEREM (HUF)
Bajcsy-Zsilinszky út 15/a. **Map** 2 E4. (302 53 93.
Well-made, hearty dishes in a simple appealing atmosphere; a favourite with locals. In the summer a terrace is set up on the pavement, although constant traffic may disturb any conversation. **V** 🍴

MIRÁKULUM ÉTTEREM ÉS KÁVÉHÁZ (HUF) | AE MC V
Hercegprímás utca 19. **Map** 2 E4. (269 32 07.
A restaurant/café with a sophisticated, pleasant atmosphere. International cuisine with some Hungarian dishes. Daily specialities in addition to the regular menu. ● *Sun.* **V** 🍴 🎵 *once a week, day varies.* 🍽 *lunch.*

VIA LUNA (HUF) | AE DC MC V JCB
Nagysándor József utca 1. **Map** 2 E4. (312 80 58.
A truly Italian place with an extensive menu. Excellent pasta dishes. Always busy so best to reserve a table. Both Hungarian and Italian wines are available. **V** ★

CAFÉ KÖR (HUF)(HUF)
Sas utca 17. **Map** 2 E4. (311 00 53.
Popular bistro-type place, so reservation is recommended. Good salad plates and Hungarian/European inspired dishes. Vegetarian food to order. A good selection of Hungarian wines to sample by the glass. ● *Sun.* **V** ★

MARQUIS DE SALADE (HUF)(HUF)
Hajós utca 43. **Map** 2 F4. (302 40 86.
An extensive menu from around the world, including interesting lamb dishes from Azerbaijan and Georgia. Basic Hungarian fare, such as *goulash*, is also on offer. Vegetarians have plenty to chose from. **V**

For key to symbols *see p187*

<table>
<tr>
<td colspan="2">
Price categories for a three-course meal for one with half a bottle of wine and including service:
(HUF) under 3,000 HUF
(HUF)(HUF) 3,000–4,000 HUF
(HUF)(HUF)(HUF) 4,000–5,000 HUF
(HUF)(HUF)(HUF)(HUF) 5,000–6,000 HUF
(HUF)(HUF)(HUF)(HUF)(HUF) Over 6,000 HUF.
</td>
<td>
CREDIT CARDS
Indicates which credit cards are accepted: AE American Express; DC Diners Club; MC Master Card/Access; V Visa; JCB Japanese Credit Bureau.
GOOD WINE LIST
Denotes a wide selection of good wines.
HUNGARIAN SPECIALITIES
Typical Hungarian fare is served.
ATTRACTIVE LOCATION
Restaurant can be found in an unusual or historic setting, or has an attractive view.
</td>
</tr>
</table>

	CREDIT CARDS	GOOD WINE LIST	HUNGARIAN SPECIALITIES	ATTRACTIVE LOCATION

MŰVÉSZ VENDÉGLŐ (HUF)(HUF)
Vígszínház utca 5. **Map** 2 E2. 339 80 08.
Located behind the Vígszínház (Variety Theatre), this is an intimate, homely restaurant. The walls display photos of theatre personalities and, with its antique furniture, it looks like a grandmother's dining room. Late breakfast served. Good home-style cooking. ● *Sun.* V ¶(HUF) ★

MC V · ▪

SIR LANCELOT LOVAGI ÉTTEREM (HUF)(HUF)(HUF)
Podmaniczky utca 14. **Map** 2 F3. 302 44 56.
Excellent kitchen preparing Renaissance-inspired dishes served by people in period costumes. Only knives and spoons are provided for the huge, substantial portions. Renaissance music in the evenings. Reservation recommended, especially for weekends. ♫ ¶(HUF)

AE DC MC V · ▪

BELCANTO (HUF)(HUF)(HUF)(HUF)(HUF)
Dalszínház utca 8. **Map** 2 F4. 269 31 01.
Eat good international and Hungarian food while hearing the waiters and some customers/opera professionals sing famous opera pieces in the evening. There is also an orchestra playing dance music. V ♫ ¶(HUF) *buffet lunch.*

AE DC MC V JCB · ● ▪

LA FONTAINE (HUF)(HUF)(HUF)(HUF)(HUF)
Mérleg utca 10. **Map** 2 E5. 317 37 15.
A real French restaurant with a French owner and chef, offering freshly made high quality French cuisine with a daily changing menu. Good salads and fish dishes. Excellent Hungarian wines and a wide selection of French wines are on offer. ● *Sat lunch, Sun.*

AE DC MC V ●

CENTRAL PEST

ALFÖLDI ÉTTEREM (HUF)
Kecskeméti utca 4. **Map** 4 F2. 317 44 04.
Popular restaurant serving tasty Hungarian food. *Pogácsa* (savoury, heavy scones) are always fresh and on the table. The menu has been extended to include a choice of salads. V ▦ ¶(HUF) *lunch.*

▪

FATÁL (HUF)
Váci utca 67. **Map** 4 F2. 266 26 07.
Often crowded, cellar restaurant serving enormous portions of standard Hungarian fare as made at home, with a huge quantity of beef and pork.

▪

GREENS (HUF)
Dob utca 3. **Map** 10 E4. 352 85 15.
Small, cheap eating place in a cellar near the Great Synagogue. It specializes in *főzelék*, the Hungarian way of preparing vegetables, but also serves meat dishes. Home-style cooking. V

QUINT ÉTELBÁR (HUF)
Bárczy István utca 1–3. **Map** 4 E1. 266 75 68.
Pleasant self-service restaurant, with a wide selection of tasty home-style dishes like *rakott burgonya* (layered potatoes), *mousaka* and *rizsfelfújt* (rice pudding). ● *weekdays after 8 pm, Sat after 3pm, Sun.* V ★

▪

CARMEL ÉTTEREM. (HUF)(HUF)
Kazinczy utca 31. **Map** 10 F3. 342 45 85.
Non-kosher Hungarian Jewish specialities and some international dishes in this atmospheric cellar restaurant. Very tasty *sólet* (cholent) with smoked goose. Reservation recommended. V ★

AE DC V ●

HANNA ORTODOXKÓSER ÉTTEREM (HUF)(HUF)
Dob utca 35. **Map** 7 A2. 342 10 72.
Orthodox kosher eating place in the courtyard of the Orthodox Synagogue on Kazinczy utca. Traditional Jewish dishes and kosher wines are served. For Sabbath meals you pay the day before or after. V

KALTENBERG BAJOR KIRÁLYI SÖRÖZŐ
Kinizsi utca 30–36. **Map** 7 A5. █ 215 97 92.
Attractively furnished beer cellar by the Museum of Applied Arts. Huge portions
of both Hungarian and Bavarian specialities. Beer is brewed on the spot and
several good wines are available. Half-price meals available on Sundays. **V** █

KÉT SZERECSEN
Nagymező utca 14. **Map** 2 F4. █ 343 19 84.
A friendly place with a pleasant atmosphere on Pest's "Broadway". A good range
of tasty salads, and Hungarian and French main courses. Most wines are available
by the glass. Booking is recommended, especially in the evenings. **V** ★

KISPIPA ÉTTEREM
Akácfa utca 38. **Map** 7 A2. █ 342 25 87.
As good as, and as it looked, 25 years ago. A wide choice of international and
Hungarian dishes. Rezső Seres, composer of "Gloomy Sunday", no longer sits
at the piano, but many of his songs are still played. **V** █ ▮█▮

VISTA CAFÉ AND RESTAURANT
Paulay Ede utca 7. **Map** 2 F5. █ 268 08 88.
Lively atmosphere with an extensive menu of contemporary tasty international
cuisine, including some excellent Hungarian specialities and fish dishes. Large area
for non-smokers. Live jazz on several evenings. ● *Jul–Aug: Sun eve.* **V** █ ▮█▮ ★

CENTRÁL KÁVÉHÁZ ÉS ÉTTEREM
Károlyi Mihály utca 9. **Map** 4 F1. █ 266 21 10.
A recently revived old time café/restaurant with an authentic, relaxed pre-war
central European feel. Open for breakfast and late night dinner. Good
Hungarian and international cuisine with excellent cakes, unusual for a
restaurant selection. **V** ★

JAZZ GARDEN
Veres Pálné utca 44/a. **Map** 4 F2. █ 266 73 64.
In effect a cellar, but really it looks and feels like a garden. Very popular
among jazz fans, not only for the daily changing music, but also for its fine
international cuisine. Booking recommended for the evening. **V** █ ▮█▮ *lunch.*

KÁROLYI ÉTTEREM ÉS KÁVÉHÁZ
Károlyi Mihály utca 16. **Map** 4 F2. █ 328 02 40.
An elegant, sophisticated restaurant in the lovely courtyard of the Károlyi
Palace. Worth trying *borjúpaprikás lángosban* (veal paprika stew in thick
potato pancake). Its attractive gardens are uncommon in the city centre.
Reservation recommended. **V** ▮▮ █ *some evenings.* ▮█▮ *lunch.* ★

SOUL CAFÉ & RESTAURANT
Ráday utca 11–13. **Map** 7 A5. █ 217 69 86.
An intimate restaurant with a pleasant and easy atmosphere on the thriving
Ráday utca, which in recent times has filled with cafes, restaurants and shops.
Well-prepared and tasty international cuisine. **V** ▮▮ ▮█▮ *lunch.*

KÁRPÁTIA ÉTTEREM ÉS SÖRÖZŐ
Ferenciek tere 7–8. **Map** 4 F1. █ 317 35 96.
First opened in 1877, this is Hungarian cuisine at its light best, set in an
elegant, beautifully ornamented interior. The beer hall serves the same dishes,
but at cheaper prices. Gipsy music in the evenings. Reservation recommended.
V ▮▮ █ ▮█▮ *Sun brunch.* ★

VÖRÖS ÉS FEHÉR
Andrássy út 41. **Map** 10 F1. █ 413 15 45.
Excellent international and Mediterranean cuisine with an extremely wide range
of wines, which can be sampled by the glass – unsurprising since the restaurant
was established by the Budapest Wine Society. Booking recommended. **V** ▮▮ ★

MÚZEUM KÁVÉHÁZ ÉS ÉTTEREM
Múzeum körút 12. **Map** 10 F5. █ 338 42 21.
Next to the National Museum, a distinguished, elegant restaurant and café,
established in 1855. It serves specialities of international and Hungarian cuisine.
Reservation is recommended. ● *Sun.* **V** █ ▮█▮ *lunch.*

SZÁZÉVES ÉTTEREM.
Pesti Barnabás utca 2. **Map** 4 E1. █ 266 52 40.
The oldest restaurant in Budapest, first opened in 1831, in a beautiful Baroque
building furnished with antique pieces. It offers Hungarian and international
cuisine which you can enjoy with Gipsy music. **V** ▮▮ █ ▮█▮ *lunch.*

For key to symbols *see p187*

	AE DC MC V		
KALTENBERG			■
KÉT SZERECSEN		●	■
KISPIPA	AE DC MC V	●	■
VISTA CAFÉ	AE DC MC V JCB	●	■
CENTRÁL	AE MC V JCB	●	■
JAZZ GARDEN	AE MC V	●	
KÁROLYI	AE DC MC V	●	●
SOUL CAFÉ	AE MC V	●	
KÁRPÁTIA	AE DC MC V JCB	●	■
VÖRÖS ÉS FEHÉR	MC V	●	
MÚZEUM	MC V	●	■
SZÁZÉVES	AE DC MC V	●	■

Price categories for a three-course meal for one with half a bottle of wine and including service:
(HUF) under 3,000 HUF
(HUF)(HUF) 3,000–4,000 HUF
(HUF)(HUF)(HUF) 4,000–5,000 HUF
(HUF)(HUF)(HUF)(HUF) 5,000–6,000 HUF
(HUF)(HUF)(HUF)(HUF)(HUF) Over 6,000 HUF.

CREDIT CARDS
Indicates which credit cards are accepted: AE American Express; DC Diners Club; MC Master Card/Access; V Visa; JCB Japanese Credit Bureau.

GOOD WINE LIST
Denotes a wide selection of good wines.

HUNGARIAN SPECIALITIES
Typical Hungarian fare is served.

ATTRACTIVE LOCATION
Restaurant can be found in an unusual or historic setting, or has an attractive view.

	CREDIT CARDS	GOOD WINE LIST	HUNGARIAN SPECIALITIES	ATTRACTIVE LOCATION

AROUND VÁROSLIGET

BAROSS ÉTTEREM (HUF)(HUF)
Baross tér 11/A. **Map** 8 D2. ☎ 343 62 38.
Beautifully restored restaurant in the late 19th-century Eastern Railway Station, Keleti pu (*see p226*). Good value for the ambiance. Live piano music in the evenings. V ♫
— DC MC V — — ■ —

MILLENNIUM RESTAURANT (HUF)(HUF)
Andrássy út 76. **Map** 5 B5. ☎ 354 05 75.
Well-prepared, Hungarian old-style food with some international dishes. Good value lunch specials. Frequented by those who enjoy a relaxed, nostalgic atmosphere. V 🍽 ♫ *Thu, Fri. Sat.* 🍴 lunch.
— MC V — — ■ —

BAGOLYVÁR ÉTTEREM. (HUF)(HUF)(HUF)
Állatkerti út 2. **Map** 5 C3. ☎ 468 31 10.
The restaurant's name means "Owl's Castle" and it offers home-style cooking of a high standard – the chef and waiting staff are all female. A cimbalom player provides music in the evenings. V 🍽 ♫ 🍴
— AE DC MC V JCB — — ■ ●

1894 BORVENDÉGLŐ (HUF)(HUF)(HUF)(HUF)
Állatkerti út 2. **Map** 5 C3. ☎ 468 40 44.
A stunning choice of over 100 Hungarian wines in this cellar restaurant, where dishes are prepared by the same kitchen as Gundel Étterem (though at lower prices) with an emphasis on quality and Hungarian specialities.
● *Sun, Mon, lunch Tue–Sat.* V 🍴 ★
— AE DC MC V JCB ● — ■ ●

PREMIER RESTAURANT (HUF)(HUF)(HUF)(HUF)
Andrássy út 101. **Map** 5 B4. ☎ 342 17 68.
International cuisine including Hungarian specialities in an elegant restaurant in the villa of the Journalists' Union. Daily specials at lunchtime. The terrace in good weather is especially appealing. V 🍽
— AE MC V — ● — ■ ●

RESTAURANT "MOSAIC CAFÉ" (HUF)(HUF)(HUF)(HUF)
Andrássy út 111. **Map** 5 C4. ☎ 462 21 89.
Mediterranean cuisine on the menu, which also offers a good selection of Hungarian dishes. Cosy setting with an attractive garden in a recently renovated building of the inter-war period, now a hotel. V 🍽 ♫ 🍴 *lunch Mon–Fri.*
— AE DC MC V ● — ■ ●

GUNDEL ÉTTEREM. (HUF)(HUF)(HUF)(HUF)(HUF)
Állatkerti út 2. **Map** 5 C3. ☎ 468 40 40.
Hungary's most famous restaurant and no longer the most expensive. Innovative Hungarian and international cuisine, including goose liver prepared in many diferent ways. Gipsy music in the evenings. The Sunday brunch buffet is excellent value. Lovely gardens. V 🍽 ♫ 🍴 *Sun brunch, Jul–Aug lunch.* ★
— AE DC MC V JCB ● — ■ ●

FURTHER AFIELD

58-AS KISVENDÉGLŐ (HUF)
"Niche" Camping, Zugligeti út 101. ☎ 200 37 73.
Attractive, interesting location in a former tram terminal inside the campsite at the bottom of the *Libegő* (Chair lift). ● *Oct–Apr.*
— — — ■ ●

FENYŐGYÖNGYE VENDÉGLŐ (HUF)
Szépvölgyi út 155. ☎ 325 97 83.
Popular small restaurant in the Buda Hills offering traditional Hungarian fare made in a lighter, healthier way. Large garden area. Booking is a good idea. V 🍽 ★
— AE MC V JCB — — ■ ●

JÓKAI ÉTTEREM (HUF)
Hollós út 5. ☎ 395 36 58.
Relaxed restaurant in a 19th-century villa in the hills near the Svábhegy cog-rail station. Attentive service and well-prepared Hungarian dishes. Pleasant terrace in the summer. V 🍽
— — — ■ ●

KERÉK VENDÉGLŐ (HLF)
Bécsi út 103. [250 42 61.
An authentic Old Buda restaurant from the 1960s offering Hungarian cuisine to the music of an accordion player. The garden is also of a nostalgic character. Booking is advised. **V** 🖼 🎵
DC MC V ▪

MAKK HETES VENDÉGLŐ (HLF)
Németvölgyi út 56. [355 73 30.
Popular and friendly family-run restaurant with well-prepared, home-style Hungarian fare. A rare speciality is *borjúláb rántva* (calf foot fried in breadcrumbs). **V** 🖼
▪

SZÉP ILONA VENDÉGLŐ (HLF)
Budakeszi út 1–3. [275 13 92.
A long established pleasant restaurant offering Hungarian and international specialities. Good garden in summer. **V** 🖼
MC V ▪

VASAS CSALÁDI VENDÉGLŐ (HLF)
Pasaréti út 11–13. [212 87 77.
Popular restaurant with a relaxed and friendly atmosphere offering home-style cooking; a family restaurant with a good menu for children. Excellent value, three-course set lunch. Booking recommended, especially for lunch.
V 🖼 🍴 *lunch.* ★
AE MC V JCB ▪

BAJAI HALÁSZCSÁRDA (HLF)(HLF)
Hollós út 2. [275 52 45.
By the Svábhegy cog-rail stop. Traditional Hungarian dishes specializing in fresh river fish. A real treat is the Baja fish soup with a huge portion of carp fillets served on the side of the soup. **V** 🖼 🎵
AE DC MC V JCB ● ▪ ●

KÜLVÁROSI KÁVÉHÁZ (HLF)(HLF)
István út 26. [379 15 68.
A gem in the north Budapest district of Újpest. International cuisine with excellent Hungarian dishes, including a three-course *Betyárleves* (bone marrow on toast, golden soup with noodles and vegetables, beef cooked in soup). Reservation is essential. **V** 🖼 🎵 ★
AE DC MC V ● ▪

NÁNCSI NÉNI VENDÉGLŐJE (HLF)(HLF)
Ördögárok út 80. [397 27 42.
A wide choice of the restaurant's own interesting, home-style interpretation of traditional Hungarian dishes. Giant *túrógombóc* (curd cheese dumplings) is a favourite dessert. Booking essential, especially for the popular garden area in summer. **V** 🖼 ★
MC V ● ▪ ●

NEFRIT CHINESE RESTAURANT (HLF)(HLF)
Apor Vilmos tér 4. [213 90 39.
Cantonese and Sechaun specialties in this pleasant restaurant in an old villa. Tasty *dim sum* are on offer. **V** 🖼 🍴 *lunch Mon–Fri.*
AE MC V ●

ÖREGHALÁSZ ÉTTEREM (HLF)(HLF)
Árpád út 20. [390 44 02.
Homely atmosphere in this restaurant where fresh river fish is the speciality. It is worth trying any fish soup from the wide range on offer, though non-fish dishes are also available. Booking recommended. **V** 🎵 ★
AE DC MC V ●

KISBUDA GYÖNGYE ÉTTEREM (HLF)(HLF)(HLF)(HLF)
Kenyeres utca 34. [368 64 02.
This restaurant has a natural, old-time drawing-room atmosphere, where guests feel at home enjoying the excellent dishes of international and Hungarian cuisine to the soft music of a piano. Reservation recommended. ● *Sun.* **V** 🖼 🎵 🍴 ★
AE DC MC V ● ▪

KÉHLI VENDÉGLŐ (HLF)(HLF)(HLF)(HLF)(HLF)
Mókus utca 22. [250 42 41.
Excellent, long-forgotten tastes of old Pest and Buda offered in large portions. Established more than a century ago in Old Buda, this was the favourite place of Gyula Krúdy, the great Hungarian gourmet writer. Reservation recommended. **V** 🖼 🎵 ★
AE MC V JCB ● ▪

VADRÓZSA ÉTTEREM (HLF)(HLF)(HLF)(HLF)(HLF)
Pentelei Molnár utca 15. [326 58 17.
Exclusive and luxurious restaurant in a beautiful neo-Baroque villa run by one family for 30 years. Soft piano music in the evenings. Lovely gardens in the summer. **V** 🖼 🎵 *except Sun.*
AE DC MC V ● ▪ ●

For key to symbols *see p187*

Cafés, Wine Bars and Beer Houses

To sample the true atmosphere of Hungary, it is essential to visit the smaller eating and drinking establishments that are scattered across the city and into the suburbs. Behind even the most ordinary of buildings there could be hiding a timeless pocket of old Hungarian culture. Equally, bright neon and loud music signify the culture favoured by Budapest's contemporary youth. Between these extremes, visitors can also find a taste of 19th-century opulence in the old coffee houses and patisseries that were once at the heart of the city's life.

Cafés and Coffee Houses

Hungary has one of the oldest coffee-drinking traditions in Europe. Introduced to Hungary by the Turks during their occupation *(see pp26–7),* the coffee culture blossomed towards the end of the Habsburg era *(see pp32–3),* when there were almost 600 *kávéházes* in the city.

The 19th-century café scene was a hotbed of intellectual activity dominated by literary and artistic circles. The **New York Kávéház** *(see p129),* which opened in 1894, was for many years the centre of this creative scene; its walls adorned with frescoes painted by the leading artists of the day. At the former Café Pilvax the seeds of the national uprising of 1848-9 *(see pp30–31)* were first sown.

Today's café scene is much changed. Almost every luxurious *cukrászda* and *kávéház* has closed down, giving way to a new variety of coffee bar. *Eszpresszó* bars first appeared in the 1930s but were most popular in the 1960s. Much cheaper than their predecessors, they catered for teenagers with a taste for western culture. These have subsequently been replaced by more modern cafés, such as **Pierrot Café**.

There are many styles of coffee in Budapest. A *kávé* is an espresso with milk and sugar, and a *dupla* is a double espresso. French-style milky coffee is called a *tejeskávé*, while cappuccinos are often served with whipped cream or Viennese-style, without either chocolate or cinnamon. Order a *koffeinmentes* for a decaffeinated coffee.

Wine Bars

Wine and wine bars occupy a very different positon in the social hierarchy in Hungary than they do in, say, Britain or the United States. Whereas the latter regard wine drinking as something of a middle-class pursuit, it was considered a workers' pastime in Hungary. Despite the fact that young men are starting to adopt beer as their favoured drink, the old tradition of wine-drinking is still reflected today in the *borozó* in Budapest.

A *borozó* is generally an unglamorous, cheap wine cellar, where wine is served straight from the barrel and sold by the decilitre. Few places have tables and chairs. In the city centre there is the more stylish **Rondella Borozó**, where wine is drawn from the barrels and served in curious jugs with a tap at the bottom.

The Castle District is home to a range of *borozós*. The Hattyú, meaning "Swan", at No. 1 Hattyú utca, and the Várfok Borozó, at No. 9 Várfok utca are of the simple kind. At the other end of the spectrum there are places like the **Hilton Hotel** *(see p180)* which has a stylish wine bar located in an authentic medieval cellar. Such establishments tend to serve expensive, bottled wine rather than wine from a barrel.

Tokaji *(see p193)* also has quite a number of wine bars dedicated to it. Arguably, the best is found in **Tokaji Borozó**, located at No. 20 Andrássy út, where customers tend to drink standing up.

Beer Houses

In recent years, beer has become a very popular beverage in Hungary. It is beginning to take over from wine as the country's favorite drink. Driven by this fashion, many wine bars have now been turned into beer houses, called *sörözős.* Several new places have also opened, modelled on the German *bierstube* and the English pub. As a result of this, beer-drinking in Budapest is considered an aspirational pastime, and prices are much higher than in *borozós,* especially in popular tourist areas.

As well as Hungarian *világos* (light) and *barna* (dark) beers *(see p192),* it is now possible to get virtually all the major international brands. Beer is measured by the *korsó,* the equivalent of a pint, and the *pohár,* a smaller glass. *Sörözős* differ from *borozós* as they offer a variety of good and moderately priced snacks and hot dishes, including smoked knuckle. Another difference is that a *söröző* will serve wine, while a *borozó* would never serve beer.

Food and Customs

Wine bars, where people can pop in for a glass of wine or a spritzer *(see p193)* at any time of day, do not generally serve food. Occasionally, however, light snacks are available. Typically these consist of a slice of bread and dripping with raw onion, sprinkled with paprika, or *pogácsa,* a yeast pan-bread with crackling, cheese, caraway seeds or paprika. Wine bars with tables sometimes serve frankfurters or knuckle, but this is rare.

Contrary to most other European countries, it is not done to clink beer glasses together in Hungary. This seemingly innocent practice was adopted by the Austrians as they executed Hungarian generals after the uprising of 1848–9. Over a hundred and fifty years later, this gesture is still frowned upon.

DIRECTORY

CASTLE DISTRICT

Cafés

Pierrot
Fortuna utca 14.
Map 1 B4.
375 69 71.
11am–11pm daily.

Ruszwurm Cukrászda
Szentháromság utca 7.
Map 1 B4 (9 A2).
375 52 84.
10am–7pm daily.

Wine Bars

Fehér Galamb
Szentháromság utca 9–11.
Map 1 B4 (9 A2).
212 56 04.
noon–midnight daily.

Móri Borozó
Fiáth János utca 16.
Map 1 A3.
214 92 16.
2–11pm
Mon–Fri, 4–9pm
Sat & Sun.

Beer Houses

Budavári Fortuna Spaten
Hess András tér 4.
Map 1 B5.
375 61 75.
11am–midnight daily.

NORTH OF THE CASTLE

Wine Bars

Bástya Borozó
Székely utca 2–4.
Map 1 C4 (10 E2).
212 38 19.
10am–10pm daily.

Kékfrankos Borozó
Keleti Károly utca 4.
Map 1 A2.
212 53 86.
10am–9pm daily.

Pince Csárda
Török utca 1.
Map 1 B1.
212 45 08.
11am–10pm Mon–Fri.

Vincellér Borszaküzlet
Erőd utca 10.
Map 1 B3.
201 15 61.
10am–6pm Tue–Fri,
8pm–midnight Sat & Sun.

Beer Houses

Alagút Sörház
Alagút utca 4.
Map 1 B5 (9 A3).
212 37 64.
24 hours daily.

AROUND PARLIAMENT

Cafés

Anna Café
Váci utca 7.
Map 4 E1.
266 90 80.
8:30am–midnight daily.

Café Firenze
Szalay utca 5a.
Map 2 E3.
331 83 99.
9am–8pm daily.

Művész Cukrászda
Andrássy út 29.
Map 2 F4 (10 E2).
352 13 37.
9am–midnight daily.

Wine Bars

Tokaji Borozó
Falk Miksa utca 32.
Map 2 D2.
269 31 43.
noon–10pm Mon–Fri,
4–11pm Sat.

Beer Houses

Tóth Kocsma
Falk Miksa utca 17.
Map 2 D2.
302 40 20.
11am–11pm daily.

CENTRAL PEST

Cafés

Auguszt Cukrászda
Kossuth Lajos utca 14–16.
Map 4 F1.
316 89 31.
10am–6pm Tue–Fri,
10am–2pm Sat.

Gerbeaud Cukrászda
Vörösmarty tér 7.
Map 2 E5.
429 90 00.
9am–9pm daily.

Grinzingi Borozó
Veres Pálné utca 10.
Map 4 F2 (10 E5).
317 46 24.
9am–1am Mon–Sat,
3pm–11pm Sun.

Károlyi "R" Café
Károlyi Mihály utca 19.
Map 4 F2 (10 E5).
266 02 44. 9am–
midnight Sat & Sun.

Café Mozart
Erzsébet körút 36.
Map 7 B2. 352 06 64.
9am–11pm Mon–Fri,
9am–10pm Sat & Sun.

New York Kávéház
Erzsébet körút 9–11.
Map 7 B2. 322 38 49.
9am–midnight daily.

Rondella Restaurant & Winehouse
Régiposta utca 4.
Map 4 E1 (10 D1).
483 08 29.
noon–midnight daily.

Söröző a Szent Jupáthoz
Retek utca 16.
Map 1 A3. 212 29 23.
noon–6am daily.

Villányi-Siklósi Borozó
Gerlóczy utca 13.
Map 4 F1 (10 E4).
267 02 41.
6am–11pm Mon–Fri.

Beer Houses

Aranyászok Sörház
József nádor tér 12.
Map 2 E5 (10 D4).
267 24 63.
11am–11pm daily.

Astoria Café Mirror
Kossoth Lajos utca 19.
Map 4 F1.
317 34 11.
7am–11pm daily.

Bécsi Söröző
Papnövelde utca 8.
Map 4 F2 (10 E5).
267 02 25.
10am–10pm Mon–
Fri, 10am–4pm Sat & Sun.

Beckett's Irish Pub
Bajcsy Zsilinszky út 72.
Map 2 E3 (10 E1).
311 10 33.
noon–1am Mon–Fri,
noon–3am Sat & Sun.

Fregatt Söröző
Molnár utca 26. **Map** 4 E2
(10 D5). 318 99 97.
11am–11pm daily.

Gösser Söröző
Régiposta utca 4. **Map** 4 E1
(10 D4). 318 26 08.
10am–midnight daily.

AROUND VÁROSLIGET

Cafés

Lukács Café
Andrássy út 70.
Map 5 A5. 302 87 47.
9am–8pm Mon–Fri,
10am–8pm Sat & Sun.

Beer Houses

Bajor Sörsátor
Kós Károly sétány.
Map 6 D3.
363 19 04.
10am–11pm daily.

FURTHER AFIELD

Wine Bars

Badacsonyi Borozó
Károlyi István utca 24 .
Map 4 F2. 269 32 07.
9am–12am Mon–Fri,
12pm–12am Sat.

John Bull Pub
Apáczai Csere János utca
17. **Map** 2 D5.
338 21 68.
noon–11pm Mon–Sat,
5–11pm Sun.

Vidocq Borozó
Lajos utca 98.
388 83 14.
noon–11pm Mon–Fri,
noon–midnight Sat & Sun.

SHOPS AND MARKETS

Shopping in Budapest has changed dramatically since the more spartan days of Communism. A huge variety of consumer goods, both foreign and home produced, are now available here. Major shopping streets include the pedestrianized and fashionable Váci utca (Váci Street, *see p127*) good for folk art and Zsolnay porcelain, and the less fashionable, but much cheaper

String of paprika peppers

Nagykörút, where locals come to do their shopping. For a more traditional shopping experience, don't miss a visit to some of Budapest's many markets. These range from stunning 19th-century food halls such as the Great Market Hall (Nagy Vásárcsarnok), to flea markets such as the huge and lively Ecseri Flea Market, for everything from bric-a-brac to furniture and antiques.

OPENING HOURS

Most shops in Budapest open from 9am to 5:30 or 6pm Monday to Friday, and from 9am to 1pm on Saturday. Department stores open at 10am, while green-grocers, bakeries and supermarkets are open from 7am until 8pm. Many shops stay open until 8 or 9pm on Thursday. Indoor markets and department stores open on Sunday, and most cafés sell milk and bread on Sunday morning. One result of the increase in private enterprise since 1989 is a large number of small shops which open 24 hours a day and sell groceries, cigarettes and alcohol.

Duna Plaza Shopping Centre on Váci út

HOW TO PAY

Credit cards and Euro-cheques can be used to pay for goods and services in many of the more touristy parts of Budapest. Outside these areas it is best to carry plenty of cash in Hungarian forints.

VAT EXEMPTION

The price of all goods in Hungary includes a value-added tax of 25% (ÁFA). With the exception of works of art and antiques, it is possible to claim back the value-added tax on anything costing more than 50,000 forints when you leave the country. First, present your goods at customs within 90 days of purchase to receive your customs certification and a refund claim form. You will need your sales receipt and currency exchange or credit card receipt, plus the customs certification, to apply for your refund within 183 days of your return home.

DEPARTMENT STORES AND MALLS

There are a number of department stores in the city, many housed in spectacular old buildings. The Secession-style **Luxus** on Vörösmarty tér offers three floors of smart men's and women's clothing, as well as accessories and perfumes. Nearby on Váci utca, the **Fontana** is a slightly down-

Traditional folk crafts, on sale around Váci utca

market version of the Luxus, with an excellent rooftop café.

More of a mall than a department store, the **Duna Plaza** on Váci út is smart but over-priced. It is equipped with an ice-skating rink, a video arcade and a bowling alley. The now refurbished **Corvin** on Blaha Lujzha tér is the closest you can get to the kitsch treasure troves of the Communist era. The old-fashioned payment system involves taking an invoice and paying at a booth before going to claim your purchase. Another store worth a look is **Skála Metro** on Nyugati tér opposite the railway station, and on Flórián tér in Óbuda.

The most exciting new mall is **Westend City Center**. Central Europe's largest, the centre has over 350 stores, including Armani, Benetton and Marks & Spencer, a 14-screen cinema and a food court.

Sausages on sale at the Central Market Hall

Delicate lace, an example of traditional Hungarian folk art

MARKETS

M ARKETS OF ALL sorts are an essential part of life in Budapest, and offer a delightfully traditional shopping experience to visitors. Perhaps the most spectacular are the five cavernous market halls which dot the city. All were built in the late 19th century and several are still used as markets. The three-level Great Market Hall (Nagy Vásárcsarnok) known officially as the **Central Market Hall** (Központi Vásárcsarnok) on

Fővám tér is the largest of all. More than 180 stalls display a huge variety of vegetables, fruit, meat and cheese, under a gleaming roof of brightly-coloured Zsolnay tiles. The market opens from 7am–6pm Mon–Fri and 7am–1pm Sat.

In addition to the covered market halls, there are open-air food markets in every Budapest neighbourhood. In many you will see country women in traditional costumes selling fruit and vegetables, as well as local cheeses, honey and sausages. Some of the best markets are at Lehel tér (district XIII), Bosnyák tér (XIV) and Fehérvári út (IX). Delicious hot sausages with mustard and fresh bread, or *lángos*, a flat bread served with cream or grated cheese, are traditional and widely available market snacks.

Beginning at 156 Nagykőrösi út in district XIX, is the **Ecseri Flea Market**. Outside, a maze of wooden tables is covered in Communist artifacts, second-hand clothes and all sorts of bric-a-brac, while from tiny cubicles inside the market, serious antique dealers sell porcelain, icons, silverware, jewellery and much more. It is necessary to obtain permission from the Museum of Applied Arts *(see pp136–7)* before you can take antiques out of the country. The flea market is open 7am–2pm Mon–Sat.

Another market well worth a visit is the extremely busy **Józsefvárosi Market**, situated close to Józsefváros pu on Kőbányai út and open 7am–6pm daily. Many of the traders here are Chinese, often with Roma assistants, using the Trans-Siberian railway to transport a huge variety of new goods from China, southeast Asia, the former Soviet Union and eastern Europe, all sold at knock-down prices. Look out for all sorts of entertaining and obvious southeast Asian fashion fakes, as well as electronic goods, Chinese silks, Russian caviar and vodka, and Stalinist memorabilia.

Marks & Spencer, which has now made it to Budapest

What to Buy in Budapest

Despite price rises since the return to a free-market economy, many Hungarian goods are still great bargains. Embroidered peasant blouses and wooden carvings make unique souvenirs, as does the distinctive porcelain produced at the world-famous Zsolnay and Herend factories. Cheap, good quality CDs and records are widely available, and Hungarian wines, salamis and other foodstuffs can be bought in the city's many lively markets. Clothes and shoes made to your specifications represent one of the city's most luxurious bargains.

FOLK ART

Hungarian folk culture is still alive and well in many parts of rural Hungary. You can buy textiles, ceramics and woodwork from flea markets (see p203) and from street vendors around Moszkva tér and Parliament (see pp108–9). Folk art shops such as **Folkart Centrum**, sell machine-made products, and, for genuine Transylvanian textiles there is **Judit Folklór**. For the cheapest authentic folk costumes, head to the second floor of the **Central Market Hall** (Nagy Vásárcsarnok).

ANTIQUES

Dominated by 18th- and 19th-century pieces in the Habsburg style, the Budapest antiques scene is concentrated in the Castle District, around Falk Miksa utca and on Váci utca (Váci Street, see p127). **Moró Antik** is a tiny shop specializing in 18th-century weapons, while the huge **Nagyházi Gallery** sells everything from jewellery to furniture. The **Ecseri Flea Market** (see p203) is also a good place for antiques.

PORCELAIN

There are two major porcelain manufacturors in Hungary, **Herend** and **Zsolnay**. Herend enjoys a reputation as the producer of the country's finest porcelain, while Zsolnay's brightly-glazed tiles can be seen on many of the city's notable buildings. Second-hand porcelain can be bought in antique shops and markets. Both companies have shops selling new pieces.

CLOTHES AND SHOES

Made-to-measure clothes and shoes, and ready made designer clothes offer some of the best bargains to be had by visitors to Budapest. With a luxurious array of velvets, silks and wools, **Merino** is both a fabric shop and a workshop, where you can choose your fabric and have it made up either here or by a local designer, most of whom are happy to oblige for a fairly modest fee. For more classic clothes, the highly-respected **Greti** is the oldest of the city's design houses, making elegant and beautifully tailored clothes for women. Shoemaker's in Budapest tend to make only men's shoes. **Vass** will make you a one-off pair of dress shoes in about a month. They cost around 50,000 Hungarian forints.

FOOD AND WINE

Food and wine in Hungary are great value and make excellent souvenirs for you to take home after your stay. Sausage is a national passion and can be bought in shops and markets all over the city. Some of the most popular types include spicy sausages from Debrecen, smoked sausages from Gyulai and a whole range of world-famous salamis. Also worth bringing home are dried mushrooms, paté de foie gras, a string of paprika or some fresh sheep's cheese. All these can be bought in Budapest's markets and in major supermarkets like **Pick**. Hungary's national beverage is wine (see pp192–3) and there is various top-quality bottles to look out for. These include fine desert wines from the Tokaji region, Muscats from Kiskunhalas on the central plain and Chardonnays from Mátraalja. Also popular are the herbal liqueur Unicum, and the strong, fiery pálinka, which is made from plums, cherries or apricots. Wines and spirits are available in supermarkets and in specialist shops such as **Wine City**, **Borház** and the **House of Hungarian Wines**.

MUSIC

Hungary's rich folk and classical music traditions make low-priced CDs, tapes and vinyl a tempting purchase in Budapest. For Hungarian folk music, from traditional Roma (Gypsy) music to recordings of village folk music, the old-style **Rózsavölgyi Zeneműbolt** is a good choice. In nearby Dob utca, **Concerto Records** offers a selection of new and second-hand vinyl and CDs, specializing in classical and opera, with some jazz, folk and funk. The state label, **Hungaroton**, has a shop in Rottenbiller utca that sells a wide range of classical music as well as some pop.

BOOKS

For illustrated books and English-language guide-books, try the **Litea Bookstore and Café**, where you can brouse through the books while enjoying coffee and cakes at tables set among the shelves. The large **Studium Libri** stocks many books in English. A wide range of English-language newspapers, magazines and novels are available at **Bestsellers**. **Írók Boltja** sells art books and some English-language books, while **Pendragon** stocks a varied assortment of fiction in English. One of the best places for maps and English-language guide books is **Párizsi Udvar**. **Librotrade-Kodex** stocks books in English, French and German. For antique books, etchings and maps a good place to try is **Központi Antikvárium**.

DIRECTORY

DEPARTMENT STORES

Corvin
Blaha Lujza tér 1.
Map 7 B3.
338 41 60.

Duna Plaza
Váci út 178.
465 16 66.

Fontana
Váci utca 16.
Map 4 E1 (10 D4).
266 64 00.

Luxus
Vörösmarty tér 3.
Map 2 E5 (10 D3).
318 35 50.

Westend City Center
Váci út 1–3.
Map 2 F2.
374 65 78.

MARKETS

Central Market Hall (Központi Vásárcsarnok)
Vámház Körút 13 (Fővam tér).
Map 4 F3.
⬜ 6am–5pm Mon, 6am–6pm Tue–Fri, 6am–2pm Sat.

Ecseri Flea Market
Nagykőrösi út 156.
282 95 63.

Fehérvári út Market
Fehérvári út 20.
Map 4 D5.

Fény utca Market
Mammut Shopping Centre, near Moszkva tér.
Map 1 A3.

Józsefvárosi Market
Kőbányai út.
Map 8 F4.

Lehel tér Market
Lehel tér.
Map 2 F1.

FOLK ART

Folkart Centrum
Váci utca 14.
Map 4 E1 (10 D3).
318 58 40.

Judit Folklór
Váci utca 23.
Map 4 E1 (10 D3).
212 76 40.

ANTIQUES

Moró Antik
Falk Miksa utca 13.
Map 2 D2.
311 08 14.

Nagyházi Gallery
Balaton utca 8.
Map 2 D2.
475 60 00.

PORCELAIN

Herend Shops
József Nádor tér 11.
Map 2 E5 (10 D3).
317 26 22.

Szentháromság utca 5.
255 10 50.

Kigyó utca 5.
Map 4 E1 (10 D4).
318 34 39.

Zsolnay Shops
Kigyó utca 2.
Map 4 E1 (10 D4).
318 37 12.

Váci utca 19–21.
Map 2F1 (5 A2).
266 63 05.

CLOTHES AND SHOES

Greti
Bárczy István utca 3.
Map 2 E5 (10 D3).
317 85 00.

Merino
Petőfi Sandór utca 20.
Map 4 E1.
318 44 78.

Vass Cipőlt
Haris köz 2.
Map 4 E1.
318 28 75.

FOOD AND DRINK

Borház
Jókai tér 7.
Map 2 F3 (10 F1).
353 48 49.

La Boutique des Vins
József Attila utca 12.
Map 2 E5 (10 D3).
317 59 19.

Coop Rt
Margit körút 6.
Map 1 A3.
212 54 07.

Rákóczi út 50.
Map 7 B3 (10 F4).
322 00 69.

House of Hungarian Wines
Szentháromság ter 6.
Map 9 A2.
212 10 32.

Pick
Kossuth Lajos tér 9.
Map 2 D3 (9 C1).
331 77 83.

Wine City
Párizsi utca 1.
Map 4 E1 (10 D4).
266 24 46.

MUSIC

Concerto Records
Dob utca 33.
Map 2 F5 (10 F3).
268 96 31.

Hungaroton Records
Rottenbiller utca 47.
Map 7 C1.
322 88 39.

Liszt Ferenc Zeneműboltja
Andrássy út 45.
Map 2 F5 (10 E2).
322 40 91.

Rózsavölgyi Zeneműbolt
Szervita tér 5.
Map 4 E1 (10 D4).
318 35 00.

BOOKS

Bestsellers
Október 6 utca 11.
Map 2 E4 (10 D2).
312 12 95.

Írók Boltja
Andrássy út 45.
Map 2 F4 (10 E2).
322 16 45.

Központi Antikvárium
Múzeum Körút 13–15.
Map 4 F1 (10 E4).
317 35 14.

Librotrade-Kodex
Honvéd utca 5.
Map 7 C3.
353 08 94.

Litea Bookstore and Café
Hess András tér 4.
Map 1 B4 (9 A2).
375 69 87.

Párizsi Udvar
Petőfi Sándor utca 2.
Map 4 E1 (10 E4).
235 03 79.

Pendragon
Pozsonyi út 21–23.
Map 2 F1.
340 44 26.

Studium Libri
Váci utca (main pedestrian precinct).
Map 4 E1 (10 D4).
318 58 60.

ENTERTAINMENT IN BUDAPEST

Budapest has been known as a city of entertainment since the late 19th century, when people would travel here from Vienna in search of a good time. Its buzzing nightclubs were frequented for their electric atmosphere and the beautiful girls that danced the spirited *csárdás* and the cancan. Nowhere else did fiddlers play such heartrending music or were the gambling casinos witness to such staggering losses as in Budapest. Between the wars the city was as famous for its glittering society balls as for its libertine delights. The half-century of Communist rule dampened the revelry, but since 1990 the Budapest music scene has flourished and theatres, cabarets, festivals, cinemas and discotheques are all buzzing. Above all, the renowned nightclubs have risen convincingly from their ashes.

ENTERTAINMENT HIGHLIGHTS

Budapest has two opera houses, an orchestral concert hall at the **Franz Liszt Academy of Music** *(see p208)*, several other concert halls, an operetta theatre, numerous cabarets and more than 50 theatres, including the fringe. Among them is the **Merlin Theatre** *(see p209)*, which performs only in English.

The greatest concentration of theatres is in district V, in Nagymező utca, which has been nicknamed "Budapest's Broadway". Along this 100-m (328-ft) stretch there are two theatres, the **Operetta Theatre** *(see p208)*, the satirical cabaret **Mikroszkóp Színpad** *(see p209)*, reputed to be the best in Hungary, and the **Moulin Rouge** *(see p209)* revue theatre. Film lovers are also spoilt for choice, as Budapest boasts a large number of cinemas.

Városliget *(see pp142–3)* offers numerous attractions,

Lavishly staged opera at the State Opera House *(see p208)*

including a permanent circus, funfair and zoo, complete with a number of small bars and beer tents in the summer.

The youth entertainment centre, **Petőfi Csarnok** *(see p209)*, stages rock concerts and hosts the largest discotheque in town. The renovated **Budapest Arena** has a capacity of 12,000, and stages a range of cultural events. Casinos and striptease clubs are the latest addition to the city's nightlife. Budapest also has its own red-light district, whose activities, although illegal, form part of a long-standing tradition.

PRACTICAL INFORMATION

There are two monthly cultural bulletins for tourists in different languages; the *Programme* contains information in English and German, while the *Budapest Panorama* is in five languages (English, German, Italian, Russian and French). Both bulletins are free and can be found in hotels and tourist information centres. They also include free-entry coupons to some casinos and nightclubs.

The *Programme* gives full information on cultural events and entertainments being held throughout the whole of Hungary, while *Budapest Panorama* informs the reader only about what is happening in Budapest. Pamphlets and bulletins are often issued in connection with festivals and other special events, and it is worth keeping an eye out for the poster pillars throughout the town. The Saturday editions of all newspapers carry a calendar of events, but only in Hungarian. There is a growing number of useful websites *(see p215)*.

CASINOS

Budapest has several casinos. Given their relatively recent reappearance, it is interesting that most of them occupy historical buildings next to smart hotels. Players can try their hand at roulette, Black Jack, poker and the wheel of fortune at any one of them.

Entrance to a popular casino, at No. 13 Deák utca

Bear in mind that only the **Las Vegas Casino** does not require you to wear evening dress.

CASINO ADDRESSES

Casino Tropicana
Vigadó utca 2. **[** 266 30 62.
Casino Várkert
Ybl Miklós tér 9. **[** 202 42 44.
Las Vegas Casino
(Hyatt Regency Hotel)
Roosevelt tér 2. **[** 266 20 81.

BUYING TICKETS

Tickets for all plays and concerts can be purchased in advance, either at the booking offices or by telephoning the venue in question direct. Addresses and telephone numbers can be found on pages 208–9. The most difficult to obtain are tickets to the **Franz Liszt Academy of Music** concerts, as these tend to be sold many days in advance. Similarly, seats at opera and operetta performances sell out quickly. The best way of securing a seat, particularly for summer performances, is via the **Central Booking Office**, which is located right in the centre of town at Vörösmarty tér 1. In Budapest, like anywhere else, you can risk it and try buying returned tickets at the last minute. A cheap alternative, but not one for the foot weary, is to buy a standing-room pass.

NIGHT LIFE

At the centre of Pest, particularly along Váci utca, numerous hawkers push pamphlets on passers-by, advertising the best places for striptease and erotic dancing. The experience can be quite unpleasant financially, as even a small beer and a packet of peanuts can set you back a fortune. There are now scores of such

Poster pillar

places to choose from. None of them are cheap, but some are quite smart and offer relatively modest prices. When choosing where to go, you should consider the places that advertise in the official information bulletins published by the tourist agencies. These include: Caligula, Dolce Vita, Tiamo bár and Aphrodite Night Club. In the last-named, scantily dressed girls dance behind the glass of the display window to lure in potential guests walking by.

CIRCUS, FUNFAIR AND ZOO

Budapest's **Great Capital Circus** *(see p211)* has been present in Városliget since 1878, but was given a permanent home only in 1971. The building is both comfortable and functional. Shows are held twice a day during the week, in the afternoon and evening, with additional morning performances on Saturdays and Sundays. It is possible to purchase tickets on the day, but it is better to book them in advance.

The **Funfair** *(see p211)* has an enormous merry-go-round, a scenic railway and scores of other diversions to entertain visitors. You have to pay separately for all the individual attractions, in addition to buying the entry pass, which can make it a relatively expensive outing. There is

Pelicans at the Zoo

enough to do here for many hours, from visiting the haunted house to playing one-arm bandits.

On the 12-ha area occupied by the **Zoo** *(see p211)*, you will find over 500 animal species, as well as hundreds of exotic trees and shrubs. There is also a palmhouse and a special enclosure for elephants and hippos.

JAZZ

Jazz was very late in reaching Hungary. The best known and revered Hungarian jazz band is the Benkó Dixieland Band, which during Spring Festivals *(see p58)* plays in various theatres and large halls. It is worth keeping an eye out around town for notices advertising their performances. The **Hades Restaurant** is a highly atmospheric venue where jazz is performed five nights a week. A large and invariably crowded club is the **Kögáz Jazz Klub** *(see p208)*, which is located at the University of Economics.

LATE-NIGHT TRANSPORT

Budapest's metro *(see p230)* runs until just after 11pm. Buses marked with black numbers and the letter E provide the night transport on busy routes. There are also night trams running on some routes, though their frequency varies from between one and three an hour. Night buses must be boarded through the front door, showing your ticket to the driver. On approaching the required stop, press the request button above the door. The HÉV train *(see p231)* that connects Budapest with its suburbs stops running at about 11:30pm.

The elegant interior of the Franz Liszt Music Academy *(see p208)*

Classical and Folk Music

THANKS TO THE GREAT composers such as Franz Liszt *(see p144)*, Béla Bartók and Zoltán Kodály *(see p144)*, as well as to the great wealth of its folk tradition, Hungary is famous throughout the world for its music. Hungarians always were, and remain to this day, a nation of music lovers and song-singers. In addition to the performances by leading Hungarian artists and ensembles, Budapest is frequently visited by revered musicians from around the world.

OPERA AND OPERETTA

THE STANDARD OF opera in Budapest is very high. Performances are at either the **State Opera House** *(see pp118–19)* or the **Erkel Theatre** *(see p151)*. At both there is a mainly classical repertoire, sung in Italian with Hungarian subtitles. The secondary focus is on Hungarian works, such as Ferenc Erkel's *Bánk Bán* and Béla Bartók's *Miraculous Mandarin*. During its season the **Operetta Theatre** *(see p115)* tends to stage Hungarian operettas by Imre Kálmán and Ferenc Lehár.

CLASSICAL MUSIC

THE LARGE HALL of the **Franz Liszt Academy of Music** *(see p129)* is the leading venue for classical music concerts. The city's largest concert hall is at the **Congress Centre** *(see p160)*.

It is worth keeping an eye out for the classical music concerts that are sometimes held in the domed hall of Parliament *(see pp108–9)*, where the acoustics are excellent.

Budapest also has a strong tradition of music festivals, including the Budapest Contemporary Music Weeks *(see p60)*.

SACRED MUSIC

CONCERTS OF organ music are held between March and December in the magnificent setting of the **Mátyás Church** *(see pp82–3)*. Among the composers whose works are featured, Bach is the most popular. **St Stephen's Basilica** *(see pp116–17)* serves sporadically as the venue for concerts of choral music. Lastly, between March and October the Musica Sacra Agency organizes concerts in the **Great Synagogue** *(see p134)*.

FOLK AND GYPSY MUSIC

PERFORMANCES OF folk and gypsy music are regularly held at the **Duna Palota** and the **Hungarian Heritage House**. Watch out for shows by the Hungarian State Song and Dance Ensemble and a Gypsy band that is part of the ensemble but also stages independent concerts. Players include top Gypsy artists and their music and dance shows are a magnificent display of Hungarian Romany folklore.

During July and August the city is visited by folk troupes from all over the country. Folklore evenings are held in the Casino-Valentine Restaurant *(see p196)* on Margaret Island.

From October to May, the city's dance houses rock to the sounds of fiddles and flutes. Some of the most renowned are **Fonó Budai Zeneház**, which stages peasant and Gypsy bands from Transylvania, the Kalamajka Dancehouse at the **Inner City Arts Centre** and the **Gyökér Klub-Vendéglő**.

DIRECTORY

TICKETS

Central Booking Office
Andrássy út 15.
Map 10 E2.
☎ 267 12 67.

Ticket Express
Andrássy út 18.
Map 10 E2.
☎ 312 00 00.

OPERA AND OPERETTA

Erkel Theatre
Köztársaság tér 30.
Map 7 C3. ☎ 333 05 40.

Operetta Theatre
Nagymező utca 17.
Map 2 F3.
☎ 472 20 30.

CLASSICAL MUSIC

Congress Centre
Jagelló út 1–3.
☎ 372 57 00.

Franz Liszt Academy
Liszt Ferenc tér 8.
Map 7 A1. ☎ 462 46 00.

Vigadó
Vigadó ter 2.
Map 4 D1 (10 D4).
☎ 318 46 19.

SACRED MUSIC

Great Synagogue
Dohány utca 2–8.
Map 7 A3. ☎ 342 89 49.

State Opera House
Andrássy út 22. **Map** 2 F4.
☎ 331 25 50.

Mátyás Church
Szentháromság tér 2.
Map 1 B4 (9 A2).
☎ 355 56 57.

St Stephen's Basilica
Szent István tér.
Map 2 E4 (10 D2).
☎ 403 53 70.

FOLK AND GYPSY MUSIC

Hungarian Heritage House
Corvin tér 8. **Map** 1 C4 (9 A2). ☎ 201 50 17.

Duna Palota
Zrínyi utca 5. **Map** 2 E5 (10 D2). ☎ 317 27 90.

Fonó Budai Zeneház
Sztregova utca 3.
Map 2 E5 (10 D3).
☎ 206 62 96.

Gyökér Klub-Vendéglő
Eötvös utca 46.
Map 2 F3 (10 E1).
☎ 302 40 59.

Inner City Arts Centre
Molnár utca 9.
Map 4 E2 (10 D5).
☎ 317 59 28.

JAZZ

Közgáz Jazz Klub
Kinizsi utca 2–6.
Map 7 A5.
☎ 217 30 33.

Hades Jazztaurant
Vörösmarty utca 31.
Map 5 A5.
☎ 352 15 03.

Theatre, Cinema and Nightclubs

Budapest has many theatres, which are worth visiting not only for their impressive repertoires, but also because they are invariably located in beautiful historic buildings. Cinemas show the latest films soon after their world premieres, although not many retain the original soundtrack. For late-night dancing the city has a wealth of popular clubs to choose from.

THEATRE

The first theatre to stage plays in Hungarian was the **National Dance Theatre** (see p73). Other established theatres include the **Madách Theatre**, **Nemzeti Theatre**, **Pesti Theatre** and **Lézerszínház**. Of particular interest to English speakers is the **Merlin Theatre**, which performs in English.

Budapest has over 30 drama and cabaret theatres. Among the most prestigious is the **József Katona Theatre**, which became famous following performances in Paris and London. Its repertoire includes Shakespeare and Gogol.

Another interesting theatre is the **Vígszínház**, meaning "comedy theatre", which specializes in musicals. During the summer memorable rock-operas are staged on Margaret Island. These shows are highly prized for their good music performed in a magnificent setting.

CINEMA

Many of Budapest's cinemas were built during the 1920s and 1930s and do not offer much in the way of luxury. But they are now being overtaken by modern multiplexes such as those in the shopping malls **Duna Plaza** and **Westend City Center**, and **Corvin Filmpalota**.

Apart from foreign films, which are usually subtitled in Hungarian, the cinemas also show native Hungarian films. The range covers both the latest releases and vintage films from a time of Hungarian cinematic glory, notably when Miklós Jancsó and István Szabó received international awards for directing. The Broadway cinema regularly shows these undubbed masterpieces of a bygone era. All cinema tickets can be bought in advance on the same day and some cinemas will also sell you tickets for the next day.

NIGHTCLUBS

Nightlife in Budapest is on its way to competing with that of other European capitals, and new clubs open daily. Among the most recent arrivals are **Dokk Jazz Bistro**, a huge, high-tech club set in a converted dry dock; **Tütü Tango**, offering a mix of live bands, hip DJs and drinking and dining; and **Complex**, in Szentendre (see p165) but worth seeking out for top-name DJs playing at Hungary's first "superclub". The first two are open daily, the latter from Thu–Sun only.

Older clubs are often centred around student venues. **Petőfi Csarnok**, a cavernous youth entertainment centre built in 1984 during the Communist era is a stage and disco complex used as a venue for local and international rock bands. **E-Klub** is open on Fridays and Saturdays and is always crowded with Technical University students. A really vibrant student club is the **Közgáz Pince Klub**, which is held in the huge hall of the University of Economics (see p138).

Budapest's chic set meet at the **Made Inn**, where the attractive patio and garden are full to bursting in summer. It boasts two dance floors and a room for live bands.

DIRECTORY

THEATRE

National Dance Theatre
Színház 1–3. **Map** 9 A3.
356 40 85.

József Katona Theatre
Petőfi Sándor utca 6.
Map 4 E1 (10 D4).
318 65 99.

Lézerszínház
Népliget, Planetárium.
263 08 71.

Madách Theatre
Erzsébet körút 29–33.
Map 7 A2. 322 20 15.

Merlin Theatre
Gerlóczy utca 4.
Map 4 F1 (10 E4).
317 93 38.

Mikroszkóp Színpad
Nagymező utca
22–24. **Map** 2 F3 (10 E1).
332 53 22.

Nemzeti Theatre
Bajor Gizi Park 1.
Map 7 B1.
476 68 00.

Pesti Theatre
Váci utca 9. **Map** 4 E1
(10 D4). 266 52 45.

Vígszínház
Pannónia utca 1.
Map 2 E1.
340 46 50.

CINEMA

Corvin Filmpalota
Corvin köz 1.
459 50 50.

Hollywood Multiplex Duna Plaza
Váci út 178. 467 42 67.

Palace West End
Váci út 1–3. **Map** 2 F2.
238 72 22.

NIGHTCLUBS

Dokk Jazz Bistro
Hajogyari Sziget 122.
535 27 47.

E-Klub
Népliget út 2.
263 16 14.

Complex
Rószá utca 8,
Szentendre.
936 77 19.

Közgáz Pince Klub
Fővám tér 8.
Map 4 F3.
215 43 59.

Made Inn
Andrássy út 112.
Map 7 A1.
311 34 37.

Petőfi Csarnok
Zichy Mihály utca 14.
Map 6 E4.
363 37 30.

Tütü Tango
Hajós utca 2. **Map** 2 F4.
321 27 15.

Sports

H UNGARIANS ARE FINE athletes, as is testified by their consistently outstanding performances at competitive events, such as the Olympic Games. Budapest's world-class sports facilities serve as venues for many of these international events, including European and World championships. Sporting opportunities for visitors to the city are both varied and accessible.

SPECTATOR SPORTS

M OST COMPETITIVE sporting events are held either in the magnificent **People's Stadium** (see p155), which seats 80,000 spectators, or in the modern, indoor **Budapest Aréna**.

Soccer remains the most popular spectator sport, although Hungarian fans can only look wistfully back to the time when their national side was highly successful. In the 1950s, for instance, Hungary beat England 6–3 at Wembley. League matches in Budapest attract big crowds. The atmosphere is particularly electric when local favourites Ferencváros, FTC, take to the pitch.

Two of the three great events regularly held in Budapest are the Welcom Marathon Hungary (see p58) and the Budapest Marathon. These are run on the last Sundays of April and September respectively. The third big sporting event of the year is the Hungarian Grand Prix (see p59), which takes place during August at the Mogyoród racing circuit.

Hungarians achieve impressive results in boxing, canoeing, swimming, water polo and fencing, which are all widely supported.

HORSE RACING AND RIDING

A S A NATION of former nomads, the Hungarians have retained a great love of horses. In Budapest this passion finds its expression in horse racing, which is enormously popular. A few hours spent at a racetrack can be a cheap and fun way of soaking up the local atmosphere. Near Keleti pu (see p227) is the Trotters' Racecourse, the **Ügetőpálya**.

Those wishing to be rather more energetic and ride themselves instead of watch horses, should contact the **National Riding School**, the **Petneházy School**, the **Kincsem Horsepark** or the **Budapest Riding Club**.

SPORTING ACTIVITIES

P RACTISING SPORT for fitness and pleasure is both cheap and popular in Budapest.

Strolling through the city's parks, particularly on Margaret Island, you will encounter scores of eager joggers, both young and not so young. The indoor and outdoor swimming pools are also full of regular visitors, who come here for an hour or so of healthy exercise. Particularly popular is the **Hajós Olympic Pool** on Margaret Island, which is named after Hungary's first Olympic gold winner for swimming, who was also the pool's architect. Busy open-air swimming options include **Komjádi Pool** and the neighbouring **Lukács Baths**, both of which can be enjoyed even in winter as the hot spring water creates a steamy atmosphere over the water's surface. For the hottest spa water in the city, head to the **Széchenyi Baths** (see p151), which is the largest bathing complex in Europe. However, the most atmospheric and beautiful baths are undoubtedly the 16th-century Turkish **Rudas Baths** (see p93).

Cycling is also gaining in popularity, particularly since the introduction of cycling lanes to the city's roads (see p228). If you want to play tennis, there are numerous courts available, but these tend to be monopolized by local Hungarians. Your best bet for a game is either to befriend a local tennis player, or to find a hotel that has its own court.

Despite the moderate climate, it is also possible to undertake winter sports in Budapest. From December until March the Városliget lake (see pp142–3) is turned into a skating ring and many people take to the ice. Sváb Hill (see p161) is generally snow-covered from December to March and has several ski runs and ski lifts.

DIRECTORY

STADIA

Budapest Aréna
Rákóczi út 42.
Map 10 F4.
(273 37 00.

People's Stadium
Stefánia út 3–5.
Map 6 F5.
(471 41 00.

HORSE RACING AND RIDING

Budapest Riding Club
Kerepesi út 7.
(313 52 10.

Kincsem Horsepark
2711 Tápiószentmárton.
(423 056.

National Riding School
Kerepesi út 7.
(210 26 61.

Petneházy School
Feketefej utca 2–4.
(397 50 48.

Ügetőpálya
Kerepest út 9–11.

SWIMMING POOLS

Komjádi Uszudo
Frankel Leó út 55.
Map 1 B1.
(212 27 50.

Lukács Baths
Frankel Leó utca 25–29.
Map 1 C1. (326 16 95.

Hajós Olympic Pool
Margitsziget. (340 49 46.

Rudas Baths
Döbrentei tér 9.
Map 4 D2. (356 13 22.

Széchenyi Baths
Allatkerti körút 11.
Map 6 D3. (363 32 10.

Children's Budapest

VISITING BUDAPEST can be great fun for children. There are several options in the way of energetic outdoor pursuits, including a funfair, a zoo and a variety of swimming venues. If the weather is poor then there are a number of historical monuments that will entertain and inform. Alternatively, there are two puppet theatres that cater specifically for younger audiences.

SIGHTSEEING WITH CHILDREN

THE BUSY centre of Pest is a difficult area in which to entertain children. However, the **Postal Museum**, set in the glittering opulence of a 19th-century mansion, is well worth a morning's visit.

Also of interest is the Royal Palace *(see pp70–71)* and the Castle District *(see pp68–85)* of Buda, where children can appreciate a sense of the city's history and tradition. Having visited the **Hungarian National Gallery** *(see pp72–5)* children usually enjoy seeing the palace courtyard with its fabulous *turul*, the giant bird that is so steeped in myths. The **Mátyás Fountain** *(see pp72–3)* is also worth a look. A must, of course, is the ride up and down Castle Hill by the funicular railway, the **Budavári Sikló** *(see p231)*.

Especially fun for children is the **Labyrinth of Budavár** in Lords' Street *(see p85)*, an underground exhibition of the town's early history that really appeals to a child's imagination. The **War Museum** will absorb those who like to see old weapons, armours and the mock-ups of battles.

RECREATION FACILITIES

THE MOST SUITABLE swimming complex for children is the **Palatinus Strand** *(see p172)* on Margaret Island. Not only does it have a number of pools with varying water temperatures, but there are also slides, artificial waves and other fun and games. Numerous nearby kiosks sell snacks, ice cream and fruit.

During the winter season take the children to the **Gellért Hotel and Baths Complex** *(see pp90–91)* instead. The large swimming pool here has artificial waves and the paddling pool's very warm water is particularly enjoyed by toddlers.

Children and adults alike love the **Zoo** *(see pp150–51)*, which is one of the largest in Europe. Attractions of particular interest for children include the large sea-water aquarium, a terrarium with splendid specimens of snakes and an impressive aviary.

The **Great Capital Circus** is an ideal way to keep youngsters occupied. Shows, which often star international artists, are held daily.

Children will also spend many happy hours at the

Vidám Park funfair *(see p151)* at Városliget, riding on the merry-go-rounds or the railway and zooming down the slides. Older children will enjoy testing their marksmanship in the shooting galleries and their luck at the game machines.

INDOOR ATTRACTIONS

THERE ARE TWO puppet theatres in Budapest, which in addition to Hungarian classics also stage such favourites as *The Jungle Book*, *Cinderella* and *Snow White*.

A great attraction, and not only for children, is the **Planetárium**, situated in the People's Park *(see p156)*. Opened in 1977, it has been equipped with Zeiss Jena optical systems, thereby creating a fascinating laser world.

SCENIC RAILWAYS

CHILDREN LOVE the trip up into the Buda Hills *(see p161)*. The first leg is a cogwheel railway up to the top of Széchenyi Hill. The track is 3,730 m (12,240 ft) long and climbs to 315 m (1,035 ft).

At the top of the hill is a playground and the first stop of the Children's Railway, on which all the signalmen and conductors are children. The train follows the ridge of the Buda Hills, taking children to the Hűvös Valley.

The Libegő chair lift has run to the top of János Hill since 1970. Its lower station is located in Zugliget, which can be reached by taking bus 158 from Moszkva tér.

DIRECTORY	**War Museum**	**Great Capital Circus**	**INDOOR ATTRACTIONS**
MUSEUMS	Kapisztrán tér 2–4. **Map** 1 A4. **(** *356 95 22.*	Állatkerti körut 7. **Map** 5 C3. **(** *343 83 00.*	**Budsapest Bábszínház** Andrássy út 69. **Map** 5 A5 (10 E2). **(** *321 52 00.*
Hungarian National Gallery Szent György tér 2. **Map** 3 C5. **(** *375 75 33.*	**RECREATION FACILITIES**		
Labyrinth of Budavár Úri utca 9. **Map** 1 A4 (9 A2). **(** *212 02 07.*	**Vidám Park** Állatkerti körut 14–16. **Map** 5 C3. **(** *363 83 10.*	**Palatinus Strand** Margitsziget. **(** *340 45 05.*	**Kolibri Színház** Jókai tér 10. **Map** 2 F3 (10 F1). **(** *311 08 70.*
Postal Museum Andrássy út 3. **Map** 2 F4 (10 E2). **(** *342 69 97.*	**Gellért Hotel and Baths Complex** Kelenhegyi út 4–6. **Map** 3 C3. **(** *466 61 66.*	**Zoo** Állatkerti körút 6–12. **Map** 5 C3. **(** *363 37 97.*	**Planetárium** Népliget. **(** *263 18 11.*

SURVIVAL
GUIDE

PRACTICAL INFORMATION

BUDAPEST was always famous for its hospitality and the Hungarians, particularly in recent years, have been emphasizing tourism as an important part of the national economy. The biggest problem in its development is the formidable barrier posed by the Hungarian language, which hinders access to information. The Hungarians are therefore trying hard to learn foreign languages.

Tourist information sign

In all tourist offices, bigger hotels and most restaurants either English or German is spoken. Information brochures and tourist pamphlets are now published in several languages. It is difficult to get lost in Budapest as the road sign system is easy to follow. The historic monuments in the city centre are best visited on foot, while the more distant sights can be easily reached by public transport *(see pp228–33)*.

TOURIST INFORMATION

PRIOR TO YOUR arrival in Budapest it is worthwhile getting in touch with your nearest **Hungarian National Tourist Office**, who can supply useful information and put you in touch with reputable tour operators.

Many agencies specialize in organizing individual trips and tours to Hungary including **Travellers Cities Ltd**, **Kirker Holidays** and **Page & Moy**. They can all provide you with detailed information on meals and accommodation and help you to make reservations.

Official tourist information centres (Tourinform) in Budapest can be found at a number of locations, including **Liszt Ferenc Square**, **Nyugati Pu**, **Vörösmarty tér**, **Sütő utca** and at **Budaörs** in the AGIP petrol station, just by the M1 and M7 motorways. General tourist information in a variety of languages is provided by these centres. You can also buy a Budapest Card *(see p216)*, as well as souvenirs, guide books and maps.

Brown tourist signs can be found at all the important points of the city to help visitors find their way around.

ADVICE FOR VISITORS

BUDAPEST HAS a favourable climate year round, but the best time to visit is between March and the end of June, and from the middle of August until October. July is generally very hot.

Various festivals and cultural programmes take place throughout the year. The end of the year is a fun time, when visitors can experience the Christmas Fair and the New Year's Eve street party.

On arriving in Budapest it is a good idea to get hold of the foreign language information booklets. The *Budapest Panorama*, the *Budapest Programme Visitor's Guide*, the *Budapest Guide* and the *Dining Guide* each contain a calendar of cultural and tourist events for the month. They are free and are easily available from tourist centres and hotel reception desks. They all contain maps of Budapest, and free city maps are also published by the Tourism Office of Budapest.

It is also worth investing in the Budapest Card *(see p216)*, which, as well as entitling cardholders to unlimited use of public transport and free admission to museums, gives reductions on the price of tickets for various cultural events.

OPENING HOURS

MUSEUMS AND galleries are open all year round. Opening times for specific venues are given under their individual entries.

One of several tourist information offices in Budapest

Horses on a tourist carriage

As a general rule, the winter season from November until March sees museums offering shorter opening hours. In the summer, from April until October, they tend to stay open a couple of hours longer, typically from 10am until 6pm. Museums remain closed on Monday, except for the National Jewish Museum (*see p134*), which is closed on Saturday instead. Most museums, both state and private tend to charge an entrance fee, though it is worth checking to see if there are any applicable discounts.

Shopping centres in Budapest are open each day of the week, grocery stores are open from 7am to 7pm and other shops from 10am until 6pm during the week. On Saturdays shops close at 1pm, while on Sundays some department stores and market halls are open, often until 2pm. Detailed information on the opening hours of particular shops and markets can be found on pages 202–5 of this guide. Hungarians tend to take lunch early, between noon and 1pm.

ENTRY TICKETS

Tickets to museums and historical monuments can be purchased on the spot.

Average prices vary from 400 to 1,000 forints per person, but some can be as much as 2,000 forints. Nevertheless, students and school children are always entitled to reductions. Opera, concert and other tickets can be bought at the Central Booking Office (*see p208*). Theatre and opera tickets are also sold at individual box offices, either for shows on the same day or in advance. Ticket prices can vary from 1,000 to 2,000 forints, depending on the show

ETIQUETTE

Casual clothes are often worn to the theatre, particularly during summer. By comparison classical music concerts and operas are much smarter affairs and even tourists will feel more comfortable wearing evening dress. Traditionally, Hungarians attach great importance to being properly dressed when going to an opera or concert hall.

DIRECTORY

TOURIST OFFICES IN BUDAPEST

American Express
1052 Budapest, Deák Ferenc utca 10.
Map 4 E1 (10 D4).
235 43 00.
FAX 235 43 03.

IBUSZ Travel Agency
1053 Budapest, Ferenciek tere 10.
Map 4 F1 (10 E4).
318 68 66.
FAX 337 03 26.

Tourinform Buda Castle
1016 Budapest, Szentháromság tér.
Map 9 A2.
488 04 75.
FAX 488 04 74.

Tourinform Budaörs
2040 Budaörs, AGIP Complex.
417 518.
FAX 417 518.

Tourinform Call Centre
438 80 80.

Tourinform Hotline
550 044 (from abroad); 06 80 66 00 44 (from Hungary).

Tourinform Liszt Ferenc Square
1061 Budapest, Liszt Ferenc tér 11.
Map 7 A1.
322 40 98.
FAX 342 93 90.

Tourinform Nyugati Pu
Left wing of main station.
Map 2 F3.
302 85 80.
FAX 302 85 80.

Tourinform Sütő Street
Deák tér / Sütő utca 2.
Map 10 D3.

Tourinform Vörösmarty Square
Vörösmarty tér / Vigado utca 6. **Map** 10 D3.

Vista Visitor Center
Paulay Ede utca 7–9.
Map 10 E3.
W www.vista.hu

TOURIST OFFICES ABROAD

United Kingdom
Hungarian National Tourist Office
Embassy of Hungary
46 Eaton Place
London SW1X 8AL.
020 7823 1032.

United States
Hungarian National Tourist Office
150 East 58th Street
33rd Floor New York
NY 10155-3398
212 355 0240.

TRAVEL AGENTS ABROAD

Kirker Holidays
3 New Concordia Wharf,
Mill St, London SE1 2BB,
United Kingdom.

020 7231 3333.
@ cities@ kirkes holidays.com

Page & Moy
56 Burleysway, Abbey House, Leicester LE1 9GZ, United Kingdom.
@ service@page-moy.co.uk

Travellers Cities Ltd.
203 Main Road, Biggin Hill, Westerham TM1 63JU, United Kingdom.
5954 0700.
@ travel@ travellerscities.com

USEFUL WEBSITES

Hungarian National Tourist Office
www.hungarytourism.hu

Tourinform
www.tourinform.hu

Tourism Office of Budapest
www.budapestinfo.hu

Additional Information

Tourists in Szentháromság tér

PASSPORT AND CUSTOMS REGULATIONS

CITIZENS OF THE US, Canada, and the European Union need only a valid passport to visit Hungary for up to 90 days. Visitors from other countries require a visa which can be obtained from any Hungarian embassy. All visitors should check their requirements prior to travelling. Only visitors on long-term visas can apply for and obtain a residency permit.

The loss or theft of a passport should be reported to the appropriate consulate or embassy as soon as possible. Carry your passport or a copy of it in order to identify yourself when needed. For safety reasons keep a photocopy in your hotel. As well as personal belongings, visitors can bring the following items into the country; 200 cigarettes, 2 litres of wine, 1 litre of liqueur, 1 kilogram each of coffee, tea and cocoa and an unlimited quantity of beer.

Signs showing facilitites and major tourist attractions in Budapest

TAX-FREE GOODS

FOREIGN TOURISTS can apply for the refund of VAT (ÁFA in Hungarian) charged on goods purchased in Hungary. To reclaim it, visitors need to present the ÁFA invoice at the border. This only applies to sums in excess of 50,000 Hungarian forints, and does not apply to works of art. The exported goods must be new and not previously used in Hungary. They must also have been bought within the last 90 days.

BUDAPEST CARD

THIS SPLENDID new facility was introduced in 1997, designed for tourists visiting the city for two or three days. The Budapest Card entitles a visitor, together with one child under 14, to use all city transport free of charge, as well as providing free entry to 60 museums, the zoo and the funfair. It also entitles the holder to a 50 per cent discount on all guided tours of the city organized by Tourinform, a 10 to 20 per cent discount on tickets to selected swimming centres and cultural events, and a 10 to 20 per cent discount in recommended restaurants. The card costs about 4,000 Hungarian forints for two days and 5,000 forints for three days.

Cards can be purchased at tourist offices, hotel reception desks, museums and at the ticket offices of the majority of the larger metro stations. Enclosed with the card is an information pamphlet, in four languages, listing its benefits.

Budapest Card

PRESS, RADIO AND TV

IN BUDAPEST all the world's top newspapers and magazines are easily accessible at hotels. A number of the larger news stands maintain a constant stock of international newspapers and magazines. The largest number of these can be found at the underpasses near Nyugati and Keleti stations. As well as these, there are also various shops around town which specialize in English-language newspapers, books and maps *(see pp204–5)*.

Bear in mind that the foreign daily newspapers on sale tend to be yesterday's editions, but even so they often sell out by lunchtime. For English-speaking tourists there are also quite a few magazines, including *Budapest in your Pocket*, *The Budapest Sun* and *NLG*. These provide the most comprehensive information on local and, in some cases, world events as well as full entertainment guides.

In addition to the state and independent Hungarian television channels, most of the larger hotels offer at least one channel in English and usually more than one channel in German. All the top hotels tend to offer various satellite stations.

English language magazines, published in Budapest

DISABLED TRAVELLERS

BUDAPEST IS BECOMING more accessible for disabled visitors, although it is best to call ahead to the sights or obtain specialist information prior to your visit to ensure it is as hassle free as possible. Many buses are now equipped for boarding and some metro stations have special lifts. For advice and help, contact the **Hungarian Disabled Association**. Many museums and monuments present difficulties for the disabled, although increasingly they are being renovated to be wheelchair-friendly.

BUDAPEST TIME

BUDAPEST USES Central European time, in keeping with the rest of mainland Europe, which means it is two hours ahead of Greenwich Mean Time (GMT) in the summer and one hour ahead in the winter.

Examples of the winter time differences between Budapest and other major cities are as follows: London: -1 hour; New York: -6 hours; Dallas: -7 hours; Los Angeles: -9 hours; Perth: +7 hours; Sydney: +9 hours; Auckland: +11 hours; Tokyo: +8 hours.

PUBLIC TOILETS

THERE ARE NOT many public toilets in Budapest. The cubicle type is found in some squares and parks and these are usually free.

In cafés and restaurants there are toilet attendants and the price for using the facility is clearly displayed. In wine bars and beer houses toilets tend to be free, which is all too often reflected in their poor level of cleanliness.

There are no public toilets in metro stations, except for Batthyány tér. Apart

Sign for the ladies' toilet

Sign for the gentlemen's toilet

from the generally understood picture symbols, the toilets are signed in Hungarian: *Hölgyek* (ladies) and *Urak* (gentlemen), or *Nők* (women) and *Férfiak* (men).

ELECTRICAL AND GAS APPLIANCES

HUNGARIAN ELECTRICITY supply is 220 V and the plugs needed are the standard continental type. Adapters can be purchased in most countries. Since sockets are generally earthed, the most commonly used plugs are the flat type.

Hungarian gas cookers are equipped with a bimetal safety device, which means that after lighting the knob should be held down until the burner warms up. This is an effective means of preventing the escape of any unlit gas.

Hungarian plug with two pins

DIRECTORY

FOREIGN EMBASSIES AND CONSULATES IN BUDAPEST

Australia
Királyhágó tér 8–9.
[C] 457 9777.
[FAX] 201 97 92.
[W] www.ausembbp.hu

Canada
Budakeszi út 32.
[C] 392 33 60.
[FAX] 392 33 90.

New Zealand
Teréz körút 38.
Map 2 F3.
[C] 428 2208.
[FAX] 428 2208.

South Africa
Gárdonyi Géza utca 17.
[C] 392 09 99.
[FAX] 200 72 77.
[@] dha@axelero.hu
[W] www.sa-embassy.hu

United Kingdom
Harmincad utca 6.
Map 2 E5.
[C] 266 28 88.
[FAX] 266 09 07.
[@] info@britemb.hu
[W] www.britishembassy.gov.uk

United States
Szabadság tér 12.
Map 2 E4. [C] 475 44 00.
[FAX] 374 00 34.
[@] usconsular.budapest@state.gov
[W] www.usembassy.hu

HUNGARIAN EMBASSIES

United Kingdom
35 Eaton Place,
London SW1X 8BY.
[C] 020 7235 5218.
[W] www.huemblon.org.uk

United States
3910 Shoemakers Street NW, Washington DC, 20008.
[C] 202 364 8218.
[W] www.huemblwas.org

INTERNATIONAL NEWSPAPERS

A Világsajtó Háza
V. Városház utca 3–5.
Map 10 E4. [C] 317 13 11. [○] 7am–7pm Mon–Fri, 7am–6pm Sat, 8am–4pm Sun

Bestsellers
V. Október 6 utca 11.
Map 10 D2.
[C] 317 12 95.
[○] 9am–6.30pm Mon–Fri, 10am–6pm Sat, 10am–4pm Sun

DISABLED TRAVELLERS

Hungarian Disabled Association
San Marco utca 76.
[C] 250 9013.
[FAX] 454 1144
[W] www.meosz.hu.

Security and Health

Police Symbol

BUDAPEST IS NOT JUST a beautiful city, it is also one with efficient and well-maintained services which help to ensure the safety and well-being of its residents. The public telephones generally work, the bus and tram stops display timetables and public transport is both clean and reliable. Nevertheless, as with all other central European countries, there are a growing number of negative social phenomena. Local people are increasingly complaining about rising crime rates, the plague of pickpockets and incidences of car theft. Visitors to Budapest will also be sadly aware of the growing numbers of homeless people living on the streets.

Police car

ADVICE TO VISITORS

DOCUMENTS AND money should be carried in a secure inside pocket or in a money belt. Traveller's cheques are widely accepted, so there is no need to carry much cash on you.

Money should be exchanged at a bank, your hotel or an exchange bureau, never on the black market. Do not leave valuables in your car.

There are three multistorey car parks in the city centre, at Nos. 4–6 Aranykéz utca, No. 20 Nyár utca and on Szervita tér. A lot of the larger hotels have an underground garage. Cars parked improperly may be clamped or towed away to a car park outside the centre. To find out where a car has been taken, call the **Removed Cars Information** line. On-the-spot fines of up to Ft2000 can also be imposed for parking offences.

Police badge

Pickpockets operate during rush hours, targeting people in crowded metro stations, buses and shopping centres. They also operate at all the main tourist sights, and on nearby public transport. When working as a group, they may surround unsuspecting tourists and jostle or distract them. For this reason it is a good idea to have a photocopy of your passport and your travel insurance. If a passport is lost call the police in Szalay utca 11–13

(373 10 00), where English is spoken. Once the appropriate police certificate is obtained, report the loss to your embassy *(see p217)*.

SECURITY

HUNGARIAN POLICE are frequently seen patrolling the streets on motorbikes, on foot or in cars. In addition, every district has its own police station. The Hungarian word for police is *rendőrség*. In the event of anything going missing, because of loss or theft, a report should be made immediately to a local police station. In the event of a lost passport, see the section under the heading *Advice to Visitors*.

All visitors should check their visa requirements prior to travelling. Australian tourists will need a visa, but Europeans and Americans can stay for three to six months without one. However, after one month make sure to check the registration requirements at a local police station. In reality, this applies mainly to tourists staying in private accommodation or with friends, since all hotels, hostels and pensions automatically register foreign guests. For more information, see the Hungarian Ministry of Foreign Affairs' website (www.mfa.gov.hu).

Tourists coming to Budapest by car are obliged to have the green insurance card, while those hiring a car need only present their driving licences. Hitchhiking, although not against the law, is not a recommended way of travelling in Hungary.

Women should not walk unaccompanied late at night in poorly lit areas and should avoid deserted streets. Rákóczi tér and Mátyás tér, in district VIII, have been infamous for their brothels since the 19th century and have a long-standing tradition as hangouts for prostitutes. Prostitution has been officially outlawed in Hungary since 1950. In recent years, however, it has been tolerated more.

Road policeman on a motorbike

MEDICAL MATTERS

WHEN TRAVELLING TO Hungary it is highly recommended that visitors take out travel insurance.

Foreign nationals are only entitled to free medical help in emergencies, such as accidents or a sudden illness requiring immediate medical intervention. Any other medical care, including hospitalization, must be paid for. The cost depends on the type of insurance policy held and the relevant agreement between Hungary and the visitor's home country. Most insurance companies expect policy holders to pay for their treatment as they receive it and then apply for a refund on their return home. All the relevant bills and police reports must be submitted with any insurance claim. Remember that, where applicable, a report must be made to the police within seven days of any incident.

Budapest's pharmacies (*Gyógyszertár* or *Patika*) are well stocked and, in case of a minor ailment, the chemist will be able to recommend a suitable treatment. Some drugs require a prescription, while others can be sold over

Pharmacy sign

the counter. If your nearest pharmacy is closed, there should be a list displayed, either on the door or in the window, of all the local chemists and it will indicate which ones are on 24-hour emergency duty.

No special vaccinations are required for Hungary and the general standard of hygiene in the country is reasonably good.

That said, allergy sufferers and people with breathing difficulties should take account of the summer smog conditions, which are particularly acute in the crowded streets of Pest. Those susceptible should consider staying in the Castle District, from which cars are banned, or retreating to the wooded Buda Hills (*see p161*)

Pharmacy shop front

or the greenery of Margaret Island (*see pp170–71*).

The water in Budapest is of good quality. It is generally considered safe to drink water straight from the tap. There are also numerous thermal baths (*see pp50–53*) which are an excellent way to relax.

Ambulance

DIRECTORY	Gas Emergency Service	Falk SOS Hungarian Medical Service	Telefon-doktor

EMERGENCY SERVICES

Ambulance
📞 104 (also 311 16 66).

Fire
📞 105 (also 321 62 16).

Police
📞 107.

Metropolitan Police
📞 443 50 00.

Tourist Police
Vigadó utca 6.
Map 10 D4.
📞 235 44 79 (24 hours).

Electricity Emergency Service
📞 40 383 838 (ask for number of local service).

Gas Emergency Service
📞 334 40 00 (24 hours).

Water Emergency Service
📞 80 200 333.

HELPLINES

Aids Helpline
📞 251 00 51 (8am–4pm Mon–Thu); 338 24 19 (8am–1pm Fri).

Alcoholics Anonymous
📞 251 00 51.

BKV Lost Property
📞 267 52 99 (lost today).
📞 461 65 00 ext. 11346 (lost prior to today).

Falk SOS Hungarian Medical Service
1025 Budapest,
Kapy utca 49.
📞 200 01 00.

Foreigners' Registry Office
Izabella utca 61.
📞 436 91 00.
🕒 8am–noon Mon–Wed & Fri, 8am–6pm Thu.

International Vehicle Insurance
📞 061 209 07 30.

Removed Cars Information
📞 383 07 00.

SOS Non-Stop Dental Service
📞 267 96 02.

Telefon-doktor
📞 317 21 11.

Vehicle Assistance and Breakdown Emergency Service
📞 088.
Mak-Magyar Autóklub
📞 345 16 87 (English spoken).

PHARMACIES

Déli Gyógyszertár
Alkotás u.1/b.
📞 355 46 91.

Teréz Patika
Teréz krt. 41.
Map 10 F1.
📞 311 44 39

Local Currency and Banking

Bureau de change sign

THE HUNGARIAN CURRENCY system is rapidly approaching the European standard. Budapest now boasts many modern banks, both Hungarian and foreign, which are located in smart and spacious buildings. The service is efficient and courteous. There are many automatic cash dispensers and bureaux de change in the town centre and around the railway stations. An increasing number of shops and restaurants now accept credit cards, but it is still more common in Budapest to pay for goods and services in cash. Most banks will now also advance money on a credit card.

Cash dispenser

CURRENCY REGULATIONS

FOREIGNERS are allowed to bring 350,000 Hungarian forints into Hungary, which at the beginning of 2000 was equal to about US $1,400 (890 pounds sterling). The same amount of money can be taken out of the country. There are no restrictions concerning the denominations of the Hungarian currency brought in or taken out.

Tourists who bring in foreign currencies totalling in excess of 100,000 Hungarian forints should declare them on arrival and ask the customs official for a receipt. This can then be presented when leaving the country, as the same limit applies to foreign currencies brought in and taken out of the country, without the need for an additional licence.

Foreign currencies can be easily exchanged into forints in banks, bureaux de change and hotels, but there is a limit of 20,000 Hungarian forints per day. To exchange any unspent forints back into a

convertible currency, visitors have to present the proof of purchase. So keep all the exchange receipts until the end of the visit. Otherwise, tourists will find themselves at home with forints that devalue quite rapidly, at a rate of 10–15 per cent relative to the major foreign currencies.

BANKS AND BUREAUX DE CHANGE

FOR THE BEST rate of exchange, take foreign currency to a bank or bureau de change, which are generally run by Hungarian banks. Before changing money, check the rate of exchange, as they do tend to vary quite widely. The rates quoted by some exchange offices can be misleading as they could apply only to sums in excess of 200,000 forints, which is stated in a very small print. The least favourable rates are in hotels and at the airport, while the best are offered by the bureaux de change near the railway stations and in the city centre, in Petőfi Sándor utca. A reasonable, average rate can usually be found at Hungarian banks.

The branches of **Budapest Bank** are open Monday till Friday, from 10:30am until 2pm. Merchant banks, such as **K & H Bank**, are open Monday till Thursday, between 8am and 3pm, and on Friday between 8am and 1pm. Most banks are closed on Saturdays and Sundays, but the bureaux de change and automatic cash dispensers remain open.

Exchanging money is only permitted in licensed, designated places. Transactions on the street are illegal, and you are likely to find youself with counterfeit money.

Most hotels, stores and restaurants accept credit cards. The most widely accepted are VISA, American Express, MasterCard and Diners Club. The logos of accepted credit cards are usually on display.

DIRECTORY

BANKS

Budapest Bank
Báthori utca 1.
(269 23 21.

CIB Bank
Váci utca 19–21.
(485 98 00.

Citibank
Vörösmarty tér 4.
(288 23 51.

K & H Bank
Vigadó tér 1.
(328 90 00.

Magyar Külkereskedelmi Bank Rt
Váci utca 38.
(269 09 22.

OTP Bank
Deák F. utca 7–9.
(486 60 00.

Posta Bank
Jósef Nádor tér 5.
(266 85 53.

Entrance to a branch of the Budapest Bank, in Váci utca

Hungarian currency

The Hungarian currency unit is the forint (HUF or Ft). Banknotes are issued in denominations of 200, 500, 1,000, 2,000, 5,000, 10,000 and 20,000 forints. Both an old and a new style of some notes are currently legal tender, but an older version of the 5,000 than the one shown here is no longer accepted.

200 HUF

500 HUF

1,000 HUF

2,000 HUF

5,000 HUF

10,000 HUF

Coins

Currently in circulation are coins of 1, 2, 5, 10, 20, 50 and 100 forints. As with the banknotes, new coins are gradually being phased in – the new 100 forint coin, with a brass disc inside a nickel ring, is now the only legal version.

1 HUF   **2 HUF**   **5 HUF**

10 HUF   **20 HUF**   **50 HUF**   **100 HUF**

Communications

Telephone symbol

T HE HUNGARIAN telephone operating system has undergone enormous changes in the last few years. Nowadays, you can easily access the telephone number you require. There are many telephone boxes throughout the city, although card-operated telephones are much more widespread than coin-operated ones. Most telephone boxes no longer contain a telephone directory. However, by dialling 199, the telephone information system provides a directory enquiry service.

Telephone box

USING THE TELEPHONE

T ELEPHONE CARDS are the best option, and can be obtained in units of 800, 1,800 or 5,000 forints. They are widely available from tobacconist shops, post offices, street vendors and some newspaper kiosks. Alternatively, coin phone boxes accept 10, 20 50 and 100 forint coins. The minimum rate for a local call is 20 forints, and 100 for an international call. To make an international call dial 00, wait for the dialing signal and then dial the country code, followed by the rest of the number.

Budapest telephone numbers consist of seven digits (when combined with the dialing code there are eight digits). There is really no advantage in using the services of a hotel operator, as this only adds to the length of the call and makes the call very much more expensive.

Cheaper off-peak rates apply throughout the night and on public holidays.

USING A CARD TELEPHONE

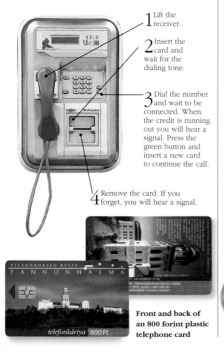

1 Lift the receiver.

2 Insert the card and wait for the dialing tone.

3 Dial the number and wait to be connected. When the credit is running out you will hear a signal. Press the green button and insert a new card to continue the call.

4 Remove the card. If you forget, you will hear a signal.

Front and back of an 800 forint plastic telephone card

USING A COIN TELEPHONE

1 Lift the receiver.

2 Insert coins and wait for the dialling tone.

3 Dial the number and wait to be connected. When the credit is running out you will hear a signal and should then insert more coins.

4 When you have finished speaking, replace the receiver. Wait for any unused coins to be returned.

10 HUF   **20 HUF**   **50 HUF**

Budapest's Districts

Budapest is divided into 23 districts. Streets of the same name may appear in several different districts, so it is important when addressing a letter to quote the four-digit postal code.

MAP OF THE CITY DISTRICTS

INTERNET CAFÉS

E MAIL IS A popular way to communicate from abroad. Budapest has several internet cafés offering coffee and snacks whilst you check your emails or search the internet.

Internet Galéria & Café
VI Szondi utca 79. **Map** 5 A5.
[C] *269 00 73.* ◯ *8am–10pm daily.*

Kávészünet Internet Café
XIII Tátra utca 12/b. **Map** 2 E3.
[C] *236 08 53.* ◯ *9am–9pm Mon–Fri, 10am–9:30pm Sat–Sun.*

Siesta Netcafé
VI Izabella utca 05. **Map** 7 B1 [C] *312 32 59.* ◯ *10am–2pm Mon–Fri, noon–2am Sat, to 12am Sun.*

POSTAL SERVICES

W HEN GOING TO a post office in Budapest, you must be prepared to spend some time there. Postage stamps cost between 60 to 130 Hungarian forints for sending a postcard, depending on the country. Apart from ordinary stamps, all post offices sell various special issues that are very pretty. Ask the cashier if you can see the different designs.

On weekdays, most post offices are open from 8am until 6pm, and they usually close at 2pm on Saturday and are closed all day Sunday. If you know the values of the stamps you require, it is easier to buy them from a *trafik* (a tobacconist shop or a newspaper kiosk), as often there are long queues at post offices. Post offices cannot be avoided, however. Airmail (*légiposta*) or registered letters have to be posted at a post office and poste restante mail has to be collected there. Telegrams can also be sent by telephone from post offices. Public fax machines can be found at most post offices.

Post office logo

Budapest postal codes are four-digit numbers. The first digit refers to Budapest, the second and third digits refer to the district number and the fourth digit defines the postal area within the district.

Post boxes are emptied daily at the times indicated on the front of the box.

POST OFFICE ADDRESSES

Bajcsy-Zsilinszky út 16. **Map** 10 E1.
◯ *8am–8pm Mon–Fri, 8am–2pm Sat.*

Baross tér 11. **Map** 8 D2.
◯ *7am–9pm Mon–Fri.*

Krisztina körút. **Map** 3 C1.
◯ *8am–8pm Mon–Fri, 8am–2pm Sat.*

Teréz körút 51. **Map** 10 F1.
◯ *7am–9pm Mon–Sat, 8am–8pm Sun.*

Városház utca 18. **Map** 10 E4.
8am–8pm Mon–Fri, 8am–2pm Sat.

Red post box for national and international mail

USEFUL TELEPHONE NUMBERS AND DIALLING CODES

- Sending telegrams: 192
- International operator calls: 190
- Inland operator calls: 191
- Inland information: 198
- International information: 199
- SDC for international calls: 00
- SDC from Budapest to other Hungarian towns: 06

- SDC from Budapest to Australia: 00 61
- SDC from Budapest to France: 00 33
- SDC from Budapest to New Zealand: 00 64
- SDC from Budapest to South Africa: 00 27
- SDC from Budapest to the UK: 00 44
- SDC from Budapest to the US: 00 1
- For Budapest from UK and most of Europe: 00 361
- For Budapest from US and Australia: 00 11 361

GETTING TO BUDAPEST

Hungarians like to boast that Budapest is the heart of central Europe – a claim with some justification as the city acts as a major crossroads linking north to south and west to east. It has excellent rail links with the whole of Europe and its two largest railway stations, Keleti pu and Nyugati pu *(see p227)* are conveniently situated in the centre of town. The country's motorway network has undergone improvements in recent years, successfully making up for decades of neglect. Budapest can now

A plane owned by the Hungarian airline, Malév

be reached by motorway from all but the northern direction. Travelling down by car from Slovakia and Poland, via Vác, is not recommended. The poorly maintained and narrow road makes for a very tedious journey, particularly at peak travelling times, such as in high season and at weekends. For sheer comfort and convenience, it is far better to make use of the air links Budapest has with major cities throughout Europe. The journey from London to Budapest, for example, takes just two and a half hours.

ARRIVING BY AIR

Airlines from around 40 towns and cities, in 27 different countries, now fly to Budapest. The city's Ferihegy airport is used by many major international airlines, including **Air France**, **British Airways**, **Northwest**, **Lufthansa** and, of course, the Hungarian national carrier, **Malév**.

British Airways and Malév each operate two daily scheduled flights between London's Heathrow airport and Budapest. There are also four code-share flights a week from Gatwick airport, which are a joint operation between British Airways and Malév. It is possible to fly to Budapest from other airports in the UK, including Manchester, but only by taking a connecting flight from another European city, such as Brussels or Frankfurt. Consequently, the

flight time and cost are both greater.

Northwest flights from the United States involve a transfer or touch down in Frankfurt or Zurich, but there is a daily direct code-share flight from New York's JFK airport with Northwest reservations on a Malév-owned plane. The flight takes around ten hours.

TICKETS AND CONCESSIONS

When planning to travel to Budapest by air, bear in mind that substantial savings can be made by purchasing APEX tickets, although they do carry certain conditions. The tickets require fixed dates for departure and return, and the stay must

Malév stewardess

include at least one Saturday and last no longer than one month. APEX tickets usually need to be bought in advance but it is worth checking purchasing arrangements with individual airlines. For those aged 2–24, British Airways offer youth fares to Budapest which, although nominally higher than the lowest APEX fare, carry none of the restrictions. Autumn and winter is an opportune time to look around for special offers, as the low season brings with it some very good deals. Look out for excellent low-price weekend flight-plus-hotel deals between September and March.

FERIHEGY AIRPORT

Budapest's international airport, Ferihegy 2, is 16 km (10 miles) from the city centre. Originally built in 1985, it was extended to accommodate more flights in 1997–8 and, in 1999 it took on all of Budapest's passenger services (an older terminal, Ferihegy 1, now handles only freight).

Terminal 2a deals with the arrivals and departures of the Hungarian carrier, Malév; Terminal 2b handles those of all foreign airlines.

Both terminals offer comfort and good amenities to passengers. Catering facilities

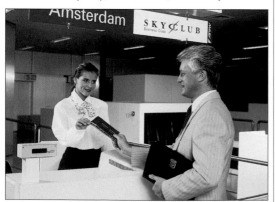

Check-in desk at Budapest's modern Ferihegy 2

A Malév aircraft parked outside Ferihegy 2

include bars, cafés and restaurants, and there are numerous boutiques and shops. They both have currency exchange facilities. All the major car rental firms have desks in the arrival halls of both Ferihegy 2a and Ferihegy 2b. The main names to look out for are Avis, Budget, and Europcar (see p228).

On departure, after passport control, you will find several duty-free shops offering attractive prices on all kinds of goods – not only Hungarian products.

Airport taxi company logo

Malév airlines' logo

GETTING TO THE CENTRE

FOR AROUND 2,100 Hungarian forints the **Airport Minibus Shuttle** will take passengers from either terminal to any address in the city centre. As well as being wheelchair-accessible, they also run a pick-up service for the return journey. BKV+ runs to Kőbánya-Kispest metro station, followed by the blue M3 metro line.

Taxis from the airport are very costly – ensure that the driver starts the meter or you may well be overcharged. As with taxis elswhere in Budapest, it is often adviseable to find out in advance how much a particular fare should be.

DIRECTORY

AIRPORT AND AIRLINES

Ferihegy 2
(296 96 96 (general info).
(296 71 55 today's info).
(296 70 00 (departures).
(296 80 00 (arrivals).

Air France
Pesti Barnabás utca 4.
Map 4 E1.
(484 50 55.

British Airways
Régiposta utca 5.
Map 10 D4.
(411 55 55.

Lufthansa
Váci utca 19–21.
Map 4 E1.
(266 45 11.

Malév
Roosevelt tér 2.
Map 2 D5.
(235 35 65.

Northwest (KLM)
East West Business Centre,
Rákóczi út 1–3.
Map 10 F4.
(373 7737.

AIRPORT MINIBUS

Airport Minibus Shuttle
(296 85 55.

BUDAPEST'S AIR LINKS WITH EUROPE

Budapest has air links with major cities in every European country. From each of the locations marked on the map you can travel to Budapest in under three hours.

Ticket offices at a main railway station in Budapest

RAIL TRAVEL

BUDAPEST has direct rail links with 25 other capital cities. Every day, more than 50 international trains, many of them express services, arrive and depart from the city's four railway stations. Some trains terminate here, while others enable passengers to join connecting services. Hungarian trains are widely considered to be a very efficient means of getting around, and their reputation is well deserved. Most importantly, they invariably depart and arrive at the right time.

Trains from Budapest to Vienna, the main communication hub for western Europe, depart approximately every three hours. The fastest trains run at top speeds of 140–160 km/h (85–100 mph). The travelling time is an efficient 2 hours 50 minutes. The "Transbalkan" train, which also has car carriages, runs from Keleti pu to Thessaloníki in Greece every day.

Detailed information on all domestic and international rail travel running to and from Budapest can be obtained from either Keleti pu or the MÁV (Hungarian Railways) ticket sales office, which is centrally located at No. 35 Andrássy út.

It is worth knowing that there are several concessionary fares available. Foreign visitors to Hungary can buy a season ticket that is valid for between seven and ten days

and offers unlimited travel throughout the country. There are also a number of Europe-wide passes that allow you to travel cheaply on trains throughout Europe and Hungary.

Local trains can be either "slow" *(személy)* or "speedy" *(sebes)*, but both invariably make frequent stops. A much better option if time is tight is for you to take the fast *(gyors)* train. There are also modern Intercity trains, which take passengers to Pécs, Miskolc, Debrecen, Szeged, Békéscsaba and all the larger cities in Hungary in around 1–3 hours. Seat reservations, costing a small extra charge, are required on these clean and **Railwayman** comfortable trains.

RAILWAY STATIONS

THERE ARE three main railway stations in Budapest – Keleti pu (East), Nyugati pu (West) and Déli pu (South). A fourth station, Józsefváros pu, handles mainly domestic

traffic, although it does cater for a handful of longer routes. Most international trains run from Keleti pu. The express train to Croatia ("Maestral") and trains to the Lake Balaton resorts leave from Déli pu, almost every hour during the high season. Most international express trains depart from Nyugati pu.

The easiest way to get to Keleti pu is by the M2 metro. The same line connects Keleti pu with Déli pu. For Nyugati pu take the M3 metro line, or trams 4 or 6. A special minibus runs between the various railway stations.

Rail information
[461 54 04 (international).
[461 59 00 (national).

COACH TRAVEL

BUDAPEST has one international coach station, called Népliget (Üllői út 131), which can easily be accessed by the M3 metro line. There are three national coach stations: Népliget (to Western Hungary), Népstadion (the People's Stadium, to Eastern Hungary), and Árpád Bridge (to Northern Hungary and the Danube Bend). Népstadion station can be reached by the M2 metro line, while Árpád Bridge is served by the M3 line. The international routes are served by luxury coaches, which have all the usual facilities. The domestic traffic is served by Volánbusz coaches, which operate routes to most of the major towns throughout Hungary.

Coach information
[317 29 66.

The imposing exterior of one of Budapest's main railway stations

Luxury air-conditioned tourist coach

TRAVELLING BY BOAT

FROM APRIL UNTIL October hydrofoils run along the Danube between Vienna and Budapest, via Bratislava.

It is also possible to take a hydrofoil or pleasure boat along to the Danube bend, to towns such as Esztergom and Visegrád (see p164). See the timetable at the departure point at Vigadó tér for exact times.

TRAVELLING BY CAR

THE LACK OF parking makes arriving by public transport preferable to travelling by car. Driving distances to Budapest are: from Vienna, 250 km (155 miles); from Prague, 560 km (350 miles); and from Frankfurt, 950 km (590 miles).

Motorways are marked by the letter "M" and international highways with the letter "E". The speed limit is 130 km/h (80 mph). Seven main roads lead out of Budapest and one, the A8, starts in Székésfehérvár. The M1 stretches from Budapest to the Hegyeshalom border crossing, where it joins the Austrian motorway network. Tolls are payable on all motorways. The M3 links Budapest to Polgár and is being extended to join up with the Slovak road network. From Budapest the M5 leads to Kecskemét (see p166), while the M7 links to the Balaton resorts.

Minor roads have three or four digits, with the first digit indicating the number of the connecting main road.

The police patrol right from the Hungarian border, so it is worth studying the traffic regulations displayed on information boards. These include: driving with the headlights on, wearing seatbelts in the back and keeping to the speed limit of 50 km/h (30 mph) in built-up areas.

Drivers must purchase a motorway sticker for the M1, M3 and M7 motorways. On the M5, a toll fee has to be paid at the motorway gates.

Vehicle assistance
C 1 88.

A road sign directing traffic to Margaret Bridge and the M3

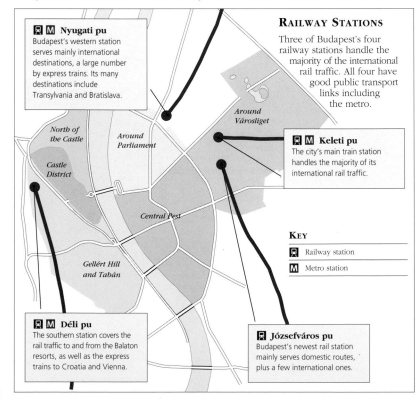

RAILWAY STATIONS

Three of Budapest's four railway stations handle the majority of the international rail traffic. All four have good public transport links including the metro.

R M Nyugati pu
Budapest's western station serves mainly international destinations, a large number by express trains. Its many destinations include Transylvania and Bratislava.

Around Városliget

North of the Castle

Around Parliament

Castle District

R M Keleti pu
The city's main train station handles the majority of its international rail traffic.

Central Pest

KEY

R	Railway station
M	Metro station

Gellért Hill and Tabán

R M Déli pu
The southern station covers the rail traffic to and from the Balaton resorts, as well as the express trains to Croatia and Vienna.

R Józsefváros pu
Budapest's newest rail station mainly serves domestic routes, plus a few international ones.

GETTING AROUND BUDAPEST

BUDAPEST IS a sprawling city with many suburban districts. However, most of its main tourist attractions are centrally located and can be easily reached by the city's public transport system, or on foot. The many choices of transport by rail, road and even water provide the visitor to Budapest with ample opportunity to travel through and around the city to reach their chosen

One of Budapest's environmentally-friendly city buses

destinations. The infrastructure of Budapest is chiefly determined by the *köruts* (ring roads), which radiate out from the city centre and into the city's suburbs. The metro system mainly operates in Pest, although the red M2 line crosses the Danube at Batthyány tér and runs just north of the Castle District. The overland HÉV train provides a service from the city centre to the suburbs.

DRIVING IN BUDAPEST

THE LARGE number of one-way streets in Budapest make it a very difficult city for visitors to navigate by car. The many changes of direction often result in unfamiliar drivers becoming lost. Any confusion brought about by the complex system of roads is further aggravated by the heavy rush-hour traffic. There are also few places to park in the city, so it is much better to sightsee on foot or by public transport.

In Hungary it is strictly forbidden to drive following

One-way traffic in direction indicated

Stop sign at road junction

End of pedestrian and cycle zone

any alcohol consumption. If any trace of alcohol is found in the bloodstream, the fine for drink-driving can be as high as 50,000 Hungarian forints (approximately US $220) and is only payable in forints.

All car occupants, both in the front and the back seats, are required by law to wear seat belts. Motorcycle drivers and passengers must wear helmets at all times.

In built-up areas the speed limit is 50 km/h (30 mph), and most of the road signs follow the European pattern. In towns the use of the horn is legally restricted to cases of imminent danger. Despite this, Hungarian drivers hoot loudly and often at both pedestrians and other drivers.

New regulations permit the use of mobile telephones by drivers only when the car is fitted with a hands-free system. Otherwise, it is advisable to pull over and stop if you wish to make or receive a call.

BUDAPEST ON FOOT

Budapest is a city in which every pedestrian will find something of interest. Visitors who enjoy rambling along leafy trails should take the railway or bus 21 from Moszkva tér to the Buda Hills *(see p161)*. Those who prefer to stroll through picturesque streets and alleyways should go to Buda's Castle District, which is closed to traffic. Váci utca (Váci Street, *see p127*) is fully pedestrianized and has seats where weary walkers can rest and watch the bustle. The promenade along the Danube is one of the most pleasant walks in Budapest.

Pedestrian zone

V. Kerület, Lipótváros
Báthori utca
2 ——— 2

New street name plate

OKTÓBER 6. UTCA

Old street name plate

Pedestrian crossing

Walk signal at a pedestrian crossing

HIRING A CAR

CARS CAN BE hired from the airport on arrival in Budapest *(see p225)*, or from one of several car hire offices, such as **Budget Hungary** who give discounts to Budapest Card holders *(see p216)*. Be prepared to leave a credit card deposit ranging between 100,000 and 800,000 forints and pay US $80–240 per day for unlimited mileage.

PARKING

BUDAPEST'S CAR parks, indicated by a blue "P", reduce the problem of on-street parking (and also relieve traffic congestion). There are more covered car parks in the centre, for example at Nyár utca, Aranykéz utca, Osvát utca and Szervita tér. There are attended and unattended car parks situated in other busy parts of the city as well. Several hotels also have car parks, and may offer spare parking spaces to non-guests. Parking charges vary from 120 to 400 Hungarian forints per hour. Parking cards for use in meters can be bought from outlets in the city.

Parking at the main tourist attractions, for example, near Hősök tere (Heroes' Square, *see pp142–3*) or the Citadel (*see pp92–3*), is free for the duration of the visit. These car parks cannot be used by people not visiting the particular sight.

When parking in a metered parking bay, the length of stay must be specified in advance. Parking without a valid ticket or overstaying the allocated time can lead to either a parking fine or wheel-clamping.

CLAMPING AND TOWING

WHEEL-CLAMPING is growing in Budapest; all illegally parked vehicles are subject to clamping. As well as paying a fine, it costs around 4,000 forints (US $18) to release a car from a clamp, and around 9,300 forints (US $40) if a car has been towed away. Parking meters often give the telephone number to contact in the event of wheel-clamping. It is also worth asking a car park attendant for advice. If the car has been towed away, details on its whereabouts and retrieval can be obtained by telephoning either 383 07 00 or 383 07 70.

Stopping and parking prohibited

FIZETŐ ÖVEZET
H · P : 08.00 –18.00
Szo : 08.00 –12.00
MAXIMUM 2 óra
Fizetés a jegykiadó automatánál.

Parking of cars allowed in this zone for a maximum of two hours

A wheel-clamped car

CYCLING

CYCLING AROUND Budapest is difficult and fairly dangerous. Cyclists have to be careful of the tram rails and the uneven, cobblestoned surface of some roads.

Budapest's main roads are closed to cyclists and designated cycle lanes continue to be in short supply. Until recently, Szentendrei út was the only road with a cycle lane. However, the provision of other new cycle routes in Budapest has made cycling an increasingly popular pastime.

The best way to see some of Budapest on a bicycle is by taking a cycling trip around Margaret Island (*see pp172–3*). There are several bike-hire shops on the island, which can provide everything needed for a day's cycling. The range of bicycles includes children's bikes, thus enabling family groups to explore the paths and avenues of this quiet, picturesque island. Many kiosks selling food and drinks can be found on the island, so cyclists can spend the whole day there.

USING A PARKING METER

2 The display panel shows the maximum and minimum parking charges. If you are using a parking card it indicates the value remaining on the card.

1 Insert coins to the value of your ticket, or insert a parking card.

3 When the display shows the correct amount of time you require, press the green button to request a ticket.

4 When using a parking card, each time the blue button is pressed, the machine deducts a fee equal to 15 minutes of parking time.

5 Turn the red button to abhort the process at any time.

6 Ticket appears here.

Getting Around by Metro

BUDAPEST HAS THREE METRO LINES *(see inside back cover)*,
which intersect only at Deák tér station. Here passengers can change trains (stamping their tickets once again),
by following the clearly marked passageways. The oldest
line, the yellow M1 line, runs just beneath the surface of
the city. Built in 1894, it is known as the Millennium Line
after the celebrations that took place two years later
(see p142). Recently it has been modernized and extended. Two more lines – the red M2 and blue M3 lines –
have been added since 1970, serving the rest of the city.

**Sign over the entrance to the M1
metro line at Oktogon tér station**

Signs for the M2 and M3 lines

door is closing and gives the
name of the next station.

Smoking and eating are not
permitted on the trains, and
music can only be listened to
through headphones. Dogs are
allowed to travel on the metro,

but only when muzzled. They
are required to have a franked
ticket for the normal fare.
This rule applies to all forms
of public transport.

The metro service runs from
4:30am until just after 11pm.

**Millennium Underground
Museum**

Deák tér. ☐ 10am–5pm Tue–Sun.

THE METRO SYSTEM

TWO WORDS to remember
when using Budapest's
metro system are *bejárat*,
meaning entrance and *kijárat*,
meaning exit, both of which
are always clearly marked.

To plan a journey, consult
the map at the back of this
guide. Most metro stations display maps of the local area,
and maps of each line are
placed over the doors inside
the trains. A recorded voice
message announces when the

A typical station on the original M1 metro line

USING A TICKET

Tickets are bought in advance and need to
be franked in a machine before a journey
is made. On the metro, the machines are
located outside the platforms. Tickets are
checked frequently, and there is a fine of
1,500 forints to be paid on the spot for
travelling without a valid ticket.

Name of
ticket
holder

**One-week travel
card for all
public transport**

**One-day
travel card
for all public
transport**

TRAVEL CARDS AND
SEASON TICKETS

The following are currently available:
travel cards for 1, 3 or 7 days (and 10
days if you are under 25 years of age);
and season tickets (for which a photo is
needed) for 7, 14 or 30 days, or one
calendar month. Prices change constantly
for all these options.

SINGLE TICKETS

Tickets are currently available for a complete
single journey, without a transfer, by metro,
bus, tram, trolley bus, funicular or HÉV, or
for a short metro journey of 3 or 5 stops. Metro
tickets are also available with a transfer option.
When changing metro lines a new single ticket
must be validated. Prices alter constantly.

Single ticket for all public transport

Travelling on the HÉV

The suburban railway logo

THE OVERLAND HÉV RAILWAY provides an essential means of transport that connects Budapest with its suburban districts. It carries residents to and from work and tourists to attractions located 20–30 km (10–20 miles) away from the city centre. The standard tickets *(see p230)* used on other forms of transport can be used to travel to the central destinations on the HÉV line, but additional fares are payable to more distant destinations. Tickets can either be bought at stations before travelling or from the conductor while on the train.

A standard HÉV train carriage

SUBURBAN RAIL LINES

THE HÉV LINE most commonly used by tourists runs north from Batthyány tér *(see p100)* towards Szentendre *(see p165)*, taking in such sights as Aquincum *(see pp162–3)* along the way. Many of the trains on this line terminate at Békásmegyer rather than running on to Szentendre. Check the destination on the front of the train before boarding. Another line runs from Örs vezér tere (at the eastern terminus of the M2 metro line)

to Gödöllő, passing the *Hungororing* Grand Prix race track *(see p59)* near Mogyoród en route. Gödöllő, a small Baroque town, was once the summer residence of the Habsburgs *(see pp28–9)*.

The third HÉV line begins at Közvágóhíd and terminates at Ráckeve *(see p167)*. Tourists who make this long journey can enjoy a visit to the palace of Prince Eugene of Savoy.

The HÉV service between Boráros tér and Csepel Island is the longest at approximately 50 km (30 miles).

OTHER TOWN TRANSPORT

THE BUDAVÁRI SIKLÓ is an old funicular railway, which takes passengers from the head of the Chain Bridge in Buda to the top of Castle Hill.

Several modes of transport operate in the Buda Hills *(see p161)*. A cog-wheel railway connects Szilágyi Erszébet fasor with Széchenyi Hill, with its picturesque walking trails, while the Children's Railway runs from there to the Hűvös Valley. A chair lift, or *libegő*, descends from the top of János Hill down onto Zugligeti út.

Getting Around by Taxi

Taxi sign

IT HAS ALWAYS BEEN EASY to find a taxi in Budapest, and now, with over 15,000 registered cabs, the competition for passengers is fierce. Nevertheless, not all taxi drivers read the meter correctly and they have been known to exploit foreign visitors, especially those unfamiliar with Budapest who are travelling to the city centre from airports or railway stations. To reduce this risk, choose a taxi whose tariffs and meters are clearly displayed.

USEFUL TAXI NUMBERS:

Budataxi 233 33 33.
City Taxi 211 11 11.
Főtaxi 0680 22 22 22.
Budapest Taxi 433 33 33.
Rádiótaxi 377 77 77.
Taxi 2000 200 00 00.
Tele5 355 55 55.
6x6 Taxi 266 66 66.

A typical taxi meter

FARES

TAXI RANKS can be found throughout Budapest and are seldom empty. Taxis can also be hailed on the street but it is often better to book one from your hotel. Before getting in to the taxi, ask

what the fare will be. Ensure that the meter is set at the beginning of the journey and get a receipt for the fare. Fares increase from year to

year but can be negotiated with unlicenced taxis. This price should always be agreed in advance. The total charge is made up of three parts; a basic charge, a per-kilometer charge, and a waiting charge.

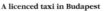

A licenced taxi in Budapest

Getting Around by Tram

THERE ARE OVER 30 tram lines in Budapest, which extend to practically every part of the city. These yellow trams are an efficient and speedy means of getting around Budapest, as they avoid traffic and run very frequently. Services start early in the morning, at around 4:30am, and run regularly throughout the day until 11pm or midnight, depending on the route. Night trams operate only on certain routes, at an average of four trams per hour. Timetables are displayed at each stop. It is worth knowing that *utolsó indul* means "last tram".

TRAM STOP

Every tram stop displays the appropriate tram numbers and the timetable.

- Tram stop symbol
- Name of the stop
- Destination
- Timetable
- Map of the route

THE TRAM SYSTEM

TICKETS FOR trams can be bought at metro stations, tobacconist shops *(trafiks)* and some newspaper kiosks. Passes valid for a week or more require a photograph and can only be bought at metro stations.

Yellow Budapest tram

When ticket offices are closed, tickets should be bought from the metro station guard. Tickets are valid for a single journey where no changes are involved, and can be used on any form of public transport. It can be cheaper and more convenient to buy books of 20 tickets.

When a tram line is closed for maintenance, replacement buses are provided. These have the same number as the tram and have the letter V preceding the number.

TRAVELLING WITH LUGGAGE

EVERY PASSENGER on the tram, just as on the bus or trolley bus, is entitled to carry two pieces of luggage. These should not exceed 40 by 50 by 80 cm (16 by 20 by 30 inches) or 20 by 20 by 200 cm (8 by 8 by 80 inches) in

size. You can also carry one pair of ice skates and one pair of skis, providing they are clean, as well as a child's buggy. If you need to transport a bicycle or a larger item of luggage, up to 100 by 100 by 200 cm (40 by 40 by 80 inches) in size, then the rack railway or the designated carriages of the HÉV trains should be used. Any items left on public transport can be traced at the Lost Property Office, at No. 18 Akácfa utca *(see p219)*.

USEFUL TRAM ROUTES

Budapest trams are possibly the most convenient form of public transport for tourists. Particularly valuable sightseeing routes are trams 18, 19 and 61 on the Buda side of town and trams 2, 4 and 6 on the Pest side.

KEY

O	Interchange tram stop
▬▬▬	Line 2
▬▬▬	Line 4
▬▬▬	Line 6
▬▬▬	Line 18
▬▬▬	Line 19
▬▬▬	Line 61

0 kilometres   1
0 miles   1

Getting Around by Bus

BUDAPEST HAS ABOUT 200 different bus routes, which altogether cover most of the city. The blue Ikarus buses generally run from 4:30am until 11pm, with departures on most routes every 10–20 minutes. Times and a list of destinations are on display at most stops. Ordinary buses are indicated by black numbers and stop at every stop. Buses with red numbers follow express routes and omit a number of stops.

THE BUS SYSTEM

BUDAPEST'S bus transport is extremely efficient and makes exploring the city easy, even for first-time visitors. Tickets can be purchased at metro stations and from tobacconist shops *(trafiks)*. They must be punched upon entering the bus.

The driver always announces the next stop, often informing the passengers about any interchanges. To ensure that the bus stops, passengers should press the button located by the door before their required stop, otherwise the bus may carry on. When arriving at or leaving a bus stop, most drivers will welcome or bid farewell to passengers. Remember that Budapest's bus drivers tend to drive fast and that the streets, particularly in Buda, can be steep. This combination makes it advisable

A clean and efficient Ikarus bus in Budapest

BUS STOP

The layout of bus stops is very similar to that of trams and trolley bus stops.

Bus stop symbol

Name of the stop

Destination

Timetable

to hang on tightly to the hand grips when standing on a bus.

It is advisable to avoid buses in the centre of town during rush hours, when traffic becomes congested. At these times it is best to take the metro or even to walk.

Getting Around by Trolley Bus

TROLLEY BUSES SERVE mainly the suburbs and as such are little used by tourists. They are a particularly uncomfortable form of transport, as they move slowly along narrow streets. In addition, their pantographs often get dislodged, causing short breaks in the journey.

Trolley bus stop symbol

THE TROLLEY BUS SYSTEM

THE SAME RULES apply to travelling on a trolley bus as to travelling on a bus. Again, remember to signal to the driver by pressing the button located above the door when approaching your stop. Otherwise, if there are no passengers waiting at the stop, the driver will not automatically come to a halt.

Trolley buses are numbered from 70 upwards and there are about 15 different routes in Budapest. Tickets must be punched upon entering the bus, and are the same type as for other forms of public transport. Failure to punch the ticket may result in an on-the-spot fine of 1,500 forints. A particularly pleasant route is trolley bus 70, which runs between Kossuth Lajos tér and Erzsébet Királyné útja.

TICKET VENDING MACHINE

Tickets are sold at tobacconist shops (trafiks), *metro stations and the vending machines at major transport junctions and HÉV railway stations. (These are often out of order.)*

Insert 1, 2, 5, 10, 20, 50 or 100 HUF coins

Press button to receive ticket

Check the amount paid

Collect the ticket and change

STREET FINDER

THE MAP REFERENCES for all the sights, hotels, bars, restaurants, shops and entertainment venues described in this book refer to the maps in this section. A complete index of street names marked on the maps appears on pages 246–8. The map below shows the area of Budapest covered by the *Street Finder* and is colour-coded by area. The *Street Finder* also includes bus and tram routes, major sights and places

of interest together with other useful information listed in the key below. As an aid to navigation, all street names, both on the *Street Finder* and in the index, are in Hungarian. Slightly confusing are the terms *utca* (often abbreviated to *u*), which means street, and *út* meaning avenue, a term mainly applied to wide, busy roads. Other commonly used terms are *körút* (ring road), *tér* (square), *köz* (lane), *körtér* (circus) and *híd* (bridge).

KEY TO STREET FINDER

■	Major sight
■	Place of interest
■	Other building
M	Metro station
⊟	HÉV station
⊟	Train station
▭	Main bus stop
▭	River boat boarding point
▭	Bus route
▭	Tram route
P	Car park
ℹ	Tourist information point
✚	Hospital with casualty unit
▨	Police station
✝	Church
✡	Synagogue
⊠	Post office
=	Railway line
►	One-way street
▬	Pedestrianized street

SCALE OF MAPS 1–8:

0 metres   200
0 yards   200

1:13,200

SCALE OF MAPS 9–10:

0 metres   200
0 yards   200

1:15,530

1

SZENT ISTVÁN KÖRÚT

MARGIT KÖRÚT

ATTILA ÚT

KRISZTINA KÖRÚT

3

ALKOTÁS U.

HEGYALJA ÚT

BUDAÖRSI ÚT

BARTÓK BÉLA ÚT

House in the leafy Tabán district *(see p94)*

Deák tér *(see p121)*, named after politician Ferenc Deák and home to the city's first ever public toilet

Flag-lined avenue in the Castle District *(see pp 78–9)*

ROBERT KÁROLY KÖRÚT

HUNGÁRIA KÖRÚT

ANDRÁSSY ÚT

ERZSÉBET KÖRÚT

KÖCZI ÚT

KEREPESI ÚT

BAROSS U.

ÜLLŐI ÚT

SOROKSÁRI ÚT

KÖNYVES KÁLMÁN KÖRÚT

0 kilometres   2

0 miles   1

Statue of King Ludwig I, part of the colossal Millennium Monument on Heroes' Square *(see p145)*, which was completed in 1929

Street Finder Index

Index

Acknowledgments

DORLING KINDERSLEY would like to thank the following people whose contributions and assistance have made this book possible:

MAIN CONTRIBUTOR

TADEUSZ OLSZANSKI was born in 1929 in Poland. During World War II, he fled with his parents to Hungary, where he attended a Polish school in Balatonboglar. He has since visited Hungary many times as a journalist and is the author of five books about the country. These include a volume of articles, Budapesztanskíe ABC. In addition, he has translated over 30 Hungarian novels and dramas into Polish. From 1986 to 1994, he lived in Hungary, working both as the manager of the Institute of Polish Culture and as a correspondent for Polish Radio and TV. In recognition of his activities in promoting Hungarian literature and culture, he was awarded the Pro-Hungarian Culture Award and the Tibor Derye Literary Prize.

ADDITIONAL CONTRIBUTORS

Sħawomir Fangrat, Mariusz Jarymowicz, Iza Mościcka, Barbara Olszaůska, Ewa Roguska.

EDITORIAL AND DESIGN

SENIOR MANAGING EDITOR Vivien Crump
DEPUTY ART DIRECTOR Gillian Allan
PRODUCTION Jo Blackmore, David Proffit
DTP DESIGNERS Lee Redmond, Ingrid Vienings
MAPS Maria Wojciechowska, Dariusz Osuch
(D Osuch i Spółka)
Elizabeth Atherton, Arwen Burnett, Lucinda Cooke, Fay Franklin, Maite Lantaron, Rebecca Milner, Rachel Symons, Anna Streiffert, Andrew Szudek, Sophie Warne.

RESEARCHERS

Julia Bennett, Javier Espinosa de los Monteros.

INDEXER

Hilary Bird.

SPECIAL ASSISTANCE

THE PUBLISHER would like to thank the staff at shops, museums, hotels, restaurants and other organizations in Budapest for their invaluable help. Particular thanks go to: the Ambassador for the Republic of Hungary in Warsaw; the Ambassador for the Republic of Poland in Budapest; Gábor Bányai; Katalin Bara and the rest of the staff at the Hungarian airline, Malév; Beatrix Basics, Tibor Kovács and Péter Gaál at the Hungarian National Museum; Éva Benkő at the Museum of Fine Arts; Zoltan Fejős and Endre Stefana Szemkeő at the Ethnographical Museum; Béla Juszel and Éva Orosz at the Hungarian National Bank; the staff of the Kiscelli Museum; Imre Kiss, Zsuzsa Mátyus and Tivadar Mihalkovics at the State Opera House; Konrad Adenauer Stifung; the staff of the Franz Liszt Museum; Zsuzsa Lovag at the Museum of Applied Arts; the Meteorological Office of the Republic of Hungary; the staff at the Hungarian Post Office; Katalin Neray at the Ludwig Museum; Anita Obrotfa at the Budapesti Turisztikai Hivatal; Csilla Pataky at Cartographia Ltd; Géza Szabó; Mária Vida at the Semmelweis Museum of Medical History; Annamária Vigh at the Budapest History Museum. Ágnes Ördög and Judit Mihalcsik and the Tourism Office of Budapest, 1056 Március 15 tér 7, for sourcing pictures and providing new information.

PHOTOGRAPHY PERMISSIONS

DORLING KINDERSLEY would like to thank the following for their kind permission to photograph at their establishments: Ágnes Bakos, Margit Bakos and Bence Tihanyi at the Budapest History Museum; the staff of the Budapesti Turisztikai Hivatal; Eszter Gordon; István Gordon at the Kurir Archive; Astoria Hotel; Dénes Józsa at the Museum of Fine Arts; Ágnes Kolozs at the Museum of Applied Arts; the Ludwig Museum; the Hungarian National Museum; the Hungarian Academy of Sciences, Tibor Mester at the Hungarian National Gallery; Béla Mezey; the Imre Varga Gallery; András Rázsó at the Museum of Fine Arts; the Semmelweis Museum of Medical History; Judit Szalatnyay at the Kiscelli Museum; Ágnes Szél; Ferenc Tobias and Erzsébet Winter at the Ethnographical Museum; Richard Wagner at the Museum of Applied Arts; the Hungarian airline, Malév.

Dorling Kindersley would also like to thank all the shops, restaurants, cafés, hotels, churches and public services who aided us with our photography. These are too numerous to mention individually.

Particular thanks are due to Marta Zámbó at the Gundel Étterem, who provided the Hungarian cuisine photographed for this guidebook.

PICTURE CREDITS

t=top; tc=top centre; tr=top right; tl=top left; cla=centre left above; ca=centre above; cra=centre right above; cl=centre left; c=centre; cr=centre right; clb=centre left below; cb=centre below; crb=centre right below; bl=bottom left; bc=bottom centre; br=bottom right; b=bottom.

The publisher is grateful to the following individuals, companies and picture libraries for permission to reproduce their photographs:

ASTORIA HOTEL: 178b.

BUDAPEST HISTORY MUSEUM: 32c, 33c, 38cb, 38b, 72t. BUDAPESTI TURISZTIKAI HIVATAL: 50cr, 50clb, 50br, 51b, 58t, 59b, 60b, 156b.

DANUBIUS HOTEL GROUP: 178b.

ESZTER GORDON: 35ca.

HUNGARIAN NATIONAL GALLERY: 16, 23b, 24cb, 26ca, 37br, 38ca, 54cla, 56cl, 74tl, 74tr, 75ca, 75cr, 75cra, 75b, 76t, 76c, 76b, 77t, 77c, 77b; HUNGARIAN NATIONAL MUSEUM: 8, 20t, 20ca, 20cr, 20cb, 20b, 21t, 21cra, 21c, 21crb, 22t, 22c, 22cl, 22br, 23t, 23c, 23cra, 23crb, 23b, 24cl, 24c, 25t, 25c, 26t, 26b, 27t, 27cra, 27crb, 27cla, 28t, 28ca, 28c, 28cb, 29t, 29c, 29cra, 29crb, 30cl, 31tr, 32t, 32cra, 32cl, 32crb, 33cr, 37cl, 130tr, 130tl, 130ca, 130cb, 131t, 131ca, 131cb, 131bc, 133t, 133c, 133b. HUNGARIAN NATIONAL TOURIST OFFICE: 218t.

JEWISH MUSEUM: 39cr.

KURIR ARCHIVE: 34tr, 34br, 35br.

LUDWIG MUSEUM: 40b, 73b; LUTHERAN MUSEUM: 41b.

BÉLA MEZEY 34ca; MUSEUM OF APPLIED ARTS: 5br, 56tr, 57bl, 136tr, 136tl, 136c, 137g, 137ca, 137c,

137cb, 137b; MUSEUM OF FINE ARTS: 39tr, 146tl, 146tr, 146ca, 146cb, 146b, 147t, 147ca, 147cb, 147b, 148tl, 148tr, 148c, 148bl, 149t, 149c, 149b.

RED DOT, BUDAPEST: 50t; Serenc Isza 51tl, 51cra, 51crb, 188cla, 188br, 188t, 189cb, 189bl, 214bl, 16bl.

SZÉCHENYI NATIONAL GALLERY: 39tl, 106tr, 110t; SZÉCHENYI NATIONAL LIBRARY: 24c, 25c, 26c, 27c, 72b; ÁGNES SZÉL: 34tl, 37br, 41c, 78bc, 84b, 160b, 190b.

JACKET
Front – DK PICTURE LIBRARY: Dorota & Mariusz Jarymowicz cbr, br, Statue of Anonymous, 1903, by Miklos Ligeti bl; GETTY IMAGES: Gavin Hellier main image. Back – DK PICTURE LIBRARY: Dorota & Mariusz Jarymowicz t, b. Spine – GETTY IMAGES: Gavin Hellier.

All other images © Dorling Kindersley. For further information see: www.dkimages.com

DORLING KINDERSLEY SPECIAL EDITIONS

Dorling Kindersley books can be purchased in bulk quantities at discounted prices for use in promotions or as premiums. We are also able to offer special editions and personalized jackets, corporate imprints, and excerpts from all of our books, tailored specifically to meet your own needs.

To find out more, please contact: (in the United Kingdom) – Sarah.Burgess@dk.com or SPECIAL SALES, DORLING KINDERSLEY LIMITED, 80 STRAND, LONDON WC2R 0RL;

(in the United States) – SPECIAL MARKETS DEPARTMENT, DK PUBLISHING, INC., 375 HUDSON STREET, NEW YORK, NEW YORK 10014.

Phrase Book

PRONUNCIATION

When reading the literal pronunciation given in the right-hand column of this phrase book, pronounce each syllable as if it formed part of an English word. Remember the points below, and your pronunciation will be even closer to correct Hungarian. The first syllable of each word should be stressed (and is shown in bold). When asking a question the pitch should be raised on the penultimate syllable. "R"s in Hungarian words are rolled.

a	as the long 'a' in father
ay	as in 'pay'
e	as in 'Ted'
ew	similar to the sound in 'hew'
g	always as in 'goat'
i	as in 'bit'
o	as in the 'ou' in 'ought'
u	as in 'tuck'
y	always as in 'yes' (except as in *ay* above)
yuh	as the 'yo' in 'canyon'
zh	like the 's' in leisure

IN EMERGENCY

Help!	**Segítség!**	**sheg**eetshayg
Stop!	**Stop!**	**sh**top
Look out!	**Tessék vigyázni**	**tesh**ayk **vid**yahzni
Call a doctor	**Hívjon orvost!**	**heev**yon **or**vosht
Call an ambulance	**Hívjon mentőt!**	**heev**yon **men**turt
Call the police	**Hívja a rendőrséget**	**heev**ya a **ren**dur **shay**get
Call the fire department	**Hívja a tűzoltókat!**	**heev**ya a **tewz**oltowkot
Where is the nearest telephone?	**Hol van a legköze- lebbi telefon?**	hol von uh **leg**kurze- lebbi **tel**efon
Where is the nearest hospital?	**Hol van a legköze- lebbi kórház?**	hol von a **leg**kurze- lebbi **koor**hahz

COMMUNICATIONS ESSENTIALS

Yes/No	**Igen/Nem**	**ig**en/nem
Please (offering)	**Tessék**	**tesh**ayk
Please (asking)	**Kérem**	**kay**rem
Thank you	**Köszönöm**	**kurss**urnurm
No, thank you	**Köszönöm nem**	**kurss**urnurm nem
Excuse me, please	**Bocsánatot kérek**	**boch**anutot **kay**rek
Hello	**Jó napot**	yow **nop**ot
Goodbye	**Viszontlátásra**	**viss**ontlatashruh
Good night	**Jó éjszakát/jó éjt**	yaw-**ayss**ukat/yaw-ayt
morning (4–9 am)	**reggel**	**reg**gel
morning (9am–noon)	**délelőtt**	**dayl**elurt
morning (midnight–4am)	**éjjel**	**ay**-yel
afternoon	**délután**	**dayl**ootan
evening	**este**	**esh**teh
yesterday	**tegnap**	**teg**nup
today	**ma**	muh
tomorrow	**holnap**	**hol**nup
here	**itt**	it
there	**ott**	ot
What?	**mi**	mi
When?	**mikor**	**mi**kor
Why?	**miért**	**mi**ayrt
Where?	**hol**	hol

USEFUL PHRASES

How are you?	**Hogy van?**	**hod**-yuh vun
Very well, thank you	**köszönöm nagyon jól**	**kurss**urnurm **noj**jon yowl
Pleased to meet you	**Örülök hogy megis- merhettem**	**ur**-rewlurk **hod**-yuh **megish**merhettem
See you soon	**Szia!**	**see**yuh
Excellent!	**Nagyszerű!**	**nud**-yusserew
Is there ... here?	**Van itt ... ?**	vun itt
Where can I get ...?	**Hol kaphatok ...-t?**	hol **kup**hutok ...-t
How do you get to?	**Hogy lehet ...-ba eljutni?**	**hod**-yuh lehet ...-buh **el**-yootni
How far is ...?	**milyen messze van ...**	**mee**yen **mess**eh van ...
Do you speak English?	**Beszél angolul?**	**bess**ayl **ung**olool
I can't speak Hungarian	**Nem beszélek magyarul**	nem **bess**aylek **mud**-yarool
I don't understand	**Nem értem**	nem **ayr**tem
Can you help me?	**Kérhetem a segítségét?**	**kayr**hetem uh **sheg**eechaygayt
Please speak slowly	**Tessék lassabban beszélni**	**tesh**ayk **lush**ubbun **bess**aylni
Sorry!	**Elnézést!**	**el**nayzaysht

USEFUL WORDS

big	**nagy**	noj
small	**kicsi**	**kich**i
hot	**forró**	**mel**eg
cold	**hideg**	**hid**eg
good	**jó**	yow
bad	**rossz**	ross
enough	**elég**	**el**ayg
well	**jól**	yowl
open	**nyitva**	**nyit**va
closed	**zárva**	**zar**va
left	**bal**	bol
right	**jobb**	yob
straight on	**egyenesen**	**ej**eneshen
near	**közel**	**kurz**el
far	**messze**	**mess**eh
up	**fel**	fel
down	**le**	leh
early	**korán**	**kor**an
late	**késő**	**kay**shur
entrance	**bejárat**	**beh**-yarut
exit	**kijárat**	**ki**-yarut
toilet	**WC**	**vayt**say
free/unoccupied	**szabad**	**sobb**od
free/no charge	**ingyen**	**in**jen

MAKING A TELEPHONE CALL

Can I call abroad from here?	**Telefonálhatok innen külföldre?**	**tel**efonalhutok inen **kewl**furldreh
I would like to call collect	**Szeretnék egy R- beszélgetést lebonyolítani**	**seret**nayk ed-yuh er- **bess**aylgetaysht lebon-yoletuni
local call	**helyi beszélgetés**	**hay**ee **bess**aylgetaysht
I'll ring back later	**Visszahívom később**	**viss**uh-heevom **kay**shurb
Could I leave a message?	**Hagyhatnék egy üzenetet?**	hud-yuhutnayk ed- yuh **ewz**enetet
Hold on	**Várjon!**	**vahr**-yon
Could you speak up a little please?	**kicsit hangosab- ban, kérem!**	**kich**it hungosh- shob-bon **kay**rem

SHOPPING

How much is this?	**Ez mennyibe kerül?**	ez **menn**-yibeh **ker**ewl
I would like ...	**Szeretnék egy ...-t**	**seret**nayk ed-yuh ...-t
Do you have ...?	**Kapható önöknél ...?**	**kup**hutaw **ur**nurknayl
I'm just looking	**Csak körülnézek**	chuk **kur**- rewlnayzek
Do you take credit cards?	**Elfogadják a hitelkártyákat?**	**el**fogud-yak uh **hi**telkart-yakut
What time do you open?	**Hány kor nyitnak?**	**Hahn** kor **nyit**nak?
What time do you close?	**Hány kor zárnak?**	**Hahn** kor **zár**nak?
this one	**ez**	ez
that one	**az**	oz
expensive	**drága**	**drah**ga
cheap	**olcsó**	**ol**chow
size	**méret**	**may**ret
white	**fehér**	**fe**heer
black	**fekete**	**fek**eteh
red	**piros**	**pi**rosh
yellow	**sárga**	**shar**ga
green	**zöld**	zurld
blue	**kék**	cake
brown	**barna**	**bor**na

TYPES OF SHOP

antique dealer	**antikvárius**	**on**tikvahrioosh
baker's	**pékség**	**payk**shayg
bank	**bank**	bonk
bookshop	**könyvesbolt**	**kurn**-yuveshbolt
cake shop	**cukrászda**	**tsook**rassduh
chemist	**patika**	**put**ikuh
department store	**áruház**	**aroo**-haz
florist	**virágüzlet**	**virag**-ewzlet
greengrocer	**zöldséges**	**zurld**-shaygesh
market	**piac**	**pi**-uts
newsagent	**újságos**	**oo**-yushagosh
post office	**postahivatal**	**posh**ta-hivatal
shoe shop	**cipőbolt**	**tsip**urbolt
souvenir shop	**ajándékbolt**	**uy**-yandaykbolt
supermarket	**ábécé/ABC**	**abay**tsay
travel agent	**utazási iroda**	**oot**uzashi iroduh

STAYING IN A HOTEL

Have you any vacancies?	Van kiadó szobájuk?	vun ki-udaw soba-yook
double room with double bed	francia-ágyas szoba	frontsia-ahjosh sobuh
twin room	kétágyas szoba	kaytad-yush sobuh
single room	egyágyas szoba	ed-yad-yush sobuh
room with a bath/shower	fürdőszobás/ zuhanyzós szoba	fewrdur-sobahsh/ zoohonzahsh soba
porter	portás	portahsh
key	kulcs	koolch
I have a reservation	Foglaltam egy szobát	foglultum ed-yuh sobat

SIGHTSEEING

bus	autóbusz	owtawbooss
tram	villamos	villumosh
trolley bus	troli(busz)	troli(booss)
train	vonat	vonut
underground	metró	metraw
bus stop	buszmegálló	boossmegallaw
tram stop	villamosmegálló	villomosh-megahllaw
art gallery	képcsarnok	kayp-chornok
palace	palota	polola
cathedral	székesegyház	saykesh-ejhajz
church	templom	templom
garden	kert	kert
library	könyvtár	kurnvtar
museum	múzeum	moozayoom
tourist information	túristahivatal	toorishta-hivotol
closed for public holiday	ünnepnap zárva	ewn-nepnap zarva

EATING OUT

A table for ... please	Egy asztal szeretnék... személyre	ed-yuh usstult seretnayk ... semayreh
I want to reserve a table	Szeretnék egy asztalt foglalni	seretnayk ed-yuh usstult foglolni
The bill please	Kérem a szamlát	kayrem uh samlat
I am a vegetarian	Vegetáriánnus vagyok	vegetari-ahnoosh vojok
I'd like ...	Szeret nék egy ...-t	seret nayk ed-yuh ...-t
waiter/waitress	pincér/pincérnő	pintsayr/pintsaymur
menu	étlap	aytlup
wine list	itallap	itullup
chef's special	konyhafőnök ajánlata	konha-furnurt oyahu-lotta
tip	borravaló	borovolo
glass	pohár	pohar
bottle	üveg	ewveg
knife	kés	kaysh
fork	villa	villuh
spoon	kanál	kunal
breakfast	reggeli	reg-geli
lunch	ebéd	ebayd
dinner	vacsora	vochora
main courses	főételek	fur-aytelek
starters	előételek	elur-aytelek
vegetables	zöldség	zurld-shayg
desserts	édességek	aydesh-shaydek
rare	angolosan	ongoloshan
well done	átsütve	ahtshewtveh

MENU DECODER

alma	olma	apple
ásványvíz	ahshvahnveez	mineral water
bab	bob	beans
banán	bonahn	banana
barack	borotsk	apricot
bárány	bahrahn	lamb
bors	borsh	pepper
csirke	cheerkeh	chicken
csokoládé	chokolahday	chocolate
cukor	tsookor	sugar
ecet	etset	vinegar
fagylalt	fodyuhloot	ice cream
fehérbor	feheerbor	white wine
fokhagyma	fokhodyuhma	garlic
főtt	furt	boiled
gomba	gomba	mushrooms
gulyás	gooyahsh	goulash
gyümölcs	dyewmurlch	fruit
gyümölcslé	dyewmurlch-lay	fruit juice
hagyma	hojma	onions
hal	hol	fish
hús	hoosh	meat
kávé	kavay	coffee

kenyér	ken-yeer	bread
krumpli	kroompli	potatoes
kolbász	kolbahss	sausage
leves	levesh	soup
máj	my	liver
marha	marha	beef
mustár	mooshtahr	mustard
narancs	noronch	orange
olaj	oloy	oil
paradicsom	porodichom	tomatoes
párolt	pahrolt	steamed
pite	piteh	pie
psertéshús	shertaysh-hoosh	pork
rántott	rahntsott	fried in batter
rizs	rizh	rice
rostélyos szelet	bifstek	steak
roston	roshton-	grilled
sajt	shoyt	cheese
saláta	sholahta	salad
só	shaw	salt
sonka	shonka	ham
sör	shur	beer
sült	shewlt	fried/roasted
sült burgonya	shewlt boorgonya	chips
sütemény	shewtemayn-yuh	cake, pastry
szendvics	sendvich	sandwich
szósz	sowss	sauce
tea	tay-uh	tea
tej	tay	milk
tejszín	taysseen	cream
tengeri hal	tengeri hol	seafood
tojás	toyahsh	egg
töltött	turlturt	stuffed
vörösbor	vur-rurshbor	red wine
zsemle	zhemleh	roll
zsemlegombóc	zhemleh-gombowts	dumplings

NUMBERS

0	nulla	noolluh
1	egy	ed-yuh
2	kettő, két	kettur, kayt
3	három	harom
4	négy	nayd-yuh
5	öt	urt
6	hat	hut
7	hét	hayt
8	nyolc	n-yolts
9	kilenc	kilents
10	tíz	teez
11	tizenegy	tizened-yuh
12	tizenkettő	tizenkettur
13	tizenhárom	tizenharom
14	tizennégy	tizen-nayd-yuh
15	tizenöt	tizenurt
16	tizenhat	tizenhut
17	tizenhét	tizenhayt
18	tizennyolc	tizenn-yolts
19	tizenkilenc	tizenkilents
20	húsz	hooss
21	huszonegy	hoossoned-yuh
22	huszonkettő	hoossonkettur
30	harminc	hurmints
31	harmincegy	hurmintsed-yuh
32	harminckettő	hurmintskettur
40	negyven	ned-yuven
50	ötven	urtven
60	hatvan	hutvun
70	hetven	hetven
80	nyolcvan	n-yoltsvun
90	kilencven	kilentsven
100	száz	saz
110	száztíz	sazteez
200	kétszáz	kayt-saz
300	háromszáz	haromssaz
1000	ezer	ezer
10,000	tízezer	teezezer
1,000,000	millió	milliaw

TIME

one minute	egy perc	ed-yuh perts
hour	óra	awruh
half an hour	félóra	faylawruh
Sunday	vasárnap	vusharnup
Monday	hétfő	haytfur
Tuesday	kedd	kedd
Wednesday	szerda	serduh
Thursday	csütörtök	chewturturk
Friday	péntek	payntek
Saturday	szombat	sombut

EYEWITNESS TRAVEL INSURANCE

FOR PEACE OF MIND ABROAD,
WE'VE GOT IT COVERED

DK INSURANCE PROVIDES YOU
WITH QUALITY WORLDWIDE
INSURANCE COVER

For an instant quote
go to **www.dk.com/travel-insurance**

Organised by Columbus Travel Insurance Services Ltd, 17 Devonshire Square, London EC2M 4SQ, UK.
Underwritten by certain underwriters at Lloyd's and Professional Travel Insurance Company Ltd.